MW00652586

MY FIGHT FOR
A NEW TAIWAN

MY FIGHT FOR A NEW TAIWAN

ONE WOMAN'S JOURNEY
FROM PRISON TO POWER

LU HSIU-LIEN *and* ASHLEY ESAREY

Foreword by Jerome A. Cohen

UNIVERSITY OF WASHINGTON PRESS
Seattle & London

For our mothers

© 2014 by the University of Washington Press
Printed and bound in the United States of America
Composed in Chaparral Pro, typeface design by Carol Twombly
17 16 15 14   5 4 3 2 1

Portions of chapters 5 and 6 draw on Lu Hsiu-lien's book *Chongshen meilidao* [Re-trying the *Formosa* case] (Taipei: Zili Wanbao Chubanshe, 1991).

UNIVERSITY OF WASHINGTON PRESS
PO BOX 50096, Seattle, WA 98145, USA
www.washington.edu/uwpress

LIBRARY OF CONGRESS CATALOGING-IN-PUBLICATION DATA
Lu, Xiulian.
    My fight for a new Taiwan : one woman's journey from prison to power / Lu Hsiu-lien and Ashley Esarey ; foreword by Jerome A. Cohen.
    pages   cm
    Includes bibliographical references and index.
    ISBN 978-0-295-99364-5 (hardcover : alk. paper)
    1. Lu, Xiulian.   2. Vice presidents—Taiwan—Biography.   3. Taiwan—Politics and government—2000-   4. Taiwan—Politics and government—1975-   5. Human rights movements—Taiwan.   6. Women politicians—Taiwan—Biography.   I. Esarey, Ashley. II. Title.
    DS799.849.L78A3   2014
    951.24905092—dc23   2013046731

The paper used in this publication is acid-free and meets the minimum requirements of American National Standard for Information Sciences—Permanence of Paper for Printed Library Materials, ANSI Z39.48–1984.8

CONTENTS

Illustrations follow pages 40 and 202

FOREWORD

Jerome A. Cohen

ANYONE WHO HAS BEEN PRIVILEGED TO TEACH AT MAJOR American law schools for several decades is likely to have taught at least a few students who have subsequently become politically prominent. Of course, many students who burn with political ambition during their law school days are later seduced by other opportunities or frustrated by the vicissitudes and uncertainties of a political career. It is difficult for any professor to predict which of his interested students is likely to climb to the top of the greasy political pole. Yet occasionally a student stands out as having the talent, determination, and courage required for political success. Lu Hsiu-lien surely met that description during the year that she spent at the Harvard Law School in 1977–78.

Unlike most graduate students, Lu Hsiu-lien came widely heralded. I had heard about her achievements from students from Taiwan as well as American protégés who had lived on the island. Lu Hsiu-lien's journalistic essays and books promoting women's rights and her social activism had already made her a well-known figure at an early age. Moreover, although the repressive Nationalist (Guomindang) regime of that era did not tolerate the public expression of Taiwan-independence sentiments, Lu Hsiu-lien was also known as an advocate of democratic development and freedoms of expression, which would inevitably give voice to such sentiments. She was plainly no ordinary master of laws (LLM) candidate. Slightly older, more mature, less interested in business law, and focused on resuming public life on her return home after graduation, she stood out, even at Harvard, as a future leader deserving of scholarship assistance.

Lu Hsiu-lien added a lot to Harvard life. She frequently exchanged ideas with American and foreign students. While learning more about constitutional and international law, human rights, and even mainland China's legal system, she wrote papers that helped me and other faculty members better understand the realities of Taiwan, which Nationalist propaganda misleadingly referred to as "Free China." Lu Hsiu-lien also participated in the weekly informal discussions that I convened as part of the extracurricular activities of Harvard's East Asian Legal Studies program.

The academic year 1977–78 was a time of great tension in Sino-American relations. The world—not only the people on Taiwan—was waiting to see whether the new administration of President Jimmy Carter would complete the process of normalizing relations with mainland China, that is, the People's Republic of China (PRC), that the Nixon administration had begun. That would require the withdrawal of formal US diplomatic recognition from the PRC's Taiwan-based rival, the Republic of China (ROC), and termination of the US-ROC defense treaty. It was obvious to all that profoundly important developments were under way that put into question not only Taiwan's security but also the nature and continuity of the island's dictatorial Nationalist government. In those circumstances one can imagine the lively debates that occurred at Harvard and elsewhere, fueled in part by the contributions of students and visiting scholars from Taiwan.

Although at that time it was still not possible for Harvard Law School to enroll students from the People's Republic, our discussions of China policy did try—more faithfully than Chairman Mao's regime had—to implement the traditional Chinese maxim "Let a hundred flowers bloom, let a hundred schools of thought contend." Lu Hsiu-lien's was not the only Taiwan voice opposed to the Nationalists, but hers was surely the most daring. Some others from Taiwan took a more moderate position, favoring reform rather than replacement of the Nationalists. The latter group included a brilliant doctoral candidate who became another star of contemporary Taiwan politics, Ma Ying-jeou, now in his second term as president of the ROC.

Ma's political views continued to differ markedly from Lu Hsiu-lien's after both returned from Harvard to Taiwan. Nevertheless, in 1985 Ma, who had already become a deputy secretary-general of the Nationalist Party and English-language interpreter for President Chiang Ching-Kuo, played a key role in winning Lu Hsiu-lien's release from prison after she had served five years of the twelve-year term to which she had been sentenced for advocating Taiwan independence. Ma's bold effort, undertaken at my request, was undoubtedly motivated by not only "the old school tie" and a desire to grant the wish of a former professor, but also the hope of improving the Nationalist image, which had recently been further tarnished by the assassination of journalist Henry Liu in San Francisco. I have always been grateful for the effective help he gave us.

If prison seems a surprising fate for a recent Harvard Law School graduate, it came as no surprise to Lu Hsiu-lien. Before deciding to return to Taiwan after winning her Harvard degree, she plainly considered the personal risks that would be incurred if someone with her views became politically active in the island's extraordinarily tense situation. Her problem in 1978 was one common to high-minded and ambitious lawyers who came from countries with oppressive governments to receive advanced legal training in the United States. After graduation, what should they do with their enhanced skills and reinforced democratic values? Returning home to fight dictatorship might well lead to detention, punishment, and even death. Yet returning home to practice corporate law or to join the ruling government elite might seem a betrayal of personal ideals and a black mark against one's prospects for future leadership. And remaining in the United States in order to organize opposition from abroad could soon lead to divorce from political developments at home, a reputation for playing it safe while others risk involvement in the struggle, and other frustrations of self-exile.

There was little doubt which choice Lu Hsiu-lien would make. She was tempted to accept a post-graduate fellowship that would have allowed further study and research at Harvard while awaiting the impending upheavals in international relations and Taiwan politics that normalization of US-PRC relations would create. But she decided instead to plunge into the furnace of history. When, shortly before we secured her release, Ma Ying-jeou and I visited her in a military hospital, Lu Hsiu-lien reminded me that on the last occasion we met before she left Cambridge for Taipei, I had told her the late President Harry Truman's famous admonition about politics: "If you can't stand the heat, don't go into the kitchen." She then smiled ruefully and said: "I didn't realize how hot the kitchen could get!"

Yet, a remarkable generation later, after great suffering and turmoil, Lu Hsiu-lien became the second-highest leader of the freest people and most democratic government ever spawned by China's political-legal culture, on an island that has made unusual social and economic progress. Appropriately, she has become a symbol of both the equal rights for women for which she has so consistently labored and the first electoral triumph of an opposition political party in China's and Taiwan's history. Given Lu Hsiu-lien's dramatic personal story, she is entitled to feel particular satisfaction. As I said to the audience that in 1997 witnessed her inauguration as chief executive of Taoyuan County, many politicians go from public office to prison, but only extraordinary ones go from prison to public office!

After completing eight years of distinguished service as vice president and surviving an assassination attempt, Lu Hsiu-lien was hardly ready to retire and rest on her laurels. Instead, she eagerly embraced a host of new challenges as Taiwan's most outstanding, "post-political" woman leader. Her devotion to the cause of protecting international human rights at home and abroad, her proposals for securing Taiwan's future and resolving disputes with its East Asian neighbors, and her specific ideas concerning how Taiwan and China might foster and regulate their relations for the coming generation have all earned widespread respect. We can be confident that for many years ahead, Lu Hsiu-lien will continue to strike sparks and launch new initiatives. Readers of this fascinating book will be better equipped to make informed predictions.

PREFACE

OUR COLLABORATION ON *MY FIGHT FOR A NEW TAIWAN* BEGAN IN THE late 1990s when Lu Hsiu-lien (aka Annette Lu) was serving as chief executive of Taoyuan County and Ashley Esarey was preparing to enter the PhD program in political science at Columbia University. In the spring of 1998, Ashley moved into an apartment next to Lu's official residence in Taoyuan, and for three months he spent hundreds of hours with Annette discussing her childhood, leadership in Taiwan's feminist and democracy movements, imprisonment, and subsequent career as a politician. These conversations served as the basis for the book, along with input from Annette on draft chapters.

As a former journalist for the International Community Radio Taipei, Ashley had opportunities to interview many of the people about whom we have written. He attended dozens of Annette's campaign rallies, press conferences, late-night strategy sessions, and one Lu family reunion with over 2,000 participants! In March 2000, Ashley flew to Taiwan to witness the DPP's historic victory in the presidential election, as a member of the Election Observation delegation from Columbia University's East Asian Institute. He attended the subsequent presidential and vice presidential inauguration on May 20 and spent July and August in Taipei conducting follow-up interviews. Ashley had the opportunity to update his knowledge of contemporary Taiwan in 2012 as a visiting scholar at Academia Sinica's Institute of Sociology, a delightful experience that spurred this book's rapid completion.

It is essential to give thanks to those individuals who have been instrumental in facilitating our efforts to complete this book over many years. Our deepest appreciation goes to Andrew J. Nathan, who read multiple drafts of the manuscript, as well as to Stevan Harrell, who read the entire manuscript, provided insightful feedback, and introduced us to Lorri Hagman, the executive editor of the University of Washington Press. Lorri has been wonderfully supportive of this project from the outset. She delighted us with perceptive suggestions for improving the manuscript and made publishing with the press a very smooth process. Jerome A. Cohen deserves our sincere gratitude for providing meticulous comments on an early draft of the manuscript and for contributing a thoughtful foreword. We also wish to thank our three anonymous reviewers for their careful consideration of the manuscript and helpful suggestions.

Lu Hsiu-lien's executive assistant Su Yen-fei deserves our heartfelt thanks. She managed to find time in Lu's busy schedule for collaboration on the book and handled our communication across oceans, continents, and time zones. We are very grateful for the efforts of our talented copy editor Lou Doucette and to Yishane Lee for her aid in drafting chapters 2 and 3. David Peattie at BookMatters helped to keep the project on schedule. Nancy Hearst, librarian at the Harvard University's H.C. Fung Library provided invaluable assistance tracking down reportage on the *Formosa Magazine* trial as well as Annette's early feminist writings in the *China Times*. The book profited from Margie Joy Walden's comments on chapter 8 as well as from her wise counsel over delicious meals in New York City.

Other colleagues, friends, and family members helped to coach us as we labored on the manuscript and provided encouragement, advice, and information that took innumerable and invaluable forms. These people include, but are certainly not limited to, the following individuals: Linda Arrigo, Crystal Ashley, Maureen Ashley, Thomas Bernstein, Jeremy Busacca, Larry Diamond, Graeme Esarey, Janna Cawrse Esarey, Jon Esarey, Chang Maukuei, Hans Chen, Chen Mumin, Ja Ian Chong, Ryan Dunch, Jo Ann Fan, Motomi Fujii, Thomas Gold, Steven Goldstein, Sheena Chestnut Greitens, Todd Hall, Nancy Hearst, Gladys Hendrickson, Jocelyn Hendrickson, Loel Hendrickson, Michael Hsiao, Teresa Hsu, A-chin Hsiau, Bruce Jacobs, Frida Lee, Chris Logan, Annie Lu, Lu Chuan-sheng, Lu Hsiu-rong (who is greatly missed), Anthony Marx, Dawn Morgan, Chris Neal, Josh Reid, Shelley Rigger, Graeme Robertson, Murray Rubinstein, Dakota Rudesill, James Seymour, Ezra Vogel, Jennifer Wei, Wu Ya-fen, and Jiunn-rong Yeh. Sole responsibility for any errors is ours alone.

LU HSIU-LIEN
Taipei, Taiwan

ASHLEY ESAREY
Turtle Lake, Minnesota

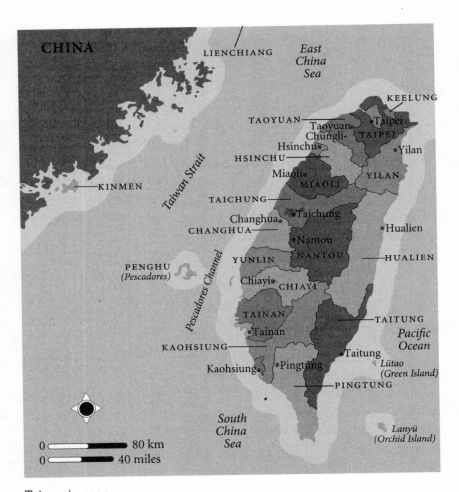

CHINA

LIENCHIANG

East
China
Sea

KEELUNG

TAOYUAN

Taoyuan
Chungli

Taipei

TAIPEI

Hsinchu

Yilan

HSINCHU

Miaoli

MIAOLI

YILAN

Taiwan Strait

KINMEN

TAICHUNG

Changhua

Taichung

Hualien

CHANGHUA

Nantou

PENGHU
(Pescadores)

YUNLIN

NANTOU

HUALIEN

Pescadores Channel

Chiayi

CHIAYI

TAINAN

TAITUNG

Tainan

KAOHSIUNG

Pacific
Ocean

Kaohsiung

Pingtung

Taitung

Lütao
(Green Island)

PINGTUNG

South
China
Sea

0 ▬▬▬▬▬ 80 km
0 ▬▬▬▬▬ 40 miles

Lanyü
(Orchid Island)

Taiwan in 2000

MY FIGHT FOR
A NEW TAIWAN

INTRODUCTION

Ashley Esarey

IN THE LAST SEVEN DECADES, TAIWAN HAS BEEN PASSED between Japanese and Chinese colonial rulers, broken free from the grip of Guomindang (Nationalist) authoritarianism, and fought to become a democracy with free and fair elections. In world affairs, Taiwan remains an outlier. Beijing asserts that Taiwan is a province of the People's Republic of China, though most Taiwanese see their home as an independent polity and have no interest in unifying with the Communist-ruled Chinese mainland. Beijing's clout meanwhile prevents most countries from recognizing the reality that Taiwan is an independent nation-state in everything but name.

All countries that travel the difficult road from authoritarian rule to democracy take a different path. Taiwan is no exception. Yet the peculiarities of Taiwan's transition and status in the international community have made the Republic of China, as Taiwan is formally called, even more difficult for outsiders to understand. In such a context, the autobiography of Lu Hsiu-lien (known in the West as Annette Lu) presents a vivid insider perspective on Taiwan's remarkable transformation since World War II.

Lu Hsiu-lien is certainly not a typical Taiwanese. Quite to the contrary, she has devoted her life to challenging traditional cultural beliefs and to promoting social values that have been considered controversial, radical, and seditious. Yet Lu has much in common with

3

other Taiwanese who grew up under Nationalist rule. Like the majority of Taiwan residents, Lu is native Taiwanese (Hoklo), whose ancestors came to Taiwan over two centuries ago. The discrimination she faced as the result of her ethnicity, and even her accent in standard Chinese (Mandarin, or Putonghua), is representative of the experiences of other Taiwanese, who were treated as second class by the mainlanders dominating Taiwan's political establishment prior to democratization.

Unlike many influential politicians in Taiwan and elsewhere, Lu Hsiu-lien does not come from an elite family. Her father, Lu Shi-sheng, ran a medium-size shop in the city of Taoyuan in northern Taiwan, and her mother, Lu Huang-chin, had more children than she could financially support. Lu Hsiu-lien's parents twice considered giving her away in hopes that she would have a better life in a more affluent home. As it was, they were too poor to buy shoes for Lu Hsiu-lien when she went off to elementary school.

To an extent remarkable for a well-known feminist, Lu Hsiu-lien holds many traditional Chinese values. In early adulthood, Lu thought her ideal husband would be tall, handsome, and her intellectual superior. She gives high status to the elderly, respects the lineage-based hierarchy of her clan, and believes in honoring proper customs concerning the funerary arrangements for one's parents; when Lu was imprisoned and unable to attend her mother's funeral, she felt searing guilt.

In other ways Lu Hsiu-lien is an extraordinary individual. Direct, immensely creative, and argumentative, she bears little resemblance to the gentle and deferent female idealized in East Asia, where women seldom hold political power. Tremendously driven, Lu has chosen to pursue objectives that her contemporaries believed were impossible. In the face of setbacks, Lu Hsiu-lien proved resilient, typically engaging in introspection that left her with a sharper sense of purpose. Throughout Lu's life, she has had a remarkably clear conception of self, although as was true of many of her compatriots in post-colonial Taiwan, Lu struggled to find answers to such questions as: Why don't my government's policies value my culture and reflect my interests?

What can be done to chart a better course for Taiwan as an independent country?

Lu Hsiu-lien's journey to understand Taiwan's place in the world and shape its future reflects Taiwan's painful history in the nineteenth and twentieth centuries. Abandoned by the Qing dynasty to Japanese rule in 1895, Taiwan was subjected to "Japanization" policies for five decades. Taiwanese were taught to revere the Japanese emperor and adopt Japanese culture and dress. Standard Japanese, not Chinese, became the island's official language, while privately people spoke in their local Chinese dialects or aboriginal languages. In World War II, Taiwanese were forced to serve as "volunteers" in Japanese imperial forces seeking to conquer China and vast territories in East and Southeast Asia.

In 1945, when Chiang Kai-shek's Chinese representatives accepted Taiwan's surrender, Taiwan had stood at crossroads politically and culturally. Relative to China, Taiwan was affluent, although by the standards of advanced countries it was crushingly poor. Yet many Taiwanese felt optimistic. Populated by a majority of Han Chinese but ruled for centuries by outsiders, including the Dutch, the Spanish, Manchus, and Japanese, islanders were eager for freedom and political equality. They believed rule by a Chinese government espousing the merits of democracy would be an improvement. Taiwan's hopes soon foundered. In Taipei, protests against Nationalist Chinese corruption and malfeasance in late February 1947 precipitated the slaughter of Taiwan's elite by Chinese soldiers, creating deep rifts between "mainlanders" and Taiwan-born residents and contributing to the rise of the Taiwan Independence Movement overseas.

Lu Hsiu-lien was a small child at the time of the "February 28 Incident." Her mother had taken her to the nearby city of Hsinchu for a wedding. The trains were not running and Lu's mother carried the infant on her back, as she walked over forty miles to return home. Lu's recollections of the journey are limited, but the pervasive sense of fear that followed the February 28 (or 2-28) Incident was burned into her memory. Thereafter "children had ears and no mouths." Incautious mention of political matters or the Nationalist government was dangerous and discouraged by her parents. The shadow of authoritarian rule had fallen over Taiwan; the coercive ideological indoctrination and military rule that followed would last four decades.

Exiled from China after defeat in the Chinese Civil War from 1946 to 1949, Nationalists led by the US-backed Chinese dictator Chiang Kai-shek set up their government anew in Taiwan and made "launching a counterattack against the Communists and restoring the country" (*fangong fuguo*) their foremost objective. Taiwan's economic development and investment in Taiwan's infrastructure were of comparatively lesser import. The Nationalists Sinified Taiwan's education system and utilized mass media to indoctrinate the public. Taiwan became "Chinese." The national language became standard Chinese; local languages were barred from public use. Native culture was considered inferior; the only history that mattered was Chinese history, in which Taiwan played a minor part.

Lu Hsiu-lien poignantly relates her embarrassment as a school girl in the 1950s at her poor pronunciation of standard Chinese as well as her unconscious acceptance of the school curriculum placing China at the center of civilization. Like her older brother and childhood role model, Lu Chuan-sheng, however, Lu Hsiu-lien proved to be an exceptional student, eventually winning entry to the highly prestigious National Taiwan University Law Department.

University life proved a springboard for Lu's growing self-confidence as a young woman and budding intellectual. She was, however, frustrated by expectations that, as a woman, she would be unlikely to have a noteworthy career. Lu sought to overcome gender discrimination through dint of hard work, seeking to become the first-ever university student to pass the examination to become a judge. Failure to achieve this objective prompted introspection and eventually the reorientation of her aspirations. She accepted a fellowship to study law in the United States.

At the University of Illinois at Urbana-Champagne, Lu began to see the culture and politics of Taiwan in a different light. Her participation in the Protect the Diaoyutai Islands movement, which asserted the Republic of China's sovereignty over the islands, provided the impetus for her awareness of Chiang Kai-shek's inability to handle Taiwan's worsening crises in foreign relations. To get a leg up in its Cold War rivalry with the Soviet Union, the United States was moving toward diplomatic recognition of the People's Republic of China. Anticipating the future direction of US foreign policy, Japan abrogated diplomatic ties with Taiwan in favor of China in 1972. The number of countries around the world officially recognizing the Republic of China plummeted in the early 1970s.

In Illinois, Lu Hsiu-lien also learned about the feminist movement in the United States and, upon her return to Taiwan, called for a reconsideration of the role of women in Taiwan's patriarchal society. A series of economic reforms, notably land reform, and the proliferation of small and medium-size businesses specializing in manufacturing that was no longer profitable in Japan or the United States helped Taiwan's economy to grow at "miraculous" rates of over 10 percent per year from 1963 to 1972. Rising prosperity improved the climate for higher education and social mobilization.

Discrimination against women in Taiwan had roots in Confucian and Japanese cultures. Compared with men, nearly three times as many women were illiterate and half as many women held college degrees. Yet in 1971, the number of women admitted to universities rivaled the number of men, sparking a national debate over whether the surge in the number of women seeking advanced degrees was a waste of educational resources. As a young bureaucrat working in the central government (Executive Yuan), Lu Hsiu-lien condemned traditional biases against women in the mass-circulation *United Daily* newspaper. Her commentary in the *China Times* on a Taiwanese man's murder of his wife for suspected adultery further solidified her fame as a prominent feminist and helped her to attract resources to found Pioneer Press, a publishing house specializing in titles on women; the Taiwan branch of the International Federation of Business and Professional Women; and counseling centers for battered women in Taipei and Kaohsiung.

Lu's activities, like those of other outspoken intellectuals in Taiwan in the 1970s, put her on the Nationalists' radar for monitoring and later for repression. Her experiences with politically motivated harassment and government-planted spies in her organizations hardened her political views and increased her growing affinity with advocates of political reform. An encounter with thyroid cancer in her late twenties strengthened Lu's commitment to public service and convinced her that she had no time to lose.

As a graduate student of law at Harvard, Lu Hsiu-lien made the choice in 1978 to leave her studies and to run for political office in Taiwan, thereby taking advantage of what were called "election holidays" (*xuanju jiaqi*), during which restrictions on freedom of speech were temporarily relaxed. It was her intention to boldly articulate calls for placing Taiwan (and not China) at the center of the Republic of China's political priorities. Lu responded to the ROC's exclusion of Taiwan from official historical narratives by writing a history of Taiwan from the perspective of the Taiwanese. Her pathbreaking book *Taiwan: Past and Future* (Taiwan: guoqu yu weilai), first published in 1978, has been hailed as one of the most systematic reconsiderations of Taiwan's position in world affairs by a member of the opposition politicians' group known as the Dangwai, or people outside the Nationalist Party. Lu Hsiu-lien encouraged the acknowledgement of China's divided status, urged acceptance of the fact that many countries had already established formal diplomatic relations with the People's Republic of China, and asserted that the Republic of China was an independent country. Such views were seen as radical in Taiwan and flew in the face of government policy, although in twenty years the Taiwan-born President Lee Teng-hui would himself adopt them.

While Lu Hsiu-lien has founded countless organizations, she has often been uncomfortable in groups led by others. Her role in the early Dangwai movement led by Yao Chia-wen, Hsu Hsin-liang, Shih Ming-teh, and others was no exception. They distrusted Lu for her service in the executive branch of the government (Executive Yuan) and brief membership in the Nationalist Party; they fretted that she could be a spy. Eventually, her skills as a public speaker and capacity as an organizer of opposition activities, including her role as the deputy editor in chief of the *Formosa Magazine* (Meilidao zazhi), impressed the skeptics. However, Lu Hsiu-lien was an outsider and would remain so, even a decade later as a member of the Democratic Progressive Party.

The political climate in Taiwan under martial law did not allow for the establishment of opposition parties, although it did permit the founding of magazines. For this reason, *Formosa Magazine* staffed by some of the most prominent members of the Dangwai movement and advocates of Taiwan independence, provided institutional cover for the advocacy of political reform via the magazine's offices in northern and southern Taiwan. Although the arrest of the *Formosa Magazine* leadership in the aftermath of a Human Rights Day demonstration in Kaohsiung was seen as a devastating blow to the democracy movement, the subsequent trial of the activists—held openly and uncharacteristically without media censorship—gave the Dangwai unprecedented exposure for their ideas. This publicity coup helped to fuel the rebirth of the Dangwai agenda as proxy candidates, the wives and relatives of those in prison, ran successful campaigns for political office.

Lu's years in prison were the most challenging of her life. Yet she emerged a committed revolutionary and found Taiwan's political environment less restrictive in comparison to the days before her 1,933-day incarceration. After a stint as a grassroots organizer of the Clean Election Coalition to reduce vote buying, Lu won a seat in the national legislature (Legislative Yuan), and she joined a breed of politicians, rare in any democracy, that focuses almost exclusively on foreign affairs, which voters rarely see as clearly beneficial to their interests. Compared with other legislators, Lu operated a large staff. She maintained two offices in Taipei, one in her home district of Taoyuan, and an office in New York City to advance her efforts to lobby for a greater role for Taiwan in international organizations, particularly the United Nations, which has barred Taiwan's membership since 1971.

While opposition leaders such as Lu Hsiu-lien pushed for political reforms, the state responded to rising pressure from society by proactively liberalizing politics and ceding space for new political competition with the Nationalist Party. In 1986, Chiang Ching-kuo, who had succeeded his father Chiang Kai-shek as president, decided against cracking down on the Dangwai movement's successor, the Democratic Progressive Party (DPP), which was founded in defiance of a ban on political parties. The following year, Chiang ended thirty-eight years of martial law and lifted restrictions on the media industry. His death in 1988 also led to a Nationalist Party leadership change with far-reaching implications.

Lee Teng-hui, a native Taiwanese, successfully consolidated his power as Nationalist Party chairman and ROC president. Lee then pardoned such leading Dangwai activists as Shih Ming-teh and Hsu Hsin-liang and invited DPP politicians to participate in the first National Affairs Conference in 1990. The capacity of opposition politicians to participate in national debates over political reform benefited from Lee's willingness to cede them a greater political role. Even more significantly, President Lee Teng-hui agreed to participate in a national election for president, which he won handily in 1996.

Ultimately, the Democratic Progressive Party opposition had to first demonstrate its ability in local politics before it won national power. Lu Hsiu-lien joined the ranks of many DPP politicians, including future President Chen Shui-bian, who served as mayors and chief executives of counties. Many voters feared the radicalism associated with the DPP's advocacy of de jure independence for Taiwan. For DPP politicians, the experience of holding local office provided opportunities to forge bonds with the grass roots and to create networks for voter mobilization.

Lu Hsiu-lien's foray into local politics in Taoyuan County, following the execution-style murder of the chief executive she ran to replace, honed her skills as a campaigner and helped to establish her record for supervising a large bureaucracy. Perhaps equally important, serving as chief executive of Taoyuan County (*Taoyuan xian xianzhang*) helped Lu Hsiu-lien develop strategies for cooperating with county government employees who had served under Nationalists for decades. These experiences would inform her efforts to stabilize the national government after her election to even higher office.

In Taiwan, perhaps more than in most democracies, politics is public performance—not only for politicians but also for citizens, whose attendance at mass rallies is seen as a crucial indicator of support. Taiwan's relatively small size permits prospective voters to attend campaign rallies in person and thereby obtain information from political candidates directly. For vice presidential candidate Lu Hsiu-lien and her running mate, presidential candidate Chen Shui-bian, rallies were intended to attract undecided voters, calm fears that long-dominant mainlanders could face marginalization, and respond to threats from Beijing that Taiwan's voters might forever regret their support for the Chen-Lu duo. Lu Hsiu-lien's tireless efforts to energize voters in the run-up to the 2000 presidential election, when she required hospital treatments by day before nightly rallies, speak to the importance of political spectacle as a source of "contagion" for voters, especially in the ten days prior to the election, when Taiwan's election laws prohibit the release of public opinion statistics.

Three days before the 2000 election, the specter of Chinese military invasion injected uncertainty into predictions of the outcome. Chinese Premier Zhu Rongji held a press conference at which he threatened those pursuing Taiwan independence and advised Taiwan's voters not to "act on impulse at this juncture, which will decide the future course that China and Taiwan will follow. . . . Otherwise I am afraid you won't get another opportunity to regret [the decision]." Broadcast on television networks throughout Taiwan, Zhu Rongji's remarks implied that victory by Chen Shui-bian and Lu Hsiu-lien, longtime advocates of Taiwan independence, could lead to war that would destroy Taiwan's fragile democracy.

Tense relations with China had defined the final years of President Lee Teng-hui's administration, as well. Just five years earlier, a "private" visit by Lee to his alma mater, Cornell University, had prompted the Chinese declaration that Lee Teng-hui was leading Taiwan toward independence. Beijing castigated the United States, broke off semiofficial talks with Taipei, and held a series of military exercises that involved firing missiles near Taiwan. In response to this "Taiwan Strait Crisis," the United States sent two aircraft carrier battle groups toward Taiwan in the largest concentration of US naval forces since the Vietnam War. Although many Western pundits believed that resentment of China's military intimidation had contributed to Lee Teng-hui's landslide in the 1996 presidential race, China's leaders had failed to learn that threatening the Taiwan electorate could backfire.

As it was, Taiwanese voters who were inclined to support Chen Shui-bian and Lu Hsiu-lien faced a difficult choice. They could embrace the champions of liberty, human rights, and political transformation at the risk of an invasion, or purchase peace at the expense of their democratic freedom and national pride. At a rally on the eve of the election, Lu Hsiu-lien sought to give her supporters courage: "Zhu Rongji was the world's ugliest man when he threatened Taiwan's democracy. . . . But Zhu Rongji was right about one thing: he was right to believe in the wisdom of the people of Taiwan and to trust that they will make the right historic choice. I share this belief and this trust. Tomorrow marks the beginning of a glorious revolution." In the end, Chen Shui-bian and Lu Hsiu-lien won the election with just over 39 percent of the popular vote, beating James Soong by two percent and Nationalist candidate Lien Chan by an astounding 16 percent. The people of Taiwan, not China, had determined that two native Taiwanese from humble backgrounds would ascend to the nation's highest offices. As the first woman to serve as vice president of Taiwan, a position that she held for eight years, Lu Hsiu-lien's improbable journey from prison to power has earned her the respect of compatriots and a prominent place in the history of East Asia's democratization.

CHAPTER 1

DREAMS COME TRUE

THE WAIL OF A THOUSAND AIR HORNS, THE CRACKLING SHOWER
of fireworks, the undulation of a sea of banners greeted us as we left
our party headquarters and approached the stage. A crowd stretched
for half a mile in every direction, claiming streets and sidewalks, jam-
ming intersections on Minsheng East Road. Bottle rockets shrieked
from the windows of nearby apartment buildings. To an outsider
observing the revelers on the night of March 18, 2000, the crowds in
the streets could have been celebrating the Taiwan national team's
victory in some sort of world championship, but the pride of the Taiwanese was participatory, not vicarious: They had voted to remove
the Nationalist Party (Guomindang) from the nation's highest office
after its fifty-five years in power and had stood up to China despite
its threats to invade Taiwan if they dared vote this way. They had cast
aside the successors of a regime that had ruled Taiwan by force and
fiat, by threat and murder, by corruption and co-optation, by autocracy and exploitation. On March 18, the Taiwanese had, through their
vote, peacefully "changed the heavens" in their homeland, as the saying went, and given birth to the feeling that Taiwan was experiencing
its finest hour, that the wrongs of the past could be righted.

What a coincidence it was! On the very same day twenty years
before, March 18, 1980, I stood in a military courtroom as one of the
eight main defendants charged with sedition for leading a demonstration on Human Rights Day. An intense man unknown outside legal
circles, Chen Shui-bian, had been among our legal defense attorneys.

Even our lawyers' valiant efforts had not prevented the court from sentencing us to lengthy prison terms on the basis of confessions elicited through torture. Who would have dared predict that two decades later, one of the defense lawyers and one of the codefendants would be elected president and vice president of the country at the crowning moment of Taiwan's struggle for democracy?

The hope that the Nationalists would one day be turned out of power had sustained me while I served five and a half years in prison for criticizing their authoritarian regime. I had been waiting for the celebration of March 2000 since my childhood, when I had denounced my schoolteacher for changing the grades of the daughter of a Nationalist official because the teacher wanted to ingratiate himself with the government. Since my recovery from cancer in the 1970s, I had sworn to dedicate my life to equal political participation for all members of Taiwanese society and for all ethnic groups. I had prayed for the replacement of the Nationalist government with a democratically elected opposition since my realization, in prison, that the shock of my incarceration had cost my mother her life.

Although I had dreamed of such a moment, somehow I'd never imagined how victory might feel when it blossomed like a flower more fragrant than the evening primrose. Certainly not during the long months of campaigning in 1999 and 2000, when I'd appeared with Chen Shui-bian at six political rallies each night, speaking until my voice grew hoarse and cracked—I was too busy fighting to win the election. Yet the moment did come, with the decisiveness of nightfall in the tropics. From school yards and post offices across the island, election volunteers counted the votes signaling the Nationalists' defeat. The Democratic Progressive Party had captured the presidential palace, formerly the bastion of power for Chiang Kai-shek and the symbol of authority for Japanese colonial governors. On the night of March 18, 2000, the specter of foreign dominance departed with the defeat of the Nationalists, a political party transplanted to Taiwan from China after World War II. For the first time in the history of Taiwan, a native Taiwanese man from a poor, landless family had become president. For the first time in five thousand years of Chinese history,

I, a woman from an ordinary family, had been elected by the public to serve the number-two position in an ethnically Chinese nation.

Twenty-two years had passed since I had first taken the podium at a political rally, challenging, among other things, the Nationalist censorship of the news media. At that time, Taiwan lived under martial law; all media organizations that did not toe the party line were promptly shut down. Now, with the president-elect, Chen Shui-bian, I stood blinking under the lights of nearly a hundred television cameras, addressing a free media, free ourselves to speak in any manner that we chose, even to speak in English, the language I used to explain the significance of our victory to the foreign press:

> Today, March 18th, 2000, the people of Taiwan have spoken, and their voice, so long muted, has sung out for the world to hear. Today, we have witnessed a glorious revolution, the culmination of a peaceful democratic transformation of our country. Today, Taiwan's people have chosen Mr. Chen Shui-bian to be their next president and me as their next vice president. They have chosen to stand up for democracy in their country and peace in the world.
>
> Taiwan can today celebrate the full flowering of her democracy. Chen Shui-bian and I will bring to Taiwan a government of the people, by the people, and for the people; a government that fosters respect for human rights and the rule of law; a government that is free of corruption and cronyism; a government that is truly accountable to her citizens. We will ensure the stability of our open and free society and the health of our country's thriving market economy. We will also create a new era of goodwill and lasting peace with China and all our neighbors. . . .
>
> To China's leaders, I wish to extend an invitation to leave behind past conflict and walk toward a future of harmonious coexistence with Taiwan and all other nations of the world. This election represents the possibility of a fresh new beginning. The historical enmity between the Nationalists and the Chinese Communist Party need no longer poison the relationship between Taiwan and China. . . .
>
> Taiwan became today the first country in the world with a

Confucian cultural heritage to elect a woman vice president. This election victory, therefore, is not just a triumph for democracy, but also a milestone for gender equality in government. With the slogan "50-50 by 2000," the 1995 United Nations Conference on Women set the goal of women's equal participation in politics and society by the year 2000. Taiwan can be proud to be one of the very few countries in the world to fulfill that goal at the highest level of government. For me personally, as well, this achievement is the culmination of thirty years of struggle for women's rights. . . .

I wish to thank the people of Taiwan for their courage and wisdom in exercising their right to determine their own fate. I also wish to thank all the leaders of the world who have supported Taiwan's democracy and the right of our people to fairly and freely choose their own leaders. And lastly I wish to thank the many members of the media from across the globe who have brought the story of Taiwan's political transformation to the world.

In 1994, after many years of struggle, black South Africans were able for the first time to vote for their country's president. I stood alongside Mr. Nelson Mandela on that election day when he cast his vote in the small rural village where the African National Congress was born. It was after the results of that historic ballot were announced that he proclaimed the birth of a new South Africa. Today, with this election, we may joyfully proclaim the birth of a new Taiwan. A Taiwan in which the people have risen above fear to speak their hopes. A Taiwan in which women and men are equal and free. A Taiwan in which democracy has come to full flower, for all the world to see.

Our presidential campaign in spring of the year 2000 had been the most hotly contested election in the history of Taiwanese democracy. The Nationalists, split by internal division, forwarded two candidates, one official and one running as an independent. Both candidates were tainted by allegations of corruption and ties to members of organized crime. This time, the party's hallmark vote buying, the strategy by which it had maintained power in elections after the introduction of democracy, failed to rekindle the traditional loyalty. Sick of the Nationalist Party corruption, the Taiwanese voted to set the country on a new course.

On March 18, 2000, more than 82 percent of eligible voters went to the polls, a much higher voter participation rate than that of many Western countries. Only two hours after the polls closed, the vast majority of twelve million votes had been counted and the Nationalist candidate, Lien Chan, had fallen in ignominious defeat with 23 percent of the vote; the former Nationalist provincial governor, James Soong, running as an independent, claimed 36 percent of the vote. The former mayor of Taipei, Chen Shui-bian, and I won the election with nearly 40 percent, a narrow mandate for reform at the dawn of a new era.

For the die-hard supporters of the Democratic Progressive Party, established in 1986 by the members of Taiwan's opposition movement in violation of a ban on political parties, the triumph of March 18, 2000, had been a long time coming. The Nationalist Party had dominated Taiwan politics since 1945. For thirty-eight years, the Leninist party-state had ruled by imposing martial law and by quashing political dissent, censoring the media, and controlling the judiciary.

Throughout Taiwan's history, foreign powers had attempted to control the fate of the island: the Dutch and Spanish in the seventeenth century, the Manchus in the eighteenth and nineteenth centuries, the Japanese from 1895 to 1945, and the Nationalists after Japan's defeat in World War II. The year 2000 proved no exception, as the Chinese Communists threatened Taiwan with war if Taiwanese voters elected us. Chinese premier Zhu Rongji held a press conference in the final days of the campaign, threatening military invasion if the Taiwanese elected a candidate committed to "any kind of independence" from China.

Although the Chinese Communists have never controlled Taiwan, China claims sovereignty over my country because Taiwanese are ethnically Chinese. Beijing's veiled reference to Chen Shui-bian and me struck fear into the hearts of some voters, but it backfired with many more, who resented China's attempt to control the island's democracy through strong-arm tactics.

Our election victory was the expression of collective aspirations for freedom from the yoke of the Nationalist Party. It was the expression of hope that Taiwan's economy will thrive through new liberalization and administrative efficiency. Fifty-five years of Nationalist rule had resulted in environmental degradation, inadequate transportation networks, complacency and nepotism in the bureaucracy, and a judiciary emasculated by corruption.

This is the story of how Taiwan came to such a crossroad in history, as well as the story of how a girl who was twice nearly given away as a child discovered a love for her country that would change her life. It is the story of how a woman who suffered from cancer, imprisonment, and torture found ways to love her country through democratic politics and to advance the cause of freedom in the world. This is the true story of my life.

CHAPTER 2

TAIWANESE DAUGHTER

WHEN THEY WERE NEWLY MARRIED, FATHER AND MOTHER ONCE came upon an old fortune-teller who, beckoning to them, offered to predict their futures. Father was skeptical, but Mother, who was curious about what the old man might say, wanted to give him a chance.

Peering first into Father's eyes, the fortune-teller said, "You have the fate to have one son." Then he turned to Mother and said, "You have the fate to have three sons." It was an unsettling prediction, but it turned out to be true. Over the years Mother ended up miscarrying two male babies, and my brother Chuan-sheng was the only son who survived.

I was born amid the D-Day news on June 7, 1944. My arrival was certainly less dramatic than a military invasion. If anything, it was something of a disappointment; my parents had been hoping for a boy. They already had two daughters, Hsiu-ching and Hsiu-rong, twelve and fourteen years my senior; and then my brother Chuan-sheng, eight years older than me. If I had been a boy, the family would have been perfect in my parents' eyes—two girls and two boys.

My parents named me Hsiu-lien, or "graceful water lily." From an early age I realized that I had let down my parents by being a girl. When I misbehaved, Mother let her disappointment show by saying things like, "Don't be naughty, or I'll give you away!" or, "Watch out or I'll put you in a trash can!" I wanted to say to them, "You are the ones who made me; it's not that I asked to come here."

We lived in the county of Taoyuan, in northern Taiwan, around twenty-five miles south of the capital of Taipei. My ancestors came from the region of Zhangzhou in Fujian, China. Nearly everyone in the large Lu clan to which I belong is descended from Lu Ting-yu, who immigrated to Taiwan around 1860 with his newly wedded wife. Since then, our family has lived in Taiwan for eight generations and has produced more than seven thousand descendants.

Mostly farmers, my ancestors were poor. My grandfather was a farmer, as was Father until he became a shopkeeper. Father sold salted fish during the Japanese Occupation of Taiwan from 1895 to 1945. In those days most Taiwanese couldn't afford to eat meat, but a little salted fish went a long way when they ate it with rice. With talent for business and sincerity in his dealings with others, Father enjoyed a measure of financial success, eventually expanding the family business to three shops in different towns with the help of partners.

Unlike many couples in their generation, my parents had married for love, rejecting the marriages arranged by their families. When they met, my parents had both already been assigned to their respective intended spouses. Mother was living in the same house with her foster family and husband-to-be. But after meeting each other, my parents refused to go through with marrying their prospective partners. It caused a big scandal, which is why I never heard the full story until both of them had passed away. I'm proud of this family rebelliousness. It explains how they endured years of hardship when our family's fortunes later turned bleak.

In those days it was common in Taiwan to give away a girl to become a *simpua*, or foster daughter, to another family. The girl helped with household chores until she was old enough to marry a foster "brother" in her household. To be a *simpua* was usually a miserable lot. The girl would have to fetch and carry things, labor like a maid, and act very meek and quiet, all from an early age. Several girls in my sixth-grade class of fifty had been adopted out or even sold to other families.

With two daughters already, my parents nearly gave me away as a *simpua*, not once but twice. When I was almost two years old, a friend of Father's wanted to adopt me because the man and his wife had no children. As a toddler I had big, round, pink cheeks, and because of that, people called me Ringo, the Japanese word for *apple*. The wife once saw me and said, "What a pretty girl you have! I wish she were mine." Father responded half jokingly, "You can have her! I already have two daughters."

The couple took his offer seriously. After a few days they sent a go-between to ask my parents again. Of course they would have preferred to have a son, but people believed this kind of daughter-in-law adoption, called a "lead in," encouraged the spirit of a baby boy to follow. After carefully considering the cost of raising another daughter, Mother agreed to allow the adoption. The couple sent over the first round of gifts, including traditional cakes made of popped rice.

When my brother and sisters heard about the planned adoption, they hatched a plot to save me. Brother, who must have been about ten years old, grabbed me when Mother wasn't looking and carried me off to the home of an aunt living in the countryside. The agreement had been made, engagement gifts received, but I was nowhere to be found. Brother was missing too; for an entire day we hid. Finally Eldest Sister told Mother what they had done. The other family, seeing how much my siblings loved me, called off the adoption, and my parents returned the gifts.

The second time I was almost given away was a few years later. Our family's finances had improved, but the interested party was a wealthy neighboring doctor. Mother believed that I would have an easier life as their only daughter. But as discussions between our two families dragged on, the doctor decided to adopt one of his brother's daughters instead.

When I was an infant, Japan still ruled Taiwan. Most Japanese looked down on Taiwanese, calling us *Shi na*, which is comparable to the epithet "Chink" in English. So when there was talk of Taiwan reverting back to Chinese rule at the end of World War II, people felt hopeful and optimistic, thinking, "At long last we will have self-rule and equality!"

High expectations led to tragic disappointment. Chiang Kai-shek, accepting Japan's surrender of Taiwan on behalf of General Douglas MacArthur, sent the dregs of his army to Taiwan. Chiang needed his best commanders and troops to remain in China to continue fighting the Communists. As stories circulated of how the new arrivals pillaged and raped, confiscating private property and mistreating people, Taiwanese enthusiasm for Chinese rule vanished.

I was almost three years old when strife between Taiwanese, demonstrating for autonomy, and Chinese troops, cracking down on dissidence, engulfed the island in violence. Chiang Kai-shek sent thirty thousand soldiers to Taiwan, where they put down unrest by spraying crowds of civilians with machine gun fire. Under orders to eliminate resistance from the island's elite, the troops dragged intellectuals from their homes and herded them together for mass executions. Thousands disappeared and an entire generation was silenced. The Taiwanese uprising and the ensuing massacre carried out by Chinese soldiers is known as the "2-28 Incident," named for the first day of Taiwanese protests on February 28, 1947.

Mother was attending a wedding ceremony in Hsinchu, with Eldest Sister and me, when news of widespread rioting reached the wedding banquet. Nervous and frightened, everyone made plans to leave, only to find that all bus and train service had been suspended. Mother had to walk all the way home to Taoyuan with me wrapped in a cloth on her back—a hilly two-day journey covering a distance of forty miles. Later, she would scold me by saying, "If I had known you would be this bad, I would have left you by the roadside, rather than carry you all the way back to Taoyuan!"

Two years after the 2-28 Incident, the Nationalists lost the civil war on the Chinese mainland, and Chiang Kai-shek and two million Chinese fled to Taiwan. Chiang called his new regime in Taiwan "Free China" to contrast with the Communist-led People's Republic of China. Chiang claimed that his government was the sole legitimate representative of all of China.

The bitter truth, however, was that "Free China" was neither free nor in China. Chiang imposed martial law in Taiwan in May 1949. The Nationalists justified this by claiming that China's "period of Communist rebellion" put Taiwan in a constant "state of siege." Under martial law, citizens could be arbitrarily sentenced to prison for vague offenses that "threatened the internal security of the state" or public order and safety. Through its network of agents and informants, the military's Garrison Command carried out political surveillance, repression of dissent, and social control.

While I attended elementary school, Nationalist-sponsored thought control was little noticed but a very strong influence on the island's children. Primary school textbooks and lessons extolled the virtues of Sun Yat-sen (the founder of the Republic of China on the mainland) and Chiang Kai-shek. These men were portrayed as saints, while the Chinese Communists led by Mao Zedong, Liu Shaoqi, and Zhou Enlai were considered monsters. The Nationalist government was obsessed with the goal of *fangong fuguo*, that is, counterattacking the Communists and recovering the mainland.

My earliest memories are of when we lived at the intersection of Peach Garden Street and Eternal Peace Avenue. Behind our house ran a small lane, where there was always a great bustle, with women leaning out of the windows and drunken men singing in the middle of the night. It wasn't until later that I learned the reason for all the activity: brothels lined the lane. We had some country relatives whose daughters were prostitutes; after checking on their daughters, they often stopped by to visit Mother.

I loved running up and down the lane and chatting with all the "aunties" there. I must have been about five years old. Soon everyone was calling me the little storyteller, because I would retell the stories that my sisters and brother told me, acting out the different parts. For such a little girl, they said, I sure talked a lot.

By the time I was nine years old, Father had saved a little money and was able to build a house behind an important social hub in town, Jingfu Temple. Located on a traffic circle in the center of town, the temple overlooked the road that came out from the railroad station plaza. On one side of our house was a movie theater, and on the other was the city market, where farmers and merchants carted in fresh vegetables and cages full of chickens and ducks. At first our home had only one floor, with a makeshift second floor where we ate. The store was in front and we lived in back. Later, when business was better,

Father added a second floor, and then a third. It was fairly prestigious at the time to have a three-story concrete house, though I never felt like our family was rich.

Father had dropped out of Japanese primary school at an early age because his family needed his help working in the fields. I remember him as very thin, with deep-set eyes, closely cropped black hair, and a severe expression on his face. This stern exterior concealed the warmth of his heart. Even though Father hadn't had much formal education, he had taught himself how to read Chinese characters and knew a great deal about Chinese literature. Sitting on his knee, I listened to him recite proverbs and tell stories that taught me how to be a good human being. "Teeth are to be used as gold" was one of Father's favorite sayings. He believed that the mouth we speak with is what others will know us by. We must be very conscientious about the words we use, he said, as our actions must achieve what we promise.

Father frequently traveled to Yilan and Keelung in northern Taiwan to buy fish. On one trip he saw a crowd of people standing around a large sea turtle for sale. The auctioneer was shouting, "Five hundred yuan, six hundred!" Father thought the turtle seemed so sad and pitiful, looking up at the crowd, about to go from the auction block to the chopping block. Turtle soup is a Taiwanese delicacy. On impulse, he decided to bid for it and won the auction. Then, in front of everyone, Father released the turtle back into the sea.

In addition to stressing the importance of ethics, Father gave me vision and ambition. He often kept the shop open while I used his desk to do my elementary school homework. Many fathers at that time discouraged their daughters from studying too much, but Father was supportive of my intellectual development and read articles from the newspaper aloud to me, analyzing political events and international affairs.

Mother was a very conservative, if somewhat nontraditional, Taiwanese woman. In my memory she always looks old-fashioned, a small woman dressed in a well-fitting, long, dark-colored *qipao* dress that covers her shoulders but leaves her arms exposed. She was superstitious and prone to irrational fears, but Mother was strong and loving. While Father minded the shop, Mother traveled to southern Taiwan to handle a variety of business transactions. Sometimes she took me with her. We rode the slow train to save money on fares, and she would drop me off with my grandmother in the town of Chiayi before attending to business. Although Mother took equally good care of household matters, she would tell my sisters, "In our family, women not only do housekeeping but man's business!"

Mother discouraged my elder sisters from continuing their education, because she believed that a woman's best fate was to be married into a good family. When I started to do well at school, Father became very proud. He boasted to his friends, "Don't think she's just a little girl. She has the best grades in her elementary school." Mother replied by saying, "What difference does it make for girls?" To her, girls were married off and left the family.

At school it was easy to see differences between myself and wealthier schoolmates. I didn't own a pair of shoes until third grade. The richer girls in primary school not only wore shoes but could afford tutorials with our teacher. Knowing he would get paid extra, our teacher saved the best material for these after-class sessions. During the day, I served as his student assistant, and once he ordered me to switch the grades between a girl from a poor family and a girl whose father was the speaker of the county council. I was furious, and though I obeyed, I told all my classmates what had happened. The teacher accused me of lying. For several days I refused to attend school, until Brother spoke to my teacher and managed to smooth things over.

Just as Japan had imposed its own language during the Japanese Occupation, the Nationalists asserted control by making standard Chinese (Mandarin) the lingua franca and banning the use of Taiwanese, Hakka, and aboriginal languages. Only two Taiwanese songs could air on TV and radio each day, and there could be no more than two hours of programming in Taiwanese. The rest had to be in standard Chinese.

Because of state censorship no one had a complete picture of what went on in society. Whispered rumors circulated in what became known as the bamboo telegraph. There was a Taiwanese saying, "You children have ears and no mouths." Under authoritarian rule, parents seldom mentioned politics, to keep children from repeating what their parents said in private and unknowingly get the family into trouble.

Beginning in elementary school, these restrictions and China-centric education slowly affected who I was and what I believed in. I believed wholeheartedly the Nationalist line that reunifying China and Taiwan was a glorious objective. I had no clearly defined sense of Taiwanese identity, although it bothered me that during speech contests my pronunciation of Chinese was not as good as that of my teachers from the mainland.

In primary school in Taoyuan we were required to speak standard Chinese, even though we spoke Taiwanese outside of class. If children were caught speaking Taiwanese in school, they had to pay a fine, a harsh penalty when most of Taiwan was poor. Even worse, as class leader, I had to enforce this rule when I felt awkward speaking Chinese myself.

Since they were so much older, my sisters helped Mother raise me. They taught me skills like sewing, knitting, and cooking. Eldest Sister, already in her twenties when I attended elementary school, had suffered from serious asthma and other illnesses as a child. Because our family wasn't wealthy, it made sense to have her stay at home and help around the house after completing only primary school. Mother didn't want Eldest Sister to marry, so she could take care of my parents as they aged. In fact, Eldest Sister didn't marry until age forty, late in life by Taiwanese standards.

Second Sister married early. She was very smart and had the chance to go to Taipei to study. But Mother was adamant that a girl could not go to Taipei alone, even for school. Second Sister liked to dress up very fashionably, sometimes wearing sunglasses. She kept mainlanders as friends in spite of ethnic tensions with native Taiwanese. Second Sister was what people at the time would call a "black cat" or a "butterfly." Paranoid that she might get into trouble, Mother wanted to marry her off as quickly as possible. So when she was twenty, Mother arranged a wedding for her with a government clerk. Because Second

Sister had a great talent for entrepreneurship, she and her husband stayed on to help Father until quarrels drove them from the family home. Father bought them a shop in which they ran their own business. They lived on the outskirts of Taoyuan, so Second Sister wasn't around much when I was growing up.

Of all my siblings, Brother played the most pivotal role in my youth. He was my childhood protector, inspiration, and role model. My greatest hope was to bring my parents as much happiness as he did. Typical of Taiwanese families, my parents had dreamed that Brother would become a doctor. So naturally I wanted to become a doctor, too. When I was about nine years old, I contracted whooping cough. Brother, then seventeen, took my prescription to a pharmacy to get it filled. Instead of improving after taking the medicine, I got much worse and my skin broke out in black blotches. We later found out that the pharmacy had dispensed placebos containing dangerous ingredients instead of real medicine. I recovered eventually. But after this experience, Brother became disillusioned with the medical profession and decided to become a lawyer to fight such wrongdoing.

I loved being with Brother as much as I wanted to be like him. He let me tag along with him when he went hiking with friends in nearby mountains. On the way, Brother told me stories about famous people in Chinese and Western history, including George Washington, Abe Lincoln, Confucius, and Sun Yat-sen. None of them were women, and most of them were politicians. The idea of aspiring to become a politician as great as they were became deeply embedded in my young heart. I totally forgot that I was not a man and incapable of similar achievements.

On our hikes there was a place where we had to cross a stream by hopping from stone to stone. The water was filled with snakes, and though they weren't poisonous, there were so many, you could see them swimming around. The first time we crossed the stream, Brother carried me over on his back. But when we came to the stream again on the way home, he said to me, "You must jump across by yourself." I stood there for a moment, gathering courage before leaping onto one stone, and then the next, before making it across. This event serves as a metaphor for my relationship with Brother. He gave me courage by leading the way and supported my efforts to tackle difficult challenges.

When I reached my final year in elementary school, I announced my desire to attend middle school in Taipei. Mother resisted at first, viewing the commute to Taipei as improper for a young girl. A debate raged around the dinner table for weeks. Second Sister, having missed the opportunity herself because of Mother's objections, weighed in on my behalf. Mother gave up in the end because Father and Brother, who was already attending school in the capital, strongly supported me. Then, I successfully passed the entrance exam to the prestigious Taipei First Girls' Middle School.

It took Mother twenty years of hard work to put Brother and me through school in Taipei. Every morning she got up at 4:00 A.M. to light a cooking fire with charcoal or wood in order to prepare lunch boxes. She insisted that we have breakfast before we got on the train to Taipei. She would cook an egg for Brother, and he would leave half of it for me. I left half of what he gave me for Mother. Every day Mother insisted on seeing us off on the 5:30 A.M. train, and she met us at the train station every night when we returned from school.

At Taipei First Girls' Middle School, I came into contact with many wealthy Chinese girls, whose families had been landed gentry in China and had come to Taiwan with Chiang Kai-shek after his forces lost the Chinese Civil War. This second wave of mainlanders had more money and better manners than the carpetbaggers and murderers who clashed with Taiwanese in the 2-28 Incident. The wealthy Chinese also had a greater sense of superiority vis-à-vis Taiwanese. To me, the mainlander girls I attended middle and high school with in Taipei were polished and worldly. Their fathers typically held important government jobs. Father, by comparison, was a shopkeeper, and though respectable in Taoyuan, our home was modest compared with my classmates' carpeted and air-conditioned houses in Taipei. Though these girls sometimes invited me to their homes, it was years before I felt comfortable enough to reciprocate.

I had also reached an age when I felt very self-conscious about my physical appearance. The many pimples I developed in high school made this even worse. I was shy and ill at ease around boys. The way Mother raised me didn't make it any easier. Afraid I would go out with boyfriends and neglect my studies, she severely restricted my social activities. Mother even controlled what I wore, buying serious, severe-looking clothes for me that, though cut from good material, were always plain and in dark colors like black, navy blue, or brown.

I was clumsy as well. Once I tried to learn how to ride a bicycle, but a truck sideswiped me the first time I ventured beyond our lane. Mother saw this and her renewed anxiety made me even more nervous. "If you really have the potential, you will become an important person," she said. "Then you can hire a chauffeur! Don't let me see you risking your life riding a bicycle!" So that was that. I never excelled at sports.

The body and sex, in particular, were mysterious topics. Many people believed that women, particularly when menstruating, were dirty. Women who had their periods could not visit Buddhist temples. To do so would offend the gods. It could also bring a man bad luck if he touched, or even saw, women's undergarments; we had to watch where we hung them up to dry. Women washed their clothes separately, because men's clothes could be tainted by contact with women's clothes.

Back then, people in rural villages didn't usually have toilet paper. They used slightly processed and flattened pieces of bamboo shavings to wipe themselves after going to the bathroom. You'd see stacks of bamboo shavings smeared with feces in country outhouses. Even in town we only had a very rough sort of toilet paper that wasn't soft or sanitary enough for prolonged use next to the body. That's how women came to use old garments cut into pieces and sewn in layers as menstrual pads. Heaven forbid that a man should have to see or touch one of these pads. We carefully kept them out of sight.

Our parents and teachers taught us that girls should avoid getting too close to men "to avoid trouble." Just what kind of trouble this was, most schoolgirls could not even begin to imagine. Once I read a satire by the famous essayist Lin Yu-tang that perfectly captured how skewed the attitudes regarding sex were at that time. Confucius had said that food and sex are both human nature. Inspired by this, Lin wrote that our ancestors had felt that food should be partaken of openly but that sex should be hidden behind closed doors, and he asked, what if these two were reversed? He brilliantly and sardonically contrasted two stereotypes: Western artlessness with food but celebration of sensuality, and Chinese denigration of sexual indulgence but flourishing culinary arts. Lin's point was that if both are human nature, why should either be taboo?

In high school, I kept busy with pen pals overseas instead of with boys. One day my English teacher came into class and gave us the assignment of writing to a hypothetical pen pal in the United States. After she corrected our grammatical mistakes, she asked anyone who wanted to have a real pen pal to sign up. The teacher, who had taught in Ohio, arranged for us to exchange letters with students at her former school. A girl named Gail Homstad became a lifelong friend, as did another pen pal living in Maryland, Karyl Bookwalter. I was soon exchanging letters and gifts with young friends in Germany, Belgium, and Nigeria. At one point, I maintained correspondence with nine different pen pals. This correspondence sparked my imagination and nurtured a desire to learn more about the countries in which my friends lived. Most Taiwanese were not allowed to travel abroad in those days. Having pen pals was as close to experiencing foreign lands as I could get. Our curiosity piqued and unquenched by these early contacts, my high school friends and I tried to meet foreigners in Taiwan. Once we went looking for an American 4-H Club representative we wanted to try out our English on, walking for hours in vain in rural Taoyuan County.

I remember the day Brother passed the entrance examination to the law department at National Taiwan University—an honor shared by very few students from Taoyuan. Friends and family came together to feast and light off firecrackers. Later that evening Father asked me, "Hsiu-lien, do you want to go to college, too?" I was then sixteen years old. "Of course I want to!" I replied, eager as always to follow in Brother's footsteps.

Instantly, Father seemed to have some misgivings. "By the time you get out of college, you'll be twenty-three years old," he said. "That's not very good for marriage, you know." His concern puzzled me. If Brother could finish college before worrying about getting married, why couldn't I?

After Brother's success gaining admission to National Taiwan University, I never doubted that I would attend college. For me the question was which one, and this would be wholly determined by how well I scored on the entrance examinations. Students spent their entire senior year of high school cramming for these exams. Graded anonymously, and given yearly on a nationwide basis, the tests gave no one an undue advantage. Girls had an equal chance.

I had to fill out a long application, listing my preferences for department and university. Only a small percentage of those who took the examination were admitted into any college. This meant that if I scored poorly, I might end up not attending university and faced with some humbling choices.

My high school literature teacher wanted me to study literature or history. My guidance counselor wanted me to choose political science. At one point I considered library science, so I could be surrounded by books all day. But, as always, I followed Brother's example, and he had chosen law. My first and second choices were National Taiwan University Law Department and National Taiwan University Department of Political Science.

The day after the examination, the newspaper published the correct answers to the test. Using these, I determined that I had scored 433 points, one more point than I had predicted. Everything depended on my ranking relative to others who had taken the exam. I told my parents I had done poorly. Father said I could take the examination again next year. Mother said I could do something besides study, meaning get married. One month after the exam, the test takers' names were announced on the radio in the order of ranking. I heard "National Taiwan University . . . Law Department . . . Lu Hsiu-lien. . . ." I stood in the living room dumbfounded—I was at the top of the class! I would enter the same school and department as Brother.

Fifty-seven people enrolled in the law department my year—

twenty-nine men and twenty-eight women. It was a surprisingly balanced number, perhaps because the male students felt the "hard" sciences like engineering held more promise for employment. Like me, most of the women in my department came from the top two high schools in Taiwan, the Taipei First and Taipei Second Girls' High Schools. This meant I was surrounded by sophisticated mainlander women. The majority of the men grew up in central and south Taiwan. Not very articulate, they had a guileless country air. They chose law because they wanted to become judges and lawyers in Taiwan, roles monopolized by the Japanese in the past, and later by mainlanders.

During the first class on constitutional law, the professor took a look at the students and exclaimed indignantly, "This many women in law class! There will be revolution under heaven!" As it turned out, in the second year about ten women switched to other departments. To me the women seemed more concerned with finding a husband than getting the best education. A college degree amounted to a generous dowry, and some women thought it would help them find a better mate. They spent more time dating, dressing up, and experimenting with cosmetics than they did studying. I kept in mind the idea of achieving something I thought of as "higher and better." I didn't make a conscious point of challenging traditional gender roles. I studied hard, maintained good marks in my classes, and wrote articles for publication in the university newspaper, gaining a reputation as an outspoken, industrious student.

After seeing an advertisement in the school paper that a Taiwanese PhD candidate in France was seeking to befriend female students at his alma mater, I picked up a pen and wrote out of curiosity. When a postcard arrived from France two months later, I had nearly forgotten the matter. "Frank" was a graduate of the law department at National Taiwan University. Frank was not his real name but the English-language name he used. He must have received many responses, because he replied by sea mail to save money. I later heard from him more and more frequently. We wrote longer letters and exchanged photographs. The postcards of different cities that Frank visited in Europe fueled my romantic fantasies. Though we never used Western-style endearments, we developed a genuine intimacy through correspondence.

About this time I experienced my first academic setback, a serious blow to my confidence. I had taken it upon myself to beat Brother's exam record by passing a series of qualifying exams to become a judge while still in university. I took the first exam one year prior to entering university. I was still wearing my high school uniform, and people thought I had wandered into the wrong room.

After passing the first five exams, I was stopped short at exam number six. I failed it, not once but also a second time—with a slightly lower score. I couldn't believe it. My world had come to an end! I cried for three days with my head under my quilt. I missed passing the exam by just a few points. Then, I got angry. The test, on standard Chinese language, was in essay form, and I felt it couldn't possibly be scored objectively. Usually the judgeship exam lasts three hours and consists of writing essays, a task requiring not only clarity of thought but good handwriting. Beautiful handwriting and brush calligraphy are viewed with special significance in Chinese culture. I have always had sloppy handwriting, in part due to a dysfunctional thyroid gland that was not discovered for another decade. The thyroid symptoms included the inability to hold a pen firmly enough in my fingers to write well, leading to poorer marks on the exam.

The taste of failure was bitter, but the experience of failing was very good for me. I'd believed that I could achieve any goal that I set for myself if I worked hard enough. After the qualifying exam, I realized that many things are beyond my control. Besides, how could I expect to always be number one? Failure forced me to rethink future plans. My pen pals had sparked in me fancies of visiting the United States or Europe, or of serving as a diplomat in Africa. Frank, the Taiwanese student studying in France, was pressuring me to travel to Europe so we could see more of each other. The combined allure of living overseas and romance made me take the idea of studying abroad seriously. The biggest obstacle to going overseas wasn't money; I realized that I could probably win a scholarship. It was my family. Relentlessly protective, Mother resisted having any of her children leave her sight for long. Allowing me to leave the country was for her unthinkable.

Also, Father's health was failing. He had asthma and digestive problems related to a bout of cholera he had contracted in his youth. During my final year at National Taiwan University, I hinted to Father of my desire to go overseas. "It is very good that you go abroad to further your studies and develop your future," he said. "Only, when you come back, you may not be able to see Father."

Father's gentle and liberal demeanor had always made my sisters and me feel closer to him than to Mother. I knew that as an uneducated and simple shopkeeper, to the outside world he wasn't anyone important. But he was a hero to me for his kindness and integrity. An enthusiastic supporter of the politicians opposing Nationalist rule, Father encouraged me to examine issues from a variety of perspectives and to seek an alternative to dictatorial rule in Taiwan.

After graduation, I worked briefly at a newspaper while I helped to take care of Father at home. For a short while we felt optimistic about his health, and Brother went so far as to order him a new car. At that time hardly anyone had cars, but Brother's law practice was doing well, and he wanted to drive Father around in comfort. Father's condition worsened. He had to be hospitalized in Taipei. I quit my job and began sleeping on the floor next to his hospital bed. Father's stay in the hospital lasted two weeks; he took a handful of pills with every meal. At last the doctor said he was well enough that we could take him home. Brother went to pay the bill and I went to pick up prescriptions. But when we returned to Father's room, he had fallen unconscious. Everyone panicked and ran to find the doctor. The interns didn't know what to do. Mother arrived at the hospital as nurses attempted to resuscitate Father.

A patient in another bed asked me in a low tone, "Did you ever think to give the doctor a *hongbao*?" I was shocked. A *hongbao*, or red envelope containing money, is the customary way of expressing gratitude or sympathy. But it had never occurred to me that the doctor at a public hospital would expect a bribe. We had very little cash left in our pockets. "Hurry up and go to the doctors' dormitories behind the hospital grounds. You'll probably find the doctor there," the patient said. We found the head doctor eating a snack in the canteen. He gave us excuses and said he had other things to do. "You have other things to do while my father is dying?" I asked in disbelief. Brother shoved the *hongbao* into his hands, and the doctor changed his tune, saying that he would come right away. We went back to the hospital, but the head doctor didn't come for another two hours, and then only to say that he would consult with the other medical staff. Probably we hadn't given him enough money. Finally, at 11 o'clock at night, another doctor came and told us what we feared. There was little that could be done.

Taiwanese believe very strongly that a person must die at home. If you are fortunate enough to do so, this means that you led a just and good life. If you die away from home, it is said you "died on the road" before you could return, and you must have sinned. Mother insisted that we take Father home immediately. He was completely unconscious.

Around 1 o'clock in the morning, Brother called a taxi, and we rode back to Taoyuan, cradling Father in our arms. Just by chance, the taxi passed by the presidential palace. The tall central tower and north and south wings of the palace were brightly adorned with lights left over from the Lunar New Year holiday. To me, the garish decoration seemed to mock our sorrow. By no means could Father have ever imagined that his youngest daughter would move into the presidential palace thirty-two years later. We arrived home in the early hours of Sunday morning and gently placed Father on the floor and covered him with a blanket. As if he had held out until that moment, Father breathed his last, and his spirit left us with no more sound than a sigh. He was sixty-seven years old.

In a Confucian society the male line is central, which means that the rituals for men and women at funerals differ widely. Married daughters, since they leave the family, are treated like water that has been dumped out. A married daughter mourning for her own parents has to cry, literally, in the streets. She starts wailing loudly some distance from the funeral location and shrieks as she enters the site, as if she is proclaiming for all to hear: "I was not home when you died. I didn't take care of you. You gave me life, but I left you."

Taiwanese believe that in the first week after death, the soul lingers around the body. The son helps to perform ceremonies that permit the soul to begin its journey. If he (or if there is no son, the male relative closest to a son) does not perform these rites, the soul will wander aimless and hungry in the netherworld. Daughters and their husbands and other relatives take over these duties in the following weeks, when the body is placed in an elaborately decorated coffin, coated with lacquer in black and red designs. Incense is packed inside around the body. Then an astrologer chooses a date for the funeral, usually one week to two months after death.

All these preparations require a large amount of crying, both to show grief and to scare away spirits that might steal food set out for the deceased. At first you really cry, and your throat chokes up and your eyes swell. Later on, you cannot cry anymore, but you still go through the motions of grief. Over the course of the period of mourning, while my siblings all returned to their jobs and daily lives, I was at home crying three times a day for one hundred days. In the middle of the night, Mother wept with her head on the coffin and I wept with her. Sometimes memories of Father brought genuine tears. But I also had to cry together with the relatives when they came to mourn. If I did not wail on these occasions, I was not a good daughter.

After weeks of this my ears began to buzz. The sound of weeping rang in my ears. No wonder people would later hire professional mourners. Some people have even used tape-recorded sounds of crying to "feed" the spirits three times a day! Father's death, as painful as it was, made me realize that some traditional ceremonies are out of sync with modern life. Most people follow them superficially, out of a sense of social propriety.

While mourning for Father, I felt a certain release from family bondage and freedom from pressure that I should attempt to imitate Brother's achievements. The dream of life abroad persisted, and I applied for two scholarships: one for nine months at the University of Amsterdam that would allow me to meet with Frank in France, and another to fund study for an LLM degree at the University of Illinois. I also secretly registered to take the entrance exam to attend graduate school in law at National Taiwan University. I didn't tell anyone about the latter because I was afraid that I would fail, having only two weeks to study after the hundred-day mourning period. Surprisingly, I was one of eighteen out of ninety-eight applicants admitted and once again received the top score.

The more that I pursued my own ambitions, the greater pressure I felt to get married. In my first two years at university, teachers and counselors had encouraged scholastic achievement. As time went on, however, they began to ask more frequently, "Do you have a boyfriend yet?" I could hear in their questions the echo of Mother's reminders: "For girls, it doesn't do any good to study so much. It's best to find a husband. Marriage is your sanctuary."

I did want to get married, at least in the abstract sense, and my whole family busied themselves with finding a suitable match for me. They took great pains to introduce me to a physics student studying in Germany. It was during the man's visit home. My sister-in-law set it up. The meeting didn't really come to anything, and I left with the feeling that awkward arranged meetings seemed ill suited for finding a lifelong partner.

Many men in Taiwan's social elite capped off their education with graduate degrees abroad. A man tried to find a bride during visits home, would decide to marry a woman after two or three meetings, and then would correspond with his bride-to-be while finishing up his studies. Marriage happened on another visit home. This type of union seemed overly superficial and utilitarian to me; in a newspaper article, I once called the dating practice "catching little chickens."

I wanted to achieve my own goals before getting married, ideally to a man who supported me as much as I did him. It seemed difficult to find such a partner among my acquaintances, and so I had paid scant attention to my classmates at National Taiwan University. At a reunion that I hosted in the presidential palace three decades later, several blushing classmates admitted they had been attracted to me but had been too intimidated to ask me out on a date. Another one said that he had even written me a love letter revealing his crush on me but that I had rejected his advance. Honestly speaking, I don't remember receiving such a letter, but I do remember one classmate whose affections I had been too timid to reciprocate.

My beau via international mail, Frank, had an elder sister who was married to a diplomat. When she and her husband came back from assignment in Lebanon, they invited me to dinner at their home in the diplomatic residence section of Peitou, a beautiful suburb of Taipei. She prepared a formal dinner just for me. It was a friendly meeting, but I returned home feeling queasy. I knew that the conversation, while relaxed, had been a very important one. Soon I got a letter of congratulations from Frank saying his sister had approved of me. Frank said he was willing to pay for my airplane ticket to Europe. To demonstrate his family's support of our relationship, Frank's father and mother made a special trip from Hualien on the east coast to see me in Taoyuan. After traveling for hours, his parents murmured a few polite phrases when they met me and said they would like me to accept an airplane ticket to go to visit their son in France. I wrote to Frank in France, telling him that I had won a scholarship to study in Amsterdam and explaining that I would secure the means myself to meet him in Europe. Delighted, Frank replied that he would arrive in Amsterdam before me, and wait for me at the Amsterdam train station at noon every day until we met. At the time, it seemed like a logical plan.

Prior to applying for the fellowship to study in Europe, I had entered another competition, to study in the United States. The scholarship was offered by the Li Foundation in New York, which granted one fellowship for two years of graduate study to the most distinguished graduate of National Taiwan University. Only those with the top scores in each department could apply. The winner was decided by a lengthy battery of written and oral exams.

Late one night about two weeks before I was scheduled to leave for Europe, I received a special-delivery letter from the president of National Taiwan University, requesting that I go to see him in Taipei as soon as possible. He informed me that, through a serendipitous series of events, the Li Foundation scholarship had been awarded to me. The original recipient had decided at the last minute to marry her boyfriend instead of accepting the scholarship. The first runner-up lived in Hong Kong, and it turned out he had skipped his two-year mandatory military duty in Taiwan and was ineligible. Suddenly, as I was to leave for Europe, this marvelous opportunity had appeared. Quickly, I made arrangements to reactivate my application to the University of Illinois, which had admitted me to a master's degree program in comparative legal studies.

Despite the scholarship's prestige, Mother remained adamantly opposed to my going abroad. Just one year had passed since Father's death. She was weakened physically and emotionally. On top of this, Mother was desperately afraid of being abandoned by her children. I was the youngest, and despite Eldest Sister's living at home, my leaving would be symbolic that the last of her children had grown up and abandoned her to old age.

Mother could accept a daughter departing from home only for marriage. Brother and an uncle who had always been proud of my achievements tried to help me assuage Mother's fears. But when she saw the luggage I had purchased, she became hysterical. "I raised you to an adult with so much labor, and now you don't want me! You are going to fly away like a bird and never come back!" she wailed. It was no use trying to convince her that I would return. Trends in Taiwan justified her fears: 90 percent of National Taiwan University graduates went abroad to study. Many found good jobs overseas and only returned for family visits.

Then one morning Mother disappeared. She had never been the same since Father had died, hardly ever leaving the house. By nightfall I was frantic. We searched the neighborhood and asked all the pedicab drivers in our area whether they had taken an old woman of her description anywhere that morning. We called the police. One distraught relative even consulted a spirit medium at a temple. The spirit medium said he saw an old woman with her hair flowing wildly in the breeze and walking by the seashore weeping. So Brother drove to the nearest coastal town, searched through the temple there, and asked the street vendors if anyone had seen Mother. Many people knew Mother because our shop had been in business near the main market in Taoyuan for many years; no one had seen her. Finally a cousin called to say that Mother was staying with an aunt who, feeling similarly abandoned by her own son, had goaded Mother into giving the family a scare. I went immediately to bring her back. I had to acknowledge Mother's authority and demonstrate my love for her. I also wanted to gain her blessing before leaving the country.

Brother, Eldest Sister, and I decided to pretend we had just happened to look for Mother at our aunt's house. Though we couldn't see Mother when we arrived, we knew that she could probably hear us from somewhere within the small house. Speaking to our aunt, we recounted in detail our concern and frantic search and told her that Mother's name had even been broadcast over the police radio network, which was true. After hearing our story, the aunt relented and opened the door to a back room and asked Mother to step out. Mother, who had been listening throughout and wanting to maintain her self-respect, launched into a tirade against me. She didn't agree with my plans to study in America, but I knew that our words and efforts had placated her.

As I prepared to fly to the United States, and not to the Netherlands, a deep anguish filled my heart. Frank had already left for our rendezvous in Amsterdam. I knew that he would be waiting for me every day at noon in front of the train station. Neither his parents in Hualien nor I had his address or telephone number in Holland. I had no way to tell Frank that I couldn't meet him there.

Lu Hsiu-lien at age five.

Lu Hsiu-lien's father (front row, right) and his three brothers.

The exterior of the Lu family store in Taoyuan (left), with farmers in the foreground bringing agricultural products to sell at a nearby market.

Second Sister (Lu Hsiu-ching, left) and Eldest Sister (Lu Hsiu-rong).

Lu in her graduation
photo from National
Taiwan University.

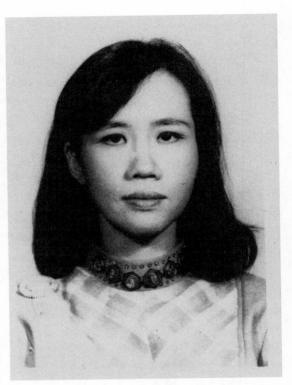

Lu in 1971, when she launched Taiwan's feminist movement.

Lu in 1978, when she returned to Taiwan from the United States to run for a seat in the National Assembly.

Lu speaking to demonstrators in Kaohsiung on the night of the Kaohsiung Incident.

一九七九年美麗島軍法大審辯護律師群

有公道的立法，才有公道的社會

來，蘇貞昌和大家一起來打拼。

The legal defense team at the 1979 *Formosa Magazine* trial. The large banner reads, "Only through justice in law does a society have justice."

LU HSIU-LIEN/ANNETTE LU

is Taiwan's most-noted advocate of women's rights. In this photograph she is shown celebrating her birthday with the Prime Minister of Taiwan, now the President, Chiang Ching-kuo.

Ms. Lu earned a Masters of Law degree from Harvard University in 1978. In December 1979, she was arrested in Taiwan after speaking at a Human Rights Day celebration. Her last words were: "We who are here today struggling for human rights, must give our utmost for our homeland." For that speech and other political activities, Ms. Lu was detained, mistreated, charged with "seditious intent," tried by a military court and sentenced to 12 years in prison.

One side of a preprinted postcard sent by Amnesty International supporters to ROC president Chiang Ching-kuo, calling for Lu Hsiu-lien's release from prison.

Date: _____

I have learned that Lu Hsiu-lien was sentenced to 12 years in prison and 10 years denial of civil rights for speaking at a Human Rights Day rally in 1979 and for other political activities, although it has been confirmed that she did not use or advocate violence. Her detention is in violation of the basic rights guaranteed by the U.N. Declaration of Human Rights, Articles 19 and 20.

I urge you to use your good will and authority to free her now.

              Sincerely,

Name: _____

Address: _____

_____

13¢ USA

28¢ Overseas

President Chiang Ching-kuo
Office of the President
Chieh Shou Hall
Chungking S. Road
Taipei, Taiwan
Republic of China

AIR MAIL

Reverse side of the postcard sent by Amnesty International supporters hoping to secure Lu's release from prison.

Lu at an Amnesty International gathering in 1986,
wearing a dress she had knitted in prison.

Lu Hsiu-lien with Eldest Sister (right) after release from prison.

Lu with villagers at her family's ancestral home in China in 1990.

CHAPTER 3

LIFTING HALF THE SKY

SO MUCH HAD HAPPENED SO FAST. ALMOST BEFORE I COULD reflect on the new direction my life had taken, the plane touched down in Chicago's O'Hare airport, where a university classmate, Chen Hen-chieh, waited to greet me. I had arrived in America. During the car ride to the University of Illinois at Urbana-Champaign, my classmate briefed me on the campus dynamics. Several hundred Taiwanese and Hong Kong students studied at the university, one of the largest ethnically Chinese student populations in the United States. There were no students from the People's Republic.

Classmate Chen told me that I could stay in the apartment building where he lived with several other Asian students. My conception of America had been shaped by movies and magazine photographs of large houses, flashy cars, and beautiful people. When I saw Chen's apartment, I was appalled. Old, small, and dilapidated, the rooms were no better than any I had seen in Taiwan. Chen dropped me off at an apartment shared by several Chinese women, one of whom popped her head out of a room to say, "It's very late now and we have to go to class tomorrow. Yes, it's inconvenient here and too crowded." Then she darted back inside like the White Rabbit in *Alice in Wonderland*. I felt a bit like Alice myself, as I realized that I was alone in a bewilderingly foreign environment without any relatives or close friends around. I decided to move into university dormitory housing the next day.

The master's degree program I entered was comparative law, my intention being to compare Taiwan's legal system with its American counterpart. I threw myself into course work to stave off loneliness. At night I heard a Haitian girl crying in the room next to mine, and sometimes we shed tears together, from opposite sides of the wall.

I often thought of Frank. In the whirlwind of leaving Taiwan, I had been unable to contact him. All I could do was write a letter to his empty dorm room back in Lyons, the only address I had. Some months after I arrived in the United States, Frank's reply came in the mail. "I waited every day until I only had enough money to take the train back to Lyons," he wrote. "Even though I understand your choice I feel betrayed." I wrote back to him and apologized again and again, saying his understanding meant very much to me.

We agreed to meet in New York City at Christmas before making any decisions about a future together. It was 1969 and I was twenty-five years old. After two years of correspondence we would finally meet in person. On the flight to New York I fussed with my hair and makeup repeatedly. I worried that he might not find me attractive enough, and wondered how this encounter might change my life.

When I walked off the airplane and saw Frank for the first time, my heart sank. He wasn't the dashing, cosmopolitan diplomat-to-be I had envisioned. Instead, he was a Taiwanese who, despite living over-seas, hadn't shed his country roots. And although he had a handsome face, he was too short. As if enamored of the idea of love rather than feeling love itself, I struggled to move beyond the stereotype of an ideal Taiwanese husband: tall, handsome, knowledgeable, protective.

Somehow Frank and I made it through the next few weeks. We went sightseeing in New York, took a trip to visit my old pen pal Karyl Bookwalter and her family in Baltimore, and went for more sightseeing in Washington, DC. At times we relaxed and felt at ease, especially at the Bookwalter's when the focus wasn't on each other. Still, whenever we were alone together, the thought kept creeping into my head, "The man I marry should be someone I can look up to, someone I can learn from." When I looked at Frank I thought, "Everything you have, I have."

Late one night in Baltimore, Frank and I talked for hours in front of the fireplace after the others had gone to bed. "I'll be going back to

Taiwan in a year, Hsiu-lien," he said. "Will you go back with me?" My first reaction was to feel flattered; this was as close as any man ever came to asking to marry me. "I can't," I replied. A tightening in my throat made me doubt my power of speech. "I just left Taiwan and I want to finish my studies."

I knew I had hurt him deeply, and it took Frank several days to respond. "Now I understand you," he said one stormy day in Washington, while we waited in the rain for the White House tour. "You are a girl of such strong will. It would be really hard to get along with you. Nothing is more important than your ambitions. Where do you put me in your priorities?" He sighed and then took my right hand, reading the lines on my palm, "You will become very powerful someday. I wouldn't dare marry you." Tears ran down my face when we said goodbye in the airport, where I took a plane back to Illinois and university life.

I saw Frank once again the following summer, while traveling in Europe with my other high school pen pal, Gail Homstad, and one of her co-workers. Frank and I both knew it was over. Each of us had fallen victim to gender stereotypes and couldn't help feeling disappointed when the other did not conform. I longed for a man I could look up to, and he for an obedient and self-sacrificing wife. Perhaps we should have been more enlightened, having had good educations and the experience of living overseas, but at heart he was a traditional boy and I an untraditional girl—with surprisingly traditional expectations.

In Taiwan, marriage was seen as a lifetime commitment, and divorce a great failure in life. While men pursued their own careers, women relied on their husbands to bring home happiness and success. And to think that in one lifetime there was only one choice of men! Sometimes when I think of Frank, I am reminded of a parable about Socrates and Plato. As the story goes, Socrates once took his students to a wheat field and said, "You can only walk across the field once, and you can only pick one ear of wheat. Each of you is to bring back to me the biggest ear of wheat that you can find." The students went into the field and then came back with ears of varying sizes. His most eminent student, Plato, came back empty-handed. Plato was not sure which ear of wheat was largest and knew that he would regret it if he found a larger one later. My entire life, I took this attitude toward men, always thinking that there might be a better choice down the road and I, too, came up empty-handed.

One positive outcome of my correspondence with Frank was the growth of my political consciousness. Soon after we started writing to each other, Frank had admitted he was only interested in meeting Taiwanese girls, not mainlanders. He had said there was something he needed to ask me that he could not mention in writing because of government monitoring of the mail. Frank had been concerned about whether I belonged to the Nationalist Party because, although he planned to work as a diplomat, as a native Taiwanese Frank held strong antigovernment views and resented the Nationalist dictatorship.

During my visit to France, Frank introduced me to Chang Wei-chia, whose prodding arguments sharpened my Taiwanese consciousness. Also a graduate of National Taiwan University Law Department, Chang had been studying in Switzerland when he decided to drop out of his academic program to dedicate himself to revolutionary change in Taiwan. Chang invited me to visit Lucerne, Switzerland, and to stay at the large apartment of a Taiwanese couple who opened their home to Taiwanese students passing through. On the way to Lucerne, Chang asked pointed questions about the political situation in Taiwan, gauging my answers and finding cracks in my defense of the government. Prior to meeting him, I had been ignorant of Taiwan's history and had been brainwashed by the Nationalists' education system.

In Lucerne, we bought groceries and I happily took the opportunity to cook Taiwanese food. More Taiwanese students studying in the area arrived. I fell into an easy routine: during the day Chang took me out sightseeing, and at night we carried on heated political debates.

"To be Taiwanese is to bear the burden of history," Chang said during one of his critiques of the Nationalists. From him I learned the true story behind the 2-28 Incident, long suppressed by the Nationalist government. Chang also told me about the Nationalist arrests, tortures, and executions during the White Terror of the 1950s and 60s, and about the movement by liberal scholars and officials—both mainlander and Taiwanese—to form an opposition party in the mid-1960s. Like most Taiwanese, I had no idea these atrocities had occurred, because of the Nationalists' control over the media and the publishing industry. Chang spoke passionately about the ideals of freedom and Taiwan independence from Chinese rule. Overseas Taiwanese had launched the Taiwan Independence Movement, he said, in order to provide an alternative to the Nationalists' China-centered politics.

Every night after our conversations, I read magazines published overseas advocating the creation of a democratic and independent Taiwan. Some nights I read until dawn. After one such night I asked Chang, in a fit of agitation, "Why are you telling me all this? Aren't you afraid I'll file a report about you?"

Chang frowned at me and answered seriously, "To share some-one's secrets means you are bound by duty to protect them." Chang meant that I must keep our conversations a secret, and that I, too, must join the struggle against injustice. His words stirred something deep inside me. By sharing the secrets about Taiwan's tragic past, I did feel duty-bound to help. He had appealed to my sense of logic and justice, to my feeling that everyone has the obligation to serve her homeland—ideals that I associated with the memory of Father.

When I returned to the United States, I found the community of Chinese students at the University of Illinois to be generally apolitical, career oriented, and focused on studies. Meanwhile, I became less interested in my academic work as I devoured the Taiwan independence magazines that Chang continued to send me from Europe.

My growing political awareness found an outlet in several events in late 1970 and early 1971. Tensions between Japan, Taiwan, and China ignited the passions of overseas Chinese and Taiwanese communities and set diverse political currents in motion. A territorial dispute erupted over a group of islands between Okinawa and Taiwan known as the Diaoyutai in Taiwan and as the Senkaku in Japan. The Nixon administration planned to cede this small knot of islands to Japan along with the return of Okinawa, even though the seas around the Diaoyutai had been traditional Taiwanese fishing grounds and the island group was claimed as sovereign territory by both Taipei and Beijing.

Indebted to Japan for continued diplomatic support of "Free China," Chiang Kai-shek only halfheartedly pressed Taiwan's claim to the islands, prompting an angry response from nationalists in Taiwan and China. That the Japanese killed so many Chinese during the course of their invasion of China in World War II made the concession seem all the more egregious. One day a friend at the University of Illinois, his voice ringing with anti-Japanese fervor, declared, "The Nationalist Party is being pushed around by Japan. We should stand up on behalf of our national rights." I promised to help organize a student group to help publicize this transgression of Taiwan's sovereignty.

On a cold blustery day, with temperatures dipping forty degrees below zero, a group of us drove to Chicago to protest outside the Japanese consulate. It was the first demonstration I had ever been in. I think we all embraced the heady sense of purpose that comes from supporting a cause in which you believe strongly. But the Nationalists, it turned out, disapproved of our attempts to draw attention to the Diaoyutai issue and, through the embassy in Washington, ordered us to give up the protest and return to our studies. Taiwanese students viewed the reprimand from the embassy as proof that the Chiang regime was buckling under the weight of pressure from the United States and Japan. Studying in America, the sons and daughters of Nationalist officials turned into shrill Red Guards castigating Chiang Kai-shek, the Nationalist government, and even their own parents as traitors. In the end, the United States did grant the right to administer the islands to Japan, although the matter remains disputed. The following year, Tokyo abrogated diplomatic ties with Taiwan in favor of China in another serious blow to the Chiang regime.

It was, ironically, a time of both burgeoning Taiwanese nationalism and Chinese nationalism among Taiwan's overseas students. I point this out because Taiwanese nationalism and Chinese nationalism are usually mutually exclusive. Taiwanese nationalists sought freedom and self-determination for Taiwan. Chinese nationalists believed that Taiwan was an inseparable part of Chinese territory and must one day reunite with its *zuguo* or "ancestral land." Yet both groups agreed the Diaoyutai were the sovereign territory of the Republic of China.

In April 1970, former chairman of the National Taiwan University Political Science Department Peng Ming-min, who had been under house arrest for advocating Taiwanese independence in 1964, escaped and was granted political asylum in Sweden. Later that same month, two Taiwan independence activists tried to assassinate Chiang Kai-shek's son, Vice Premier Chiang Ching-kuo, in front of the Plaza Hotel in New York.

Meanwhile, an affinity for "the real China," or the People's Republic, was developing among overseas Chinese on the heels of President Richard Nixon's historic visit in 1972. This romantic feeling of a connection was propagated by China itself during its Cultural Revolution, then at its midpoint. It is significant that few Chinese students were allowed out of the People's Republic during those years and thus were unable to tell University of Illinois students just how incredibly misguided the Communists' policies actually were.

As Chinese nationalism increased apace with the Cultural Revolution in China, Taiwanese nationalism gained strength among the native Taiwanese students at American universities. We heard that George Chang, head of the Taiwan Independence Movement in the United States, and several others had mortgaged their homes in order to raise the bail money for the two Taiwanese accused of trying to murder Chiang Ching-kuo. Taiwanese students in America felt they had to do something to show their commitment as well. With classmate Chen Hen-chieh, I drafted the charter for the Taiwanese Students' Association, an organization separate from the Chinese Students' Association dominated by Nationalist sympathizers.

Then, armed with a master's degree in comparative law earned by writing a thesis comparing Taiwanese and American interpretations of self-defense in criminal law, I secured a fellowship to study for a doctorate at the University of Washington in Seattle, and I went back to Taiwan for the summer, intending to return to America in the fall.

Back home in Taoyuan, I was surprised to find that Mother's resentment of my study abroad had evaporated. Mother had even learned to enjoy traveling. Brother had taken her on a trip to Taiwan's east coast by airplane so that she could see firsthand what flying was like. The view of the clouds and the mountainous scenery from the airplane delighted her. Later, she flew to the Penghu Islands, or Pescadores, an hour away from the west coast of Taiwan. If Mother had no objections to my traveling oversees, she still had strong views about my future. "Your mother is already so old, how can you leave again?" she cried after hearing of my plans to study in Seattle.

I began to think that she was right. By the summer of 1971 I was twenty-seven, and I had been a student my entire life. I needed to do something to prove myself outside of an academic environment, so I visited a career planning service set up by the Ministry of Education for students returning from abroad. The first interview was with the Ministry of Justice's Bureau of Investigation, an organization comparable to America's FBI in terms of both its intelligence-gathering functions and its shadowy reputation. More than anything, I was curious about what the Bureau of Investigation had to offer.

The director met me personally at the headquarters in Hsintien, a suburb north of the capital. He very formally described the organization and functions of the Bureau of Investigation before cutting to the chase. "Our main role is to protect state secrets and ward off spies," he said. "This is a grave responsibility. We administer an examination and accept just one hundred recruits each year, only the best. Ten are women. Our personnel are very talented and competent." He went on to describe special training in the use of firearms and other weapons, and in intelligence-gathering techniques, the sort of thing I had only read about in spy novels.

"Every year more and more patriotic youth want to enter the service; this is a very competitive and honorable calling," the director said. "However, a highly qualified youth such as you would be exempt from the entrance examination." Apparently my background in law and my degree from an American university made me an especially attractive candidate.

"What exactly do the new agents do?" I asked him. He replied that they receive training for six months before receiving an assignment. "You received a master's degree in criminal law in the United States, right? So we would probably send you on a mission to the United States."

He paused before continuing, "You are a native Taiwanese? There is a small band of Taiwanese abroad, the separatists, who have caused a great deal of damage to the prestige of our government. You would be given a nominal title at one of our consulates and take on the important work of countering the Taiwan Independence Movement."

So that was it: They wanted to use me against other Taiwanese, not to mention order me to actively oppose a cause I believed in. Later that day, I told Brother about the interview. "Why on earth would you go to a place like the Bureau of Investigation? That's like working for the king of hell!"

I don't know why the director spoke so frankly about what he had in mind for me. Indeed, if he hadn't spelled out how I would work to undercut free-thinking Taiwanese, I might even have accepted the job, if only to learn how the organization operated.

I do know, though, that my brief encounter with the Bureau of Investigation didn't go unnoticed. Eight years later when I was arrested, the interrogators—all from the Bureau of Investigation— brought up my job interview repeatedly: "Our director met with you personally to invite you to join our organization. How can you say that our government ever wronged you? And still you rebelled. If you had only understood how magnanimous we are, you would be standing here with us instead of sitting there a prisoner!"

Around that time, I ran into a friend who had graduated from university a year ahead of me. He had taken a job at the Executive Yuan's Law and Regulations Commission and said there might be openings. The Executive Yuan is the branch of the Taiwanese government that includes many important bureaucratic agencies. It proposes policy and drafts laws for passage in the legislative branch of government, the Legislative Yuan. After my friend arranged for an interview at the Law and Regulations Commission and after receiving a strong recommendation from the dean of the National Taiwan University Law Department, the commission offered me a position beginning in the fall of 1971.

Within a few days at the Law and Regulations Commission, I learned that only a few of us on staff had actually studied law and earned law degrees. The rest were former military officers who had "retired" into government jobs. In spite of the commission's reputation as one of the highest legal authorities in the nation, it was saddled with the deadweight of mainlander retirees who had poor training.

The commission's primary function was to review all drafts of laws proposed by government ministries before they were submitted to the Executive Yuan Council and eventually to the Legislative Yuan. It also acted as the final institution to which administrative appeals could be made after prior appeals elsewhere had failed. During my four years there, I handled cases concerning such issues as environmental pollution, trademark and patent infringements, and land acquisition review.

It soon became clear to me that the various layers of Nationalist bureaucracy protected one another rather than providing administrative oversight. One of my superiors very plainly spelled out the basic rule governing the actions of our committee. "The law is a tool in the service of politics," he stressed during a departmental meeting. In other words, enforcing the law only mattered inasmuch as it served Nationalist political objectives. Even the people charged with upholding the law didn't respect it.

I worked hard at the Law and Regulations Commission and was promoted to section chief, becoming the third woman ever to hold such a high position in the central government. For a young, newly graduated student of law, the job provided useful training and allowed me to gain familiarity with the workings of the national government. I saw firsthand many of the government's failings and understood the need for sweeping political reform, which would be difficult to implement without deposing the Nationalists.

Taiwan in the early 1970s was undergoing tremendous change. Its agriculturally based economy was giving way to urbanization and industrialism. Dramatic increases in living standards created a host of opportunities for men as well as women to pursue careers in industry, manufacturing, and the service sector. Traditional ideals faced fresh challenges as more women earned college degrees and competed with men in the job market.

In the summer of 1971, a debate was raging over the possible enactment of gender-based quotas for college placement. A conservative faction of educators believed that women had taken up too many spots in academic departments such as literature and history and journalism, to the point where women made up the majority of students in some subjects. This development had no doubt been aided by Taiwan's nondiscriminatory entrance exam system. But rather than congratulating women on their achievement and discussing how women could make good use of their education, conservative voices raised the question of whether men should have departmental spots reserved for them. Quotas, they proposed, would ensure male dominance, or at least equal participation, in the humanities.

The proposal was clearly ridiculous, and I wrote an op-ed piece for the *United Daily News* defending the right of all women to equal placement in education. I based the piece on a presentation on women's rights I had given at the University of Illinois following the fiftieth anniversary of American women's suffrage and the announcement of a second drive for women's liberation. The feminist perspective and arguments for equality between the sexes there had intrigued and inspired me.

Letters streamed in, supporting my op-ed piece. Most were from women, but one man wrote that he was delighted to see my article because he thought that Taiwanese women deserved emancipation. "I regret that I'm not a woman because I wish I could speak for them," he wrote. "I support you without reservation, and I would like to meet to discuss your plans." He was a mainlander whose father was a member of parliament. He said his beliefs stemmed from watching his elder sister waste her talent after marriage.

Invitations to speak followed as well. The first one came from one of my former professors, inviting me to give a talk on Women's Day,

March 8, 1972. If I had to pinpoint the launch of the Taiwanese feminist movement, I would single out my speech that day at National Taiwan University. I was the first one to ask why women should accept the stereotype, perpetuated by male patriarchal society, of *nan wai nu nei*, or men outside the home and women inside. No one had ever questioned in public the idea that it is the duty of men to work while women handle the tasks of child rearing and cooking. Brother attended with his daughters, and during the question and answer period following the speech, without revealing his identity, he asked me thoughtful questions. "Someone is taking these ideas seriously," went the murmur through the audience.

The events of the following summer galvanized growing concern for securing women's rights. The murder of a Taiwanese woman living in the United States by her jealous husband sparked a debate that brought women's issues to the fore. Attractive and vivacious Tang Ming-yu met her husband-to-be, a doctoral student studying for his degree in San Diego, during an arranged meeting on one of his trips back home. Tang wasn't interested in Chung Chao-man, but her mother thought it was a good match. Tang consented to accompany Chung to the United States and was unhappily married for about a year before she started having an affair. When Tang asked for a divorce, Chung exploded in rage. Neighbors heard sounds of a violent struggle in their apartment. Later, police found Tang Ming-yu's body bundled in a sleeping bag in the trunk of a car parked near the Los Angeles International Airport.

Chung Chao-man flew back to Taiwan, where he confessed to having murdered his wife and received the light sentence of eight years in prison—approximately the same sentence given to criminals convicted of arson. Apart from the criminal case, Tang's family filed a civil case to win compensation for wrongful death in an attempt to clear Tang's name. Brother served as one of the lawyers representing the victim's family in the civil suit.

At first, I mistakenly believed media reports that described Chung not as the perpetrator of a horrific crime, but as the victim of a licentious wife. Then newspapers began to portray Tang as a slut, saying she'd had her breasts enlarged and printing a photo of Tang with them partially exposed. The sexism underlying the double standard for the promiscuity of men and women, so clearly fueling the one-sided media coverage of the murder case, became unbearable. I knew that if anyone had released that photo to the public, it was Chung or his family—in effect, engaging in Tang's character assassination after Chung had taken her life. One editorial opined that it was a tragedy he ended up with such a woman. At the trial, people cheered for Chung like a hero and hissed at Tang's family. Unable to restrain myself, I wrote a furious commentary for the *China Times* newspaper.

Which is more important, life or chastity? I asked. If society approves of Tang's murder for infidelity, then let's put the shoe on the other foot. How many wives would be justified for killing their unfaithful husbands? I didn't exonerate Tang for her infidelity but asked whether a woman deserves to lose her life for adultery.

After the mass-circulation *China Times* published the article, so many people wrote letters supporting my position that the newspaper offered me a job. I was flattered but asked them, "Why me? I'm only twenty-seven years old; I'm a nobody." The editor in chief replied, "The article has already attracted so much public notice that we would like you to have your own column!" Thereafter, I wrote a weekly column for the *China Times* that would continue for five years and serve as the rallying point for a fledgling women's movement.

In addition to writing the *China Times* column and working at the Law and Regulations Commission, I started teaching classes at the Minchuan Girls' Commercial School in Taipei. This school, like a community college in the United States, combines the senior years of high school with two years of college-level instruction and prepares women for practical work as secretaries, technical assistants, and other vocational positions. As a government employee I was allowed to teach two afternoons a week, so I lectured on civil and commercial law, telling my students that life for women meant more than love, marriage, and child rearing. "Are traditional restrictions on women fair?" I asked them. "Should Taiwanese women be expected to handle all household affairs—to cook, clean, and look after children—while holding a job? What kind of person do you want to marry? What are your views about having a career? What kind of future do you want to have? As Mao Zedong once described it, men and women should each lift up half the sky. The question we face as women is how to achieve that." Women should take their careers seriously, I advised, and seek partners who would accommodate their ambitions. Though I wasn't much older than they were, I counseled them that women should seek their own destiny rather than waiting for men to determine the course our lives as wives and mothers.

Eventually, I synthesized my views in two books on feminism. One book, an anthology of my newspaper columns, went into eight printings. The other was *New Feminism*, an exposition of my feminist beliefs and a critique of male chauvinism rooted in Confucian philosophy. In Taiwan's Confucian tradition, women like Mother were taught to be virtuous wives and loving housewives. People of her generation believed that a woman's role in the family should be confined to household affairs. I argued that women have a right to equal participation in all social, political, and economic activities. The feminist ideas I espoused, while common in the West, were perceived by many in Taiwan as heresy.

The attack from traditionalists was swift and vicious. People misconstrued the points I made in *New Feminism*, and I was accused of advocating promiscuity—the same charge leveled against many early feminists in the United States. Several newspaper articles portrayed me as a woman inciting sexual licentiousness and prurience by challenging the institution of marriage. My championing of women's rights stemmed, they contended, from a deep sexual perversion. Something had happened to make me hate men, they said, and I vented my anger by denigrating those happily married.

As the newspapers hurled attacks at me, so too did some angry readers of my book. Every night I returned home and nervously opened dozens of letters, not knowing which ones contained filth. In *New Feminism* I had written, "A woman must first be a person"; one letter recast this as "a woman must first make people," that is, babies. (In Chinese the verb *to be* has various shades of meaning, including "do" and "make.") Disparaging letters ended with insults like "I wouldn't 'make people' with you even if you were on your back with your legs up." Some insulting letters even had women's signatures on the bottom, as if male writers had tried to give more weight to their words by having the message come from "one of my own." I did receive warm letters of encouragement, however. These helped me endure this rough time. In the end, in order to protect myself, I published a book containing all the responses I had received, good and bad, rational and irrational, and I printed the letters in their original handwriting to reveal the identities of the authors. The obscene letters stopped coming shortly thereafter.

In May 1972, while attending a government-sponsored family life symposium, I met a woman who would become one of my most staunch supporters and allies in the feminist movement. Su Chih-kuan headed the government's family planning program, and since she was an early advocate of birth control, Su had also suffered severe social censure. After I spoke at the symposium, Su came over to me and said, "Little sister, I'm really glad to meet you today and impressed by your position on women's rights. We should work together."

Su told me to keep up my courage in the face of criticism. Both of us wanted to do something more for the women's movement—to organize and mobilize women—and soon we began talking about founding a women's organization.

Under the Nationalist martial law regime, all voluntary associations had to be registered with the government. This included seemingly harmless organizations like the Red Cross and the Lion's Club. If an organization failed to register, its founders could be accused of sedition or any number of trumped-up charges.

After considerable discussion, I filed an application for a women's organization in Su's name because she was a well-known member of the Taipei City Council, and I thought that would help win government approval. Instead, the government rejected the request on the grounds that "there are already many other women's groups in existence." True, there were a number of women's groups, but these were primarily upper-class social forums for the wives of Nationalist officials and not in the least bit oriented toward feminism. The rejection was another example of the "law as a tool in the service of politics," a practice I was getting to know too well.

The Nationalist leadership had labeled Su a troublemaker. Not long after the rejection of our application, she quit the party after it refused to nominate her for another term on the Taipei City Council. Su later ran as an independent, becoming a firebrand critic of the Nationalists and surviving a car crash that many believed was a Nationalist attempt on her life.

After the government threw cold water on our initiative to establish a women's organization, I began to consider other means by which feminists could meet and discuss their ideas. Martial law restrictions circumscribed our freedom of assembly. A women's center like one I'd seen in the United States seemed the obvious choice, but it would be too expensive to maintain. Someone suggested a café or a coffee shop. At the time, teahouses and coffee shops in Taipei were emerging centers of avant-garde intellectual and artistic activity.

Unlike a women's center, a coffee shop had the potential to be self-supporting. One young mainlander, who had written me a letter expressing his desire to help, invested a small sum of money in the coffee shop. In recognition of his enthusiasm, I agreed to make him the shop manager, and we found a location near National Taiwan University, not far from where I lived. The students at Minchuan Girls' Commercial School helped me decorate the place.

The Pioneer Coffee Shop opened on Women's Day, March 8, 1973, exactly one year after my first speech on women's rights at National Taiwan University. Running a business proved more difficult than I thought. The manager, though well intentioned, didn't have much experience in business. We always seemed to lose money. Busy working at the Executive Yuan, I was unable to oversee the management of the coffee shop myself. Myriad worries plagued me: I had no way to be sure that my employees honestly accounted for expenditures and charged everyone, including their friends who came to visit, for the food and drink they had. The coffee shop's location near the university made for fruitful political discussions but bad business. Though young intellectuals gravitated to the Pioneer, they were often the starving-scholar type with little money to spend. After the young mainlander, the coffee shop had a series of managers, with none proving satisfactory.

I took to discussing my problems with my landlord, a man surnamed Chen, from whom I rented a room in a large, one-story Japanese-style home. A graduate of Peking University, Chen had retired from his job as a general manager with the Taiwan Sugar Corporation. I appreciated his advice, and he treated me like a daughter. Chen had encouraged my work for women's rights from the start. "I read your column, Hsiu-lien," he said. "My wife and I support you."

Chen had another lodger, Lai Chun-ming, who moved into the back bedroom with his wife a few months after I moved in. Lai was a member of Taiwan's Hakka minority group, tall and handsome and well mannered. Since his wife had graduated from Minchuan Girls' Commercial School, the two of them took to calling me Teacher when we were all together in the house. When Lai heard that I needed a manager for the Pioneer, he offered to help. Lai said that he had money to invest and that he would try to make the café profitable. Grateful for the assistance, I agreed.

Shortly after the coffee shop was set up, Lucille Dunham, an American representative of the International Federation of Business and Professional Women (BPW) telephoned me during a visit to Taiwan. Ms. Dunham wanted to set up a chapter of BPW in Taiwan. She also contacted the general secretary of the Young Women's Christian Association (YWCA), Yu Hsiao-chun, whose father had once been Taiwan's prime minister. It didn't occur to Ms. Dunham that Yu, a fervent Nationalist supporter, and I might have radically different political views. Yu and I soon found ourselves thrown together to work for this common cause. Yu applied for government approval while I wrote the charter for the organization and coordinated activities with other interested women. Suddenly I had an officially registered women's group through which I could push for programs like establishing a women's legal aid center.

Yu's faction of women wanted the BPW to be like the Nationalist

Party's other organizations for women: a social group for well-to-do Nationalist wives meant to advance personal prestige. The activities they sponsored, such as benefit banquets for ranking military personnel and galas at fancy hotels, had little practical use. My feminist friends and I couldn't afford the pearls and diamonds. Gradually the feminists dropped out of the group.

In spite of the organization's schizophrenic leadership, I persevered with one goal in mind: eventually it would be my turn to run the group, and then I could take some real action on behalf of all women. But as I gained more influence outside the BPW from my columns and lectures on women's rights, the Nationalists intensified their attempts to block my ascension to the helm of the BPW. One night, after a particularly bitter clash at a meeting, I came home and told Chen that I was ready to quit the organization entirely, that I was tired of the Nationalist wives merely using me for my organizational skills. "Chen," I said, "I can't really understand why these people are so malevolent. I've worked so hard for them and they don't appreciate it."

Listening sympathetically, Chen motioned for me to sit down, and then got up to check that we were alone in the house. "Hsiu-lien, there's something I've been dying to tell you," he whispered, with a glance over his shoulder. "I've wanted to say something for a long time. If I don't tell you today, my conscience will never rest."

His manner made me immediately apprehensive. "What, Chen? What is it?" I asked.

He took a deep breath and then spoke in low, rushed tones: "Lai Chun-ming, the one running the Pioneer Coffee Shop—he's from the Bureau of Investigation. The Bureau forced me to rent out the back part of my house so it could have someone watch you. I wasn't supposed to tell you this, but I can't stand lying to you either. Lu Hsiu-lien, please forgive me."

"I don't believe it!" I exclaimed. "Why me?"

"The Bureau approached me a year ago and demanded my cooperation," Chen said mournfully. "I felt I had no choice but to comply. I've known you for a while, Lu Hsiu-lien, and I can't see any reason that they would do this to you. Please be careful!"

I felt sick. I had treated both Chen and Lai Chun-ming as friends and confidants. I had even hired Lai to manage the Pioneer Coffee Shop! To find out that a friend or supporter is a spy actively collecting information to be used against you—betrayal is a terrible feeling. I didn't confront Lai openly, because that would risk exposing Chen to the wrath of Nationalist secret service organizations. I also realized that if I fired Lai, the Bureau of Investigation would send another spy to take his place. Better to have a spy you know than one you don't. In the future, I would watch Lai carefully. As my mind swirled with this discovery, I couldn't help wondering if any other friends would prove turncoats.

Lai had already been manager at the Pioneer for several months. The things Chen told me started adding up: The money Lai offered to invest had not come through. A waitress told me he regularly invited his friends to the Pioneer without charging them. Lai always volunteered to mind the shop during my meetings and activities with other feminists—doubtless to keep tabs on me. The only solution was to close the coffee shop. Running the Pioneer had never been profitable, so it was easy for me to justify closing it down without arousing Lai's suspicion. I also quietly arranged to move out of Chen's house.

As it turned out, the discovery that I had been living with a spy preceded a greater and more life-threatening crisis. In late May 1974, I went for a routine physical exam. A blood test revealed that something was amiss with my thyroid. In a follow-up exam, the thyroid specialist asked me, "Are you married yet?"

Taken aback by the question, I stammered, "No, I'm not."

"Well, then, we won't go for surgery," said the doctor. "We'll try medicine first."

The specialist had discovered a lump in my throat near my thyroid gland. I took medicine for a month, but the lump didn't get any smaller. I was ravenously hungry, ate huge meals, and still lost weight. I felt lethargic and slept poorly. During one of my TV appearances, my family watching the program saw the lump bobbing up and down in my throat as I spoke. Brother telephoned me immediately and demanded I go see a doctor. "I thought it wouldn't be good for your marriage possibilities if you had a scar on your neck," the doctor said when he saw me. "The medicine doesn't seem to be taking effect. We have no choice but to operate." He took an X-ray, after which he wrote something down for me to take to the National Taiwan University Hospital. I took the slip of paper, put it in my desk drawer at work, and forgot about it.

Mother, knowing I might neglect my health, sent Eldest Sister to Taipei to take me to the hospital for more tests. Eldest Sister arrived at my office at the Law and Regulations Commission one day as I was tying up the loose ends of various legal cases. Too busy to leave the office, I asked her to go to the hospital and do the preliminary paperwork. Taking out the piece of paper the specialist had given me, I looked at it for the first time. "Cancer," it said, in English.

As my heart pounded and my palms grew slippery with perspiration, my first thought was not to alarm Eldest Sister. I slipped the paper into an envelope and asked her to take it to a friend at the hospital, attaching a note asking for my friend's assistance in keeping my condition secret. But when my friend at the hospital read the cancer diagnosis, her face changed color, and Eldest Sister forced her to admit the gravity of the situation.

I was just about to turn thirty. Facing a disease that could end my life seemed a challenge that I didn't have time for. Even saying "cancer" aloud was difficult. That night I went out to dinner with my former roommate at the University of Illinois, Fanny Lo. She was the first person I told. Would it be fatal? I didn't know. There was so much more that I wanted to achieve. What if I only had a few more months or years left to live? We stayed out late at the restaurant as she tried to console me. When I returned to my room, I found that my family had left messages for me to telephone home. I was too tired to respond. The next morning the telephone rudely awakened me at 5:00 A.M. It was Brother. He was angry that I had been out late the night before. "Your health is bad and you're out straining yourself!" he yelled. "Come home to Taoyuan at once to see a thyroid specialist! The whole family is waiting for you."

"Yes, yes," I said sleepily, "I know, I have cancer."

"What? You already know you have cancer?" he exclaimed. Eldest Sister apparently didn't know that I had read the diagnosis. "Then don't fool around any longer!"

I hung up the phone and went back to bed. I went into work later and cleared off my desk, feeling strangely calm until I told my boss Hu Kai-cheng that I had to undergo cancer treatment. "Don't worry about your cases," Hu said, his voice quivering with concern. "Your health is more important." I could feel tears rising to my eyes and quickly left the office.

The specialist Brother had found in Taoyuan was affiliated with the military hospital. Usually government doctors encouraged you to see them at their private clinics, so they could earn a higher fee. But this one was just the opposite: knowing that I was entitled to government insurance, the doctor suggested I visit him at the military hospital, and not at his clinic. I liked him immediately.

The operation fell on a Monday, so I checked in the weekend before for preliminary tests. Eldest Sister and Mother wanted to stay with me at the hospital, but I asked them to leave so I could have some time alone. I waited fifteen minutes, then got dressed and walked out of the hospital to catch a taxi to Taipei. I went to attend a last meeting of the Chinese Comparative Law Society, where I didn't say a word about my impending surgery. I wanted to hang on to the last shreds of normalcy. Mentally I bid each of several friends "farewell."

The woman sharing my hospital room was a high school teacher my age who had just been through one round of surgery on a malignant tumor. When her husband and children came in and tried to comfort her, she wept while urging them to "be strong and carry on without mother." In a few days, the woman was scheduled for another operation. She wrote her will. As I watched her preparing to die, I wondered if I had done anything that would leave a mark on the world I might soon depart. I had no children of my own, no husband, and no money to leave my family. My struggle for women's rights had failed to create significant changes, attracting only a smattering of support from women, accompanied by a rash of personal attacks. The battle for gender equality would be a hard fight. I simply hadn't done enough, or lived long enough to achieve my goals.

During surgery, I remember dreaming that someone was calling out my name, "Lu Hsiu-lien, Lu Hsiu-lien, Lu Hsiu-lien." I couldn't make out the person's face, but the sound of my name seemed to echo from every direction. I awoke to the sound of the doctor's voice, "Lu Hsiu-lien, please wake up, can you hear me? Please say something." The tumor had affected only half of my thyroid gland, which the surgeons had removed during three and a half hours of surgery. The voice had been that of the doctor wanting to check my vocal cords. If the operation had gone badly, I might lose my ability to speak. "Yes, doctor, I hear you," I replied, surprised that my voice sounded lower and husky. For three weeks I recuperated in the hospital before going home to Taoyuan. Mother and Brother brewed great quantities of ginseng tea for me to drink to help me recover. Before the operation I had reflected on the things I had yet to achieve. With the removal of the cancer, I had gained a second life. This life, I felt, was owed to others.

The women's movement had temporarily hit a wall. I had closed the Pioneer Coffee Shop. The Nationalists had stymied my efforts to change the direction of the BPW. I began to consider going abroad to research women's movements in countries where intellectual freedom was permissible. America had a solid women's movement, but what about other Asian nations that were also battling the chauvinism of patriarchal belief systems? Because 1975 was International Women's Year, under the aegis of the Asia Foundation, I drafted a proposal to research the American, Japanese, and Korean women's movements. The Asia Foundation not only agreed to finance the project but arranged an internship for me with a women's organization in San Francisco.

After making plans to leave the country, I found myself waiting weeks for a passport. When I mentioned this to my boss at the Executive Yuan, Hu Kai-cheng, he offered to find out why the process was taking so long. A week later he called me into his office. "Ms. Lu, I'll be blunt. What is your relationship with the Taiwan Independence Movement?"

The question left me puzzled and surprised. "No relationship at all!" I retorted without thinking of my friend Chang Wei-chia in Europe. My boss said the government had confiscated Taiwan independence literature that had been mailed to me from abroad. Considering my response, Hu agreed to do his best to help me.

A few weeks later, however, Hu asked me why I hadn't joined the Nationalist Party. After all, most bureaucrats were party members. But I had never been presented with the opportunity to join; the party had always recruited men more heavily than women, and usually registered them during Taiwan's mandatory military service. Hu asked if I would consent to join the party. I thought it unwise to decline. A refusal would have been seen as suspicious.

"The Nationalist Party is like a company about to declare ideological bankruptcy!" Brother exploded, when he heard that I planned to join. "Why would you want to be a partner in a bankrupt company?"

Fearing that I might never leave the country if I didn't join the Nationalists, I filled out the application form, took it to my local Nationalist coordinator, and paid the membership fee. Shortly thereafter, an official called to inform me that my passport was ready. My boss at the Executive Yuan had been right. Joining the party had been enough to fool the individuals holding up my passport. I never attended a Nationalist meeting or registered with the party's overseas branches. Years later, I mailed back my membership card with a letter accusing the party of fraud after I discovered the local party coordinator had recorded my attendance at meetings while I had been out of the country. The Nationalist Party then "expelled" me for this show of disrespect.

From a Western perspective, my efforts to start a women's movement in Taiwan might seem odd. As a young single woman I had not personally undergone the hardships other women had, such as divorce, domestic abuse, or raising a family alone. When people asked me why I gave the movement so much time, I answered that it was my desire to counteract the tendency of women to undervalue their own abilities.

During my trip to America, sponsored by the Asia Foundation, I visited several women's centers and spoke with feminist leaders. For ten months I helped out at a women's center in San Francisco, observing how grassroots operations assist those in need. Then, at the invitation of Yang Mei-huei, a woman who translated great works by feminist authors such as Simone de Beauvoir and Betty Friedan into Chinese, I gave a speech at the University of Missouri. Other invitations to speak followed, and I traveled around the United States giving speeches on the women's movement in Taiwan.

My research on feminism coincided with my increasing interaction with advocates of Taiwan independence living abroad. I began to see the establishment of a democratic and independent Taiwan with new enthusiasm when I realized that democratization and feminist activism are two sides of the same coin. To achieve true democracy, all citizens—male and female—must enjoy equal rights. Moreover, women do not win respect, recognition, or support from men if they fight exclusively for women's rights. Women should participate in a wide range of political, economic, and social debates and activities. Similarly, democracy advocates who preach equality but cannot rectify gender biases in their societies fail as champions of democracy.

At a summer camp at Silver Lake in New York state sponsored by the World United Formosans for Independence (WUFI), I urged linkage of the feminist and Taiwan independence movements. "If we encouraged more women to become politically active," I said, "the independence movement would benefit from additional talent and resources. Women, in turn, would feel empowered as equal participants."

"Don't listen to her!" a woman shouted. "She is a spy for the Nationalists! Get her out of here!" A few others jumped to their feet and began shouting and pushing their way toward me.

"She was sent to destabilize the independence movement!"

"It's all a trick!"

"How can she criticize the Nationalists and then return to Taiwan to work for them?"

"She must be a spy!"

Caught off guard, I worried they would attack me physically, so intense was the atmosphere. In their eyes, by working with the Executive Yuan's Law and Regulations Commission, I was in the service of the enemy.

My suggestion that day proved so controversial that the friends who brought me to the conference refused to give me a ride to Boston, my next destination. I was left standing alone outside the conference venue. Eventually a Taiwanese couple felt sorry for me and drove me to Boston, only to be ostracized later for their kindness.

I understood some of the reasoning behind the harsh reception—constant state harassment of independence advocates led to justifiable paranoia—but I felt some hypocrisy in the actions of my accusers: among these overseas Taiwanese advocating democratization and independence, who had actually returned to Taiwan to affect change? Too many activists, content to criticize from the safety of the United States, had never faced the dangers of political activism at home.

"You cannot know me by what I have done so far," I told critics at another meeting of Taiwan independence advocates. "Give me five years and I will prove my loyalty to your cause." Indeed, in five years, I would serve a prison sentence for my role in the democracy movement.

The Nationalist auxiliary organizations in the United States invited me to conferences as well. At one that I attended in Lake Tahoe, Nevada, a man surnamed Sung approached me, claiming to be a fan of my feminist writings. Something about his manner made me suspicious, so I pestered him with questions until Sung admitted that he worked for the Bureau of Investigation. He had been sent to file a report on me. Since Sung had been so forthright, I decided to share my thoughts about the women's movement, enough to give him the information to write his report. Sung told me that his wife and children were forced to stay at home when he went abroad. They were used as "leverage" to deter him from defecting to another country.

In the summer of 1975, the United Nations held the first World Conference on Women in Mexico City. I planned to attend the conference, a historic occasion for the advancement of women's issues. The Asia

Foundation helped me to get an invitation from the United Nations. However, pressure from China prompted the Mexican government to deny me a visa. This was the opening salvo of Chinese attempts to bar my participation in international conferences. Although I had no way of knowing it at the time, this kind of Chinese strong-arm diplomacy would hinder me for decades.

My next internship was in Seoul, Korea. One reason I traveled to Seoul stemmed from an encounter I had had with a Korean woman activist, Tai-young Lee, two years earlier in Taipei. Tai-young Lee was the first Korean woman to attend law school, the first woman lawyer and judge. She had connections with the opposition in Korea, and had been jailed several times. At her office in Seoul, we talked openly about our mutual frustrations attempting to advance a feminist agenda in patriarchal societies, and the time allotted for my appointment seemed to go by much too quickly. Lee enjoyed the conversation so much that she asked me to stay through her next appointment. Her visitor was Chien Jian-chiu, the director of the Chinese Women's Anti-Communist League in Taipei. I agreed to stay but asked Lee not to bother introducing me to Chien.

Chien wore a Chinese *qipao* dress and looked like the wife of a Qing dynasty official. She filled the air with niceties about Korea and Lee's work in feminism there. "And what about the women's movement in Taiwan?" Lee asked her, flashing me a quick smile.

"Under the leadership of the Republic of China," Chien responded, "women have obtained a high status. In fact, in Taiwan our status is almost equal to that of men."

Sitting nearby, unrecognized by Chien, I was amazed by Chien's glib dishonesty. She probably thought I was a South Korean student or one of Lee's secretaries. After their brief meeting, Lee turned to me and said, "That woman is pure politician."

In Korea, Lee introduced me to the leaders of several women's organizations and opposition political activists. For three weeks I interned at an organization that Lee had founded, the Korean Legal Aid Center for Family Relations. Though I couldn't understand a word of Korean, the images of desperate, weeping women made an indelible impression. I saw what I had to do in Taiwan: provide practical help for women experiencing personal crises.

As soon as I returned to Taipei in late September 1975, I made plans to launch the New Feminist Movement. I formally quit my job at the Executive Yuan, from which I had been on leave, to devote myself full-time to the effort. The first window of opportunity came when a doctor in Kaohsiung, Taiwan's second-largest city, established a social welfare center and invited me to give a speech on women's rights. My speech was a hit. I liked the doctor and his welfare center so much that I offered to base future activities out of his center in Kaohsiung. With the center already established, we easily won official approval for a telephone hotline to assist troubled women. I quickly trained a group of volunteers; on Women's Day of 1976, the Women's Protection Hotline began offering anonymous advice to rape victims and battered women.

To publicize and raise funds for the hotline, we organized activities that were designed to switch stereotypical gender roles, including a men's cooking contest and a "tea and conversation outside the kitchen" party for women to discuss career aspirations. Both activities were successes, and with support from the Asia Foundation, we raised enough funds to start a hotline in Taipei, as well as a reference library. The hotline was a hit with the media, which made finding more volunteers easy. Soon, psychologists, professors, lawyers, and professional social workers were providing services to the women who called our hotlines.

The women's centers also conducted a poll of some 1,000 women, yielding results about the institution of marriage. The survey asked married women whether they felt satisfied with their spouses. Very few were, and even fewer women felt they could ask for divorces. "Would you marry your current husband again if you had the choice?" we asked. Only a few more than a quarter of the respondents answered "Yes." Armed with this information, we organized seminars to discuss the challenge of finding happiness in sex, love, and marriage. "Why should women maintain their chastity? For men and marriage?" I asked the audience. "No. They should maintain it for self-respect. Women do not owe men their chastity, they owe themselves self-respect."

I had several memorable experiences while working for our hotline service in Taipei. One day I received a phone call from a woman who was weeping hysterically. "I've just arrived from Hsinchu. Can I see you please?" she asked. Hsinchu is an industrial city to the south of the capital.

"Of course," I answered. A few minutes later a plump woman in her thirties wearing a short skirt arrived at the office. She couldn't stop crying, and she kept mumbling, "I should kill myself, I want to die, what can I do?"

"What is wrong? Please, sit down!" I said, pouring her some tea. A few minutes later she was able to speak.

"I married a man in Hsinchu, but my family was so poor we couldn't provide a good dowry. My mother-in-law treated me badly because of this, and my husband beat me. After many years I escaped to Taipei, where I found work as a housekeeper. I left my son behind because I couldn't afford to take him with me." She had returned to Hsinchu on the day people pay respects to their ancestors, only to discover her family had disappeared.

"There was no one there, no one at all! Only after inquiring at the police office did I find out that my husband had divorced me, deleted my name from the family register, and taken my son away," she said, sobbing. In those days, women in Taiwan had no legal rights to custody over their children. Legally, children were the father's "property."

"All I wanted to do was earn enough money to take care of my son," she continued. "Now he is gone and I have no purpose in life!"

I calmed her down as well as I could and asked her if she had any long-term career interests. A smile slowly crept over her tear-stained face. "I'd like to get a license to be a cook, so that I can go to the United States and work in a Chinese restaurant."

"I'll see what I can do to get you started in Taipei," I replied, and after a few phone calls, I lined up a job for her at a friend's restaurant.

One disturbing experience concerned another woman who came to see me at the hotline office. She was oddly dressed and smelled of pig manure. I learned that her husband beat her so much that she took to hiding among the hogs on their farm.

Our hotlines often dealt with rape cases. To respond to the need for services, the women's centers started offering self-defense classes, formed support groups, and published a booklet on rape prevention. These opportunities for rape victims to seek comfort and to receive counseling and training were some of the first of their kind in Taiwan. In my column for the *China Times*, I criticized the courts' embarrassment of rape victims by their suggestion that women brought the crime on themselves through their licentious appearance or conduct: "Women should not be accused of 'asking for rape' by dressing 'inappropriately.' Many male police are too poorly trained to handle these issues with appropriate sensitivity. Women police officers should be present during questioning. The problem stems from the lack of respect men hold for women throughout society. Men too frequently denigrate women both professionally and sexually."

At the time, I believed that educating the public at large was the best way to change traditional attitudes. I wanted to publish Chinese translations of the classics of feminist philosophy in the West. Although I was reluctant to go into business again, two talented women convinced me to found the Pioneer Press, a publishing house dedicated to publishing material we thought other publishers would not. These two women, who became my business partners, were Wang Chung-ping and Shih Shu-ching.

Wang Chung-ping became involved with the feminist movement after the difficult breakup of her marriage. She had moved to Pittsburgh and there encountered women's groups that helped her through a very rough time. We had met in the United States, where Wang said she wanted to move back to Taiwan to support the feminist movement. With a business background and English-language skills, Wang seemed well suited to become the manager of Pioneer Press. The editor was Shih Shu-ching, a writer with connections to the group of opposition politicians called the Dangwai, or "outside the party," meaning non-Nationalist. I was the publisher. Wang and Shih each invested one-third of the initial capital, while I agreed to raise the final third necessary to get the business license.

Pioneer Press published some fifteen books the first year. We focused on translations of theoretical feminist works criticizing traditional views of gender relations. But I soon found that Taiwanese women have different cultural reference points from those of Western women. The experience of Taiwanese women, for socioeconomic and cultural reasons, is different from that of women in the United States, Britain, or France. I decided to commission the writing of books specific to the Taiwanese experience.

Their Tears, Their Sweat, Their Blood chronicled the lives of rural Taiwanese girls, industrial working-class women, and prostitutes, and highlighted the problems each had to overcome. Publishing it led to my first brush with censorship. The Nationalists charged that the book aimed to "reveal the dark side of society to promote social disorder," and the government banned the book's sale in stores. Far from discouraged, we published a second book, entitled *Rape: Sex + Violence*, which was also banned. A third controversial book, *What Made Them Famous?* traced the careers of several famous women. Instead of using success as the standard of inclusion in the book, we used fame, and failing that, infamy. One of the book's profiles was of Ho Hsiu-tze, better known as Madame Ho. During the Japanese Occupation, she had married a doctor. The marriage had failed and she had become a barmaid, a prostitute, and eventually a madam. Beautiful and smart, Ho understood men's desires, and she became a wealthy entrepreneur by running a very exclusive brothel in Taipei. A popular joke at the time was that foreign VIPs paid their respects to Madame Chiang Kai-shek in the light of day, and their respects to Madame Ho at night.

Our interview with Ho ended up being the last one she ever gave. She died soon after Wang Chung-ping interviewed her for the book. Apparently, Madame Ho underwent surgery for fat removal that led to fatal complications. Wang decided to sell Madame Ho's story to the publishers of the *United Daily News*, which angered the *China Times* (I had long published with them.) The *China Times* took revenge by attacking our book in a newspaper editorial asking, "Why is a feminist like Lu Hsiu-lien affirming the accomplishments of a bad woman like Madame Ho? Is Lu Hsiu-lien encouraging women to become prostitutes?"

State agents also contacted the women portrayed in *What Made Them Famous?* and told them, "Lu Hsiu-lien wants to sully your reputation by associating you with Madame Ho." Several women we had interviewed forbade our publication of their stories.

Fearing that this book too would be banned, I decided not to include the chapter on Ho. Instead, I published the interview with Ho separately, together with another batch of angry letters denouncing our feminist work, and offered *The Ho Hsiu-tze Incident* free with every purchase of the abridged version of *What Made Them Famous?* A little ingenuity goes a long way.

Unfortunately, with two of our books banned after only one year in operation, the coffers at the Pioneer Press ran dry. Both Wang and Shih lost interest and dropped out. I was feeling state pressure at the hotline, as well. I asked a professor of social work, Tang Hsueh-pin, to help manage the Taipei hotline. At first I heard complaints that he criticized me behind my back, and then stories of how he harassed young female volunteers. It turned out that Tang Hsueh-pin, too, secretly worked for the Nationalists.

Memories of the closure of the Pioneer Coffee Shop and Lai's betrayal still weighed heavily on my heart. Unbeknown to Tang, I arranged to transfer the hotline to the sponsorship of the Taipei branch of the Lion's Club. Soon, even the apolitical Lion's Club came under attack from the state, and it became difficult to convince them to continue.

The pressure I felt and my sense of isolation were nearly unbearable. Members of the independence movement thought I was a spy for the Nationalists, while the government was in fact spying on me. My attempts to elevate the status of women through business ventures had been financial failures. Servants of the authoritarian regime has sabotaged my attempts to staff the hotlines with people interested in the improvement of women's lives. I had trouble confiding in anyone, and I feared the emotional fragility of the hotline leadership might scare the volunteers away. Once again, I felt boxed in. Every attempt to advance feminism had encountered resistance. I sensed that changing the ancient Confucian-based male patriarchy might prove even more difficult than toppling the Nationalist autocratic government.

CHAPTER 4

A MOTH FLYING TOWARD FLAME

SOME PEOPLE SAY CHANCE, SERENDIPITY, OR EVEN DIVINE intervention determines our friends and foes in life. Taiwanese believe very strongly in a concept called *yuanfen,* meaning a special destined relationship. To possess both *yuan* (destiny) and the *fen* (opportunity) is auspicious. This is perhaps why I attribute encounters and relationships more to fate than to chance. My friendship with Harvard Professor Jerome Cohen is one example of *yuanfen.* Jerome Cohen proved to be an inspiring teacher, undaunted supporter, and indirectly, my eventual liberator from prison.

When I met Professor Cohen in the autumn of 1976, he was one of very few Western experts on Chinese and Taiwanese affairs. A mutual friend and Cohen's former student, Chang Fu-mei, had written Professor Cohen a letter explaining the nature of my activities in Taiwan. I decided to take a chance and call on him at his office in Cambridge without an appointment.

Tall, with a firm handshake and deep lines creasing his forehead, more an indication of his intensity than his age, Professor Cohen was in his office when I arrived. During our conversation, he quickly pumped me with questions concerning my aspirations as a social activist, and encouraged me to apply to Harvard's Master of Laws (LLM) program. I filled out the application on the spot.

In February 1977, I was admitted to Harvard Law School with a tuition waiver, and in the fall of that same year, my research focused on constitutional provisions for codifying women's rights. The following spring, when I received my degree, Professor Cohen offered me a grant to continue my research. I accepted.

My choice to remain at Harvard proved an unsettling one for a number of reasons. Rumors trickled down from policy circles that the United States might soon end diplomatic relations with the Republic of China in favor of new ties with the People's Republic of China. This would be a crushing blow to Taiwan, as it would inevitably involve the abrogation of the US-ROC Mutual Defense Treaty. It might also mean that many nations would follow suit by cutting off diplomatic ties. At the time, state censorship of the media kept Taiwan completely in the dark about the fragility of the US alliance and the risk of a diplomatic crisis.

The partnership between the United States and the Republic of China goes back to World War II, when President Franklin Delano Roosevelt, seeking to discourage the Republic of China from negotiating a separate peace with Japan, promised to grant possession of Taiwan to Chiang Kai-shek following the Allied victory. Japan's surrender in 1945 placed Taiwan under the thumb of a Chinese regime. After the Nationalist defeat to the Chinese Communist Party in 1949, the island became the fallback point for Chiang Kai-shek, then in exile. Following the outbreak of the Korean War in May 1950, the Communists threatened to attack Taiwan by sea; the United States sent the Seventh Fleet to block an invasion.

In the 1950s, the US government called Taiwan "Free China," bolstering Chiang Kai-shek's claims to represent, not just the area of Taiwan, the Pescadores (Penghu), and Quemoy (Kinmen), but all of China as well. A mutual security treaty formalized the alliance, and Taiwan's economy profited from American aid and investment, while serving as a base for American troops in Asia.

In the words of General Douglas MacArthur, Taiwan became an "unsinkable aircraft carrier" and an essential part of the US defense perimeter directed against halting the spread of communism. By the late 1960s, rising casualties in Vietnam and a renewed interest in halting the arms race with the Soviet Union prompted US policy makers to consider alternative strategies for negotiating a withdrawal from Vietnam and for turning up the heat on the Soviets.

The answer, developed by President Richard Nixon and National Security Advisor Henry Kissinger, was to exploit the tensions between China and the Soviet Union. In 1971, Kissinger made a secret visit to China that built the foundation for Nixon's groundbreaking visit to Shanghai in January of the following year and the establishment of diplomatic relations with the People's Republic. China insisted that the United States withdraw its troops from Taiwan and renounce formal diplomatic ties with America's longtime ally. US policy makers agreed.

When word of Henry Kissinger's secret visit to China leaked out, the Americans could no longer hold together a coalition of votes in the United Nations supporting Taiwan's possession of the China seat as a permanent member of the Security Council. With the tables turning against him, Chiang Kai-shek ordered his representatives at the United Nations to walk out, rather than face the humiliation of defeat. This collapse of American support marked the beginning of a retreat into isolation by Nationalist diplomats. Increasingly, Taiwan was forced to quit its membership in such international organizations as the General Agreement on Tariffs and Trade (GATT) and the World Health Organization. Resistance by US conservatives made the formal diplomatic recognition of China a difficult final step, but also a move seen as essential by President Jimmy Carter in the late 1970s. At Harvard, the rumors I heard about the impending US abrogation of diplomatic relations with Taiwan contrasted sharply with silence on the issue in Taipei.

In the summer of 1978, I met with several Taiwan independence activists in New York, who suggested that I consider returning to Taiwan to run for the legislature or the National Assembly in the elections that fall. The Dangwai had begun to organize as a de facto opposition party for the first time ever—a historic milestone for democratization in Taiwan. Initially, I dismissed the activists' encouragement of my political career as the sort of praise that is both ubiquitous and meaningless in Chinese culture.

But the visit to Beijing by US Secretary of State Cyrus Vance in late August 1978 convinced me that the rumors of a diplomatic breakthrough might prove true, and that Taiwan's welfare would be sacrificed on the altar of US-China rapprochement. To lose diplomatic ties with the United States would jeopardize Taiwan's national security. Moreover, the shock of such a development, unanticipated by the Taiwanese public, might even lead to political instability. I did not want the riots and revolution of South Vietnam in 1975 to occur in my homeland. The time had come to act, and the freedom of speech afforded to candidates during election time, known as the "election holiday," represented the ideal opportunity for me to warn the Taiwanese public of the impending diplomatic crisis.

It was with some trepidation that I went to Professor Jerome Cohen's office to discuss my reasons for returning to Taiwan. Professor Cohen had, after all, just arranged my fellowship at Harvard. I thought he might be offended if I gave it up.

Professor Cohen's reply took me completely off guard: "Why not? You are nobody here but you could be somebody at home. Why not go home and work for your people?"

"You know the situation in Taiwan," I replied. "I might be jailed if I go into politics."

A smile creased his cheeks. "Then I will wave a flag for you in Taipei!" he said.

We both laughed. I left his office resolved to do my best in the election, even though I expected my chances for winning were slim.

My goal as a candidate was to educate voters as much as to win a post in government. In order to marshal some facts to use in the campaign, I embarked on intensive research of Taiwan's history at Harvard-Yenching Library. The Taiwanese, like any nation, had to understand their past in order to understand the challenges that might lie ahead. With the help of several Taiwanese living in Boston, I began writing the book *Taiwan: Past and Future*. It became the first book ever to examine Taiwan's history from a Taiwanese perspective, representing a pathbreaking departure from the China-centric texts printed under martial law.

Since the early seventeenth century, foreign rulers have dominated Taiwan: from the Dutch and Spanish colonial rule of the 1600s, to the corrupt Qing dynasty rule until 1895, and to the five-decade Japanese Occupation that ended with Japan's defeat in World War II and the arrival of the Chinese Nationalists in 1945. While my book did not explicitly call the Nationalist government a "foreign" regime, my meaning was clear: the party-state was foreign in the eyes of the Taiwanese it continued to dominate and exploit. Taiwan's fate throughout history was not unlike the life of a *simpua*, or an adopted daughter, that I narrowly escaped in my youth. Competing world powers, like parents bargaining with the lives of Taiwanese girls, had passed the island around in exchanges of blood and treasure. Taiwan had had little choice in determining her present, not to mention her future, form of government.

With the date of the election fast approaching, other candidates had already begun to campaign, at least informally, while I worked to get the facts straight for my book in order to make a persuasive argument. In the two months that I worked on the monograph, I kept my election plans secret, even from my family, for fear the Nationalists might prevent my return. In those days, government agents read almost all mail from abroad. I had little doubt that the secret service had wiretaps on Brother's telephones, and probably on those of other members of my family, too.

In September, I returned to Taoyuan ready to test the waters in my home county. My plans for the campaign, however, quickly ran into trouble. Brother read a draft of the book and nearly gone through the roof with concern for my safety. The message, he pointed out, was apt, albeit extremely provocative. Government censors would almost certainly ban the book and could have me thrown in jail for "seditious" intentions.

I went to Taipei to discuss my campaign with one of the important opposition leaders at the time, Yao Chia-wen. Tall, handsome, and determined, Yao was gatekeeper to the growing Dangwai candidate coalition, and a fellow graduate from the law department of Taiwan National University. Together we had worked to found the

Chinese Comparative Law Society. I hoped Yao would welcome me into the Dangwai coalition, but when I mentioned my plans to run as an opposition candidate for legislator in Taoyuan County, Yao suddenly turned cold. "The Dangwai already has a strong candidate for legislator in Taoyuan, Chang Teh-min," he said. "Perhaps you should reconsider!" Yao doubted I had sufficient qualifications for the post, and even suggested that I could be a spy sent by the Nationalists.

Brother's reluctance about my strategy was troubling, but Yao's suspicion came as a shock. In my mind, at least, my intentions were pure and simple: I hoped to deliver a warning to the Taiwanese and had even given up a prestigious fellowship at Harvard to do so. I knew that convincing democracy activists like Yao that I was on their side might not be easy. But I had banked on my contact with the independence movement abroad to bring me closer to the Dangwai leadership. I had even arranged for Yao Chia-wen to meet Jerome Cohen earlier that year. To assure Yao of our common objectives, I mentioned my recently completed book and numerous friends in the United States who were advocates of Taiwan independence.

As the word spread that I planned to run for a Taoyuan County seat in the national legislature, the Lu clan—extended family members numbering in the thousands—began putting pressure on Brother to convince me not to enter the race. One of the region's incumbent legislators was a Nationalist politician named Lu Hsueh-yi, who was also a Lu clan member. From the clan's perspective, if we both ran in the election, the Lu clan's votes would be divided, and in a multiple-member electoral district, this might cause both Lu Hsueh-yi and me to lose.

When Lu Hsueh-yi heard I might enter the campaign, he came with his wife to visit me in person. According to a complex generational formula, known as *beifen*, he was of a lower rank than I was in our clan and so was obliged to be deferential to me. At any rate, political calculation had prompted his visit. Lu practically begged me not to run for legislator.

In addition, the local Nationalist Party organization tried to convince me to abandon the race. Its emissary was a man from the

Taoyuan County branch of the Nationalist Party, Lai Kuo-feng. Lai had been one of Brother's boyhood friends. The three of us had gone hiking together in the mountains on numerous occasions. Since childhood Lai had discovered that joining the Nationalists could have very real financial advantages. Lai approached Brother first, to probe him about the chances of convincing me to quit the campaign. "My sister is not easily persuaded!" Brother warned him, with characteristic firmness.

A few days later, Lai Kuo-feng approached me directly and asked, "How much money will it take to get you to drop out of the race?" I refused his offer of a bribe with the suggestion that he leave.

The Dangwai leadership opposed my candidacy, clan members grumbled about clan unity, even my family only grudgingly supported me. In those days, the Taoyuan legislative district encompassed parts of two other neighboring counties. With a lot of ground to cover and too little time, I decided to drop my plans to run in the legislative race and to compete for a spot in the National Assembly. The Legislative Yuan, which handles legislation for the Republic of China, was a more important post. Yet winning a seat in the National Assembly, which at the time elected the president and handled constitutional reform, would provide a forum for the expression of my political views.

I borrowed US$25,000 from the bank with the help of Brother and Eldest Sister. While I had some fame nationally as a result of my column and feminist activities, in rural Taoyuan County I was relatively unknown. As a result, I planned to launch my campaign at a fundraiser in Taipei and then take the momentum southward to Taoyuan.

This was the first time ever that a candidate in Taiwan raised money from the public for an electoral campaign. Instead, most Nationalist candidates gave money to voters as a means of solidifying their grassroots support network. They "bought" votes and subsequently raised funds through corruption. My rationale for seeking public funding was that if voters provided financial support up front, I would serve them without corruption after winning the election.

The fund-raiser was to be held at the Ambassador Hotel, an aging but somewhat classy property in northern Taipei. My invitations were not unlike those to a wedding banquet. I rented a hall and asked dozens of old friends, colleagues, and a few politicians to come for dinner, with the expectation that guests would make donations. Also, just as with a wedding banquet, when all preparations should have been completed, new complications arose.

The night before the fund-raiser, my friend and Dangwai insider Chen Chu telephoned to say she was having a hard time getting the dinner tickets out. When I probed her for more information, it turned out the problem was personal, rather than technical. "Lu Hsiu-lien," she started, " a lot of people, especially Yao Chia-wen, disapprove of your decision to run for office. What have you done to alienate Yao, anyway?"

"I haven't done a thing," I replied. "He asked me not to run for legislator; now I'm running for National Assembly."

Chen Chu suggested that Kang Ning-hsiang, a national legislator and senior Dangwai member, might be more understanding. She asked me to appeal to him for support and to invite him to attend the fund-raiser.

I went to see Kang at his home in hopes of winning his support and perhaps that of other Dangwai politicians with whom I hoped to collaborate. Like me, Kang Ning-hsiang arose from humble circumstances, and he had encountered many political obstacles en route to his many electoral victories. Our meeting began with a discussion of my affiliation with the Nationalist Party, or rather with my denial that I backed the dictatorship. My circumstances were complicated because I had, in fact, been a member of the Nationalist Party. I assuaged Kang's fears by explaining the circumstances under which I had joined the party—in order to get a passport to leave the country—and mentioned my recently authored history of Taiwan.

My qualifications for candidacy impressed Kang, but he warned that Dangwai politicians feared I had ties to the Nationalists and consequently were unwilling to support me. I showed him a copy of an article from the *United Daily News*, in which I had announced my "non-Nationalist" status in an interview. This appeared to allay his suspicions.

"What's wrong between you and Yao Chia-wen?" he asked. "Weren't you classmates at National Taiwan University?" The question kept coming up and I had no good answer for anyone. When I professed that I bore Yao no antipathy, Kang looked surprised and agreed to attend my fund-raising party the following evening.

The supporters who came to the Ambassador Hotel were largely my acquaintances from the women's movement—people without a militant stance on the emerging Nationalist-Dangwai conflict. When I took the podium to speak, none of the important Dangwai leaders were in attendance. Whatever his reasons, Yao and his friends still opposed my candidacy.

The only well-known guest at the fund-raiser was Tao Pai-chuan, one of the most respected mainlanders and a Nationalist. Tao had worked hard to improve Taiwan's human rights conditions and bolster social justice. A Harvard graduate, Tao approved of my campaign literature centered on the theme "I Love Taiwan." I treated him as a guest of honor, even though I knew that doing so might further compromise my position with the Dangwai.

My sense of discouragement was evident as I addressed the dinner guests. I had given up my studies at Harvard to warn the Taiwanese of an imminent international crisis, but the Dangwai coalition I hoped to join had ostracized me. I was nearly in tears and gave a miserable speech. My despair proved premature. Toward the end of the banquet, Kang Ning-hsiang made a brief appearance, followed by that of the most senior Dangwai leader, Legislator Huang Hsin-chieh.

Huang Hsin-chieh was one of the few opposition leaders who possessed the clout to criticize the Nationalists with impunity, having been elected as a "permanent" legislator some years before. At the time, mainlanders who had been elected in China in 1947 held nearly all of Taiwan's legislative seats. This "parliament in formaldehyde" then extended its own term indefinitely. Huang Hsin-chieh was one of very few Taiwanese who had been elected to fill positions vacated by deceased Chinese legislators. Previously, Huang had supported my women's center fund-raisers by purchasing tickets for the "men's cooking contest." He had even bought a whole set of my books. Still, I was very surprised and a little puzzled by Huang's appearance. He was the leading Dangwai figure at the time; Huang's support of my political career would prove invaluable.

In the end, the dinner at the Ambassador Hotel was a great success. Not just for the money it raised, but because it was the first-ever public fund-raiser for a political campaign. Previously the trend had been for large, private donations, or for candidates to pay for their own campaigns. This banquet-style political fund-raiser became a widely imitated means of raising funds for opposition campaigns.

A week later, I started campaigning in Taoyuan with my "I love Taiwan" campaign literature, which emphasized my strong affinity to Taiwan and desire to share its destiny. I described myself as bucking the winds of "toothbrush-ism," the pejorative term for Nationalist officials who emphasized "reunification with the motherland" but kept a suitcase and toothbrush packed so they could make a quick getaway if the Chinese invaded. One of the most serious flaws of Nationalist rule in Taiwan, even when compared with that of the Japanese, was its lack of investment in the island's infrastructure. For decades the Nationalists had neglected investment in Taiwan in favor of building up the military, a manifestation of the increasingly hollow objective of "retaking the mainland." The Nationalist resolve to retake China was not matched by an affinity for the island it ruled. The "I love Taiwan" theme attempted to reverse this trend by encouraging mainlanders and Taiwanese to identify with the island and its culture. The message was simple: appreciate, protect, nurture, and support the community in which you live, accomplished in our case by "loving" Taiwan.

In the first wave of my campaign, friends in the feminist movement and members of my clan helped me distribute my literature in the thirteen towns and villages of Taoyuan County. I soon realized that I needed local volunteers because I could not expect my feminist friends from Taipei to come to Taoyuan to help campaign on a daily basis. Feminism was still my rallying banner when I recruited the first group of local volunteers at an outdoor gathering in Taoyuan. I invited famous women writers such as Tsao Yo-fang and Tan Fei to speak on my behalf, attracting a crowd of two or three hundred people.

There is a definite snowball effect to the crowd mentality in Taiwan. People enjoy an atmosphere that is *renao*, or hot and noisy, an expression that implies a lively and carnival-like spirit. The venue can be a temple or a school yard, a town hall or a city park, but the dynamic is always the same: the more people that turn up out of genuine interest, the more people are attracted out of curiosity. And as the crowd grows, venders appear with little food stands, selling ice cream, tempura-fried vegetables, or grilled sausages.

My first gathering was large enough to be *renao* and turned out to be a magnet for attracting volunteers. At first, I was reluctant to discuss my message about the impending abrogation of US-Taiwan diplomatic ties. The volunteers had, after all, been recruited as a result of their interest in feminism. Fortunately, the volunteers suggested I discuss issues with a broader political appeal, including criticism of the Nationalist party-state. Although I didn't know it at the time, the aide of the well-known Dangwai politician Hsu Hsin-liang, then chief executive of Taoyuan County, had heard my speech the previous evening and with his brother had joined my first group of volunteers. The two of them had experience campaigning for Hsu Hsin-liang and later came to my house every night to train the volunteers.

In Taoyuan, almost without exception my political competitors were better known and had better connections to local organizations. In contrast, I had spent years abroad and had to prove I was not a "home-wrecking" feminist or prissy elite academic who didn't understand the average Taiwanese. To increase my appeal, I designed an apron displaying the island of Taiwan, "Hello, compatriot," and "I love Taiwan," and my name. The idea was a little wacky but eye-catching. I arranged to make 6,000 large shopping bags with a similar logo design, which my campaign volunteers distributed in local vegetable markets.

The vegetable market was the preferred shopping place for most city dwellers. Open before dawn, the marketplace could be all but invisible from the street, except for the stream of shoppers pouring out the alley or gate that led to passages filled with hundreds of venders. Fruit and vegetable hawkers would holler out specials, while the butcher sliced pork loin or killed a chicken for a waiting customer. Housewives haggled over prices on everything from clothes to furniture. Clusters of school children would stop by to gossip over steaming rice rolls wrapped in bamboo leaves, soy milk, and red bean dumplings. The marketplace provided daily entertainment and was the social hub of Taiwanese society.

Most of the people in the marketplaces had no idea who I was, but the items we distributed were useful and practical, and citizens in the marketplaces accepted them gladly. Soon the vendors were wearing my aprons in their stalls and people were walking around with shopping bags that bore my name. It was a somewhat comical sight. Few people knew about the anti-Nationalist bent of my campaign. In the hypersensitive language of martial law era politics, the message "I love Taiwan" implied love of Taiwan *surpassing* the love for China—the latter most definitely being the preferred sentiment from the regime's viewpoint. I was also running as an explicitly non-Nationalist candidate, if not as a candidate sanctioned by the Dangwai political organization.

Looking back, distributing gifts in this manner may appear unethical because in Taiwanese culture, generosity and gift giving confer on the recipient an obligation to reciprocate. Vote buying, whether explicitly financial, consisting of free meals, or by the giving of gifts, plays upon this cultural obligation. Hopefully, my campaign activities will be seen as a somewhat unorthodox grassroots publicity strategy, which was undertaken at a time when giving gifts to voters was a common, even expected, part of campaign culture.

After my foray into the urban marketplaces, the campaign moved on to rural, hinterland areas. Here, Brother became worried. He thought that my progressive ideas would meet resistance from conservative farmers, and that people would oppose the idea of women in politics. The opposite proved true. Everyone was courteous and friendly. Because rural voters had so little personal contact with politicians, I was occasionally associated with the female opposition politician Huang Yu-chiao. In Taoyuan, Huang was known as the "tough woman" for her fierce criticism of the Nationalists. She participated in politics, winning office, sometimes losing, but vigorously active until the ripe age of eighty years. When people met me they would say, "Oh good, another tough woman like Sister Yu-chiao." Apparently they accepted the idea of women in public office although such women were seen as mean or aggressive, as if to compensate for the lack of masculine poise.

According to government regulations, after declaring my candidacy, I needed to appoint an official campaign manager. At first, it was difficult to find anyone willing, considering the controversial nature of my campaign. With some arm-twisting, I convinced one of my elementary school teachers, Teacher Chuang, to take on the job. Teacher Chuang was well thought of by the community and had many former students in Taoyuan.

By late October 1978, my campaign was in full swing. We hosted two campaign rallies per night at temples, houses, and school yards throughout the county. I insisted on speaking to people in language they could understand, and attempted to link political arguments with everyday analogies. I might begin by saying:

I went to the marketplace this morning and saw grandmothers
shopping for vegetables to feed their families and buying hens to
make soup for daughters-in-law who had just given birth. Grandfathers were buying sweets for their grandsons. It is right that
the Taiwanese people are concerned with the well-being of their
homes and families. But have you ever considered that the reason
we can live so harmoniously and happily is because we are a nation
at peace? If China decided to invade Taiwan one day, prices in the
markets would go up, fear would strike deep into our hearts, and
our brothers and husbands could be killed on the battlefield. Why
would this happen? In a word, because of politics—the murky,
oppressive, and sometimes corrupt realm of activities that affects
each and every one of us, and to which we are all, directly or indirectly, connected. You can't ignore politics, it concerns us all.

Then, I would hit my main points: the impending crisis in US-Taiwan relations and the legacy of foreign domination throughout Taiwanese history.

In nearly all speeches, I switched back and forth between Taiwanese and standard Chinese to hold the interest of a diverse audience. Election time provided the only opportunity to speak Taiwanese in public. Usually the language was banned from public use, including in schools, but during campaign time government controls relaxed, giving candidates freedom to use the language that appealed to voters. Taiwanese appealed to the Hoklo majority that immigrated to Taiwan from Fujian in China beginning in the sixteenth century. When I used standard Chinese, it was to appeal to the mainlander soldiers and bureaucrats. Unfortunately, I speak little of the dialect of Taiwan's other major ethnic group, the Hakka people, who immigrated to Taiwan from south China, and thus could not address them in their own tongue.

One memorable campaign rally occurred in the town of Daxi, the site of Chiang Kai-shek's summer mansion. My speech coincided with a religious festival held once every twelve years. Local residents had erected an altar in the center of a school playground and in front of it lay several roasted pigs, slain in a sacrifice to a folk deity. I remember feeling very sentimental, standing on the stage overlooking a crowd of men and women of all different ages, some praying religiously, some pushing small vending carts, some eating, and some just looking on curiously. A deep sadness came over me. I was here to speak about Taiwan and political problems that could affect these people's lives, but almost no one appeared interested in what I had to say: "Today is the great festival in Daxi. Why do we pray and make sacrifices to the gods? Because we want to thank the gods for all the fortune we have had so far and to pray for protection in the future. But if we want Taiwan to be stable and harmonious, we must do much more. Taiwan is facing immediate danger. Without seeking to comprehend the political situation of our country, we will have no stability and harmony regardless of how many pigs we sacrifice."

At this point, people paused to listen, some out of curiosity, others out of irritation at the distraction. A small number—presumably the curious—started walking in my direction. I paused briefly to allow them time to approach and continued.

If you don't believe me, consider for yourselves that in 1895 our ancestors were also sacrificing and praying to the gods. But the Qing dynasty government signed the Treaty of Shimonoseki that ceded Taiwan in perpetuity to Japan. When the Japanese came, some 20,000 of our ancestors fought and died in an attempt to ensure that the people of Taiwan would have the power to determine Taiwan's destiny. All to no avail. The stronger, more modern Japanese forces won, and the five-decade Japanese Occupation ensued. We must not dishonor the legacy of our ancestors by neglecting the affairs of our nation. The Taiwanese must take control!

At this point, tears started to course down my cheeks. How could they be so naive and unconcerned on the eve of a great disaster? Did they imagine that feasting on roast pig could save them? I continued by lashing out at the corruption and shortsightedness of Nationalist rule, until a county prosecutor monitoring the rally passed me a written warning to restrict my comments. By criticizing the government, I had violated the speech regulations of martial law, but the crowd had swelled and hundreds of people were listening. I continued speaking until I received a second and then a third notification from the prosecutor. I had no choice but to stop. After the rally, my campaign staff said many people in the audience had wept when I concluded. They had even seen the prosecutor wiping his eyes.

In other speeches, I compared Taiwan's fate to that of women, contrasting the awakening of a woman's consciousness with the emergence of the Taiwanese democracy movement:

The fate of the Taiwanese people is like that of the woman in traditional society. Women were forced into passive roles in society. They were made second-class citizens. Women make up one-half of the population. Why have they accepted the inferiority? Men can be very repressive, but many women don't speak up for themselves. The Taiwanese have been passive in politics in the same way that women have accepted traditional roles. Foreign powers have always determined the fate of Taiwan, and its people have not united in struggle to overcome this oppression. From this day forth, let the women speak out and let the Taiwanese stand up with dignity. Let the entire society rise up in protest against injustice and the iron-fisted rule of many by the few!

Afterward, I received dozens of phone calls from women exclaiming, "You are the pride of Taoyuan. The entire county is crazy about you!"

Another type of campaign rally was held by the government's Election Bureau, the agency ostensibly serving to promote fair elections, but in reality serving as an instrument of repression. At the government-sponsored rallies, all candidates were required to attend so the audience could hear and compare the candidates at the same time. Because there were so many candidates—eight National Assembly candidates in my race—the speakers had only a few minutes to explain their campaign platforms. At my own rallies, I could speak as long and as much as I wanted—or as long as the prosecutors allowed—but at the government rallies I could appeal to a broader range of people. Nationalist candidates seldom held private rallies. They knew that an embarrassingly small number of people would attend. My clan member, the Nationalist legislator Lu Hsueh-yi, had a rally in front of a temple. Fewer than two hundred people showed up, even though they were paid to attend.

The first government-sponsored rally in Taoyuan County that year was held in Fuxing Village, a small settlement in the mountains populated by aborigines and mainlander soldiers. Sadly, both groups had lengthy experience in being alternately controlled and manipulated by the Nationalists. My principle Nationalist Party rival, Chao Chang-ping, spoke before I did. He was already a familiar sight for me because he often stood in the front row at my rallies taking notes. In Chao's own speech, he moved swiftly to discredit me: "In these elections there is a young woman who recently returned from abroad. She says the fate of Taiwan is like that of a boat. I think this boat is a beautiful, flawless boat. Don't be deceived by her. Who knows how much money and property she has hidden in America? If you vote for her and she goes back to America, your vote will be wasted."

When it was my turn to speak, I raised my foot, to show the cheap sneakers I was wearing. "Take a look at these shoes and the clothes I am wearing. Do I dress the part of the wealthy elite?" I listed the names of Nationalist officials I had encountered in the United States and the locations of their luxurious homes. The audience applauded vigorously. Then I continued:

> Chao's words echo many Nationalist speeches we have heard before. The party is fond of saying we are all in the same boat, in the wind and in the rain. But I say our boat has a huge hole in the bottom and a typhoon is coming. The captain of the boat won't tell us where we are headed, so we can't change the course. It's time for Taiwanese to pull out navigational charts and take the helm!
>
> Chao Chang-ping tells us that he wants to improve the welfare of Taoyuan County by building new bridges and roads. Look at our constitution. Do you know what the National Assembly is for? It is a rubber stamp body to elect the president and vice president. It has no other function. If there is a candidate who tells you he wants to build bridges and roads after he gets elected to the National Assembly, tell him that he's running for the wrong position. He should be running for county chief executive. The Nationalists never mean what they say!

I finished my speech and was preparing to leave for another town, when something very strange happened. As soon as I left the auditorium, almost everyone got up and followed me out. They jogged along behind my campaign car, cheering and lighting off firecrackers. This event marked a change in the momentum of my campaign.

Although the Bureau of Investigation had compiled reports on my role in the women's movement and on my activities overseas, my dossier had never been transferred to the local government's election committee. Apparently, the Taoyuan branch of the Bureau of Investigation moved a step too slowly in this respect. Investigators' attention had been focused primarily on the candidate that Dangwai County Chief Executive Hsu Hsin-liang had publicly endorsed. Because my campaign had started out late and on an unusually small scale, the Nationalists were caught off guard by my rapidly rising popularity. Now the regime prepared its response.

As the crowds at my rallies grew larger day by day, Nationalist nervousness shot up. Someone told Eldest Sister that the government compared my supporters to bean sprouts that didn't stop growing. Secret police, wearing long shirts and dark slacks, appeared at rallies and around my campaign headquarters. I suspected that one of my campaign volunteers was a secret agent. The man was always present but never willing to give his name. Later my suspicions were confirmed.

Campaign supporters had built a "Democracy Wall" across from my campaign office, echoing the sentiment of democracy advocates in China that same year. My staff pasted the length of the wall with *dazibao*, or big-character posters, bearing various campaign slogans. Almost every night the posters were defaced or torn down. I began to receive threatening phone calls. Then another wall-type forum for posters suddenly appeared next to my office. We guessed it was a Nationalist trick, so one of my friends came up with a plan to prove it. We knew the Bureau of Investigation had a wiretap installed on the office phone because of the crackling sound it made. My friend went out and called me from a public telephone pretending to be a regular supporter. "Ms. Lu," he said, "I am delighted that you have come back from the United States to run in the elections. I think the Democracy Wall across from your office is wonderful, but there doesn't seem to be enough space. I am donating another wall to your campaign, the one next to your office."

It was a great idea. I would use the new wall freely, and if anyone ever asked, I could say that a supporter donated it to me. We covered it with my slogans before the Nationalists got a chance to use it. They were, of course, afraid to come out and claim the wall.

As the election date drew closer, new and more-threatening slogans appeared on my Democracy Wall, along with epithets such as "traitor," "rebel," and "America's running dog." One night my supporters caught some people painting over the wall and got into a brawl with the perpetrators. Fortunately, Brother rushed out and stopped the fight. Since I had occupied their intended space, the Nationalists went to a site near the county government building to build a "Patriotic Wall," where they put up more posters deriding me.

The Nationalists also actively courted my campaign manager, Teacher Chuang Ah-teng. Although he didn't participate much in strategy-making sessions, Teacher Chuang was very fastidious about detail, coming in to the office very early each morning. His job was coordinating the campaign publicity trucks—modified vehicles bearing campaign signs and loudspeakers—to which he gave daily routing assignments.

One day, a friend mentioned to me, "Have you noticed where Teacher Chuang goes in the afternoon?" I had been so busy that I had never noticed. "Every day he meets agents from the Bureau of Investigation for lunch, and then they take him to bars and hot springs in Beitou" (a place well known for brothels). The agents got Teacher Chuang drunk and tried to extract information from him, although I don't imagine he had many secrets to divulge. The Nationalists had unknowingly latched on to the wrong person, thinking that because he had been my teacher, Teacher Chuang was the campaign's main strategist.

My relationships with the leaders of the Dangwai political organization were rocky for the first weeks of the campaign. At the first general meeting of Dangwai candidates held at the Zhongshan Auditorium, I was seated in one of the back rows like any of the hundreds of other supporters, while other leaders and candidates in the election, like Kang Ning-hsiang and Huang Hsin-chieh, sat in the front rows. After the meeting, I bumped into Lin Yi-hsiung, whom I knew from the Chinese Comparative Law Society, the organization I had once stolen away from my hospital bed to attend. "Lawyer Lin," I said, "I'm running in the election. Please support me."

His face changed color and he waved his hand nervously, as if to banish an unpleasant apparition. "You're a Nationalist," he said. "I would never support you!" Disappointed, I swallowed my frustration to avoid worsening the situation. Clearly, he, too, had been influenced by the rumors about me.

I continued to participate in all the meetings held by the Dangwai candidates, and even put up posters of the Dangwai in my campaign office. Only gradually did I earn their trust, and slowly their resistance to my candidacy subsided. Dangwai elder Huang Hsin-chieh began speaking for me at campaign rallies. Chang Chun-hung's wife secretly sent supporters to assist my campaign. She had heard the rumors circulated by male Dangwai, but as a woman, she felt obligated to support me. The Taoyuan county chief executive, Hsu Hsin-liang, gave me his de facto backing after members of his staff became enthusiastic volunteers in my campaign. A member of Taiwan's Hakka minority, Hsu Hsin-liang supported me openly after a successful rally in the heavily Hakka-populated city of Chungli. The venue in Chungli was a large night market—a place where rows of small stalls sell food, clothing, and offer entertainment late into the night. My speech focused on Hakka identity and the role of Hakka in the democracy movement. At that time, the use of Hakka language was as severely restricted as Taiwanese.

Even more than the Hoklo people, the Hakka have suffered the pain of exclusion and the denigration of their culture. Fewer than two million mainlanders have long controlled Taiwan and imposed their language upon a diverse country. The more than two million Hakka in Taiwan deserve the dignity of speaking their own language and listening to it broadcast on television and on the radio.

One year ago, in an event now known as the Chungli Incident, the Hakka members of this community proved themselves determined to throw off the yoke of Nationalist oppression, when they rose up against the electoral manipulation, the vote rigging, and vote buying perpetrated by the Nationalists against Chief Executive Hsu Hsin-liang and against the people of Taoyuan County. Even while at Harvard University, I heard of the bravery of protestors from this community who marched on the police station and demanded a new election once the Nationalist Party's attempt to annul the democratic results of the county chief executive election were revealed.

You should be proud of yourselves for your contribution to Taiwan's democracy movement. You have inherited the Hakka tradition of revolution and resistance, and your accomplishments have received international recognition. The Chungli Incident taught the Nationalists a lesson. The party learned that the people of Chungli are not easily deceived. But the Nationalist habit of stealing the fruits of democracy is so deeply ingrained that it has not been completely uprooted.

By this time, the stalls in the market were empty and hundreds of listeners clustered around the podium. The swelling of the crowd, which covered several city blocks, bolstered the confidence of my campaign staff, and they refused to pass me repeated warning notes written by the vigilant prosecutor.

Deep down, I was afraid. I knew that a bullet could fly through my head at any moment. I concluded my speech by implying that the time had come for another Chungli Incident, and quietly stepped away from the microphone to the resounding cheers of the crowd.

Hsu Hsin-liang, listening in the audience, whispered to a friend, "She will be the next county chief executive."

The campaign, at long last, had taken off. The message I hoped to convey began to reach a broader audience. Yet dark clouds had gathered above Taiwan's ship of state, and the fires of democratic enthusiasm that I had fanned were soon to suffer the deluge of a political storm.

Although the essential points I made at rallies varied only slightly, we heard story after story of fanatic supporters who attended my rallies night after night. In one instance, a married couple from a rural area said they had been quarreling over which one would attend my rally and which one would stay at home. They both went and when they came home, they found that a thief had stolen all their chickens. My hairdresser told me of a factory owner addicted to gambling who apparently kicked the habit by going to my campaign rallies at night, and then abruptly picked it back up again with the cessation of campaign activities.

Early on the morning of December 16, while I was napping in my campaign headquarters, an excited man rushed in asking to see me. He said that although he had donated his house as office space to my rival Chao Chang-ping, after hearing me speak the previous evening, he ran home and tore the Nationalist candidate's billboard down. He wanted one of my signs to put up in its place. I had nearly lost my voice after all the speaking engagements and could barely croak out my appreciation. I was still dozing at my desk about an hour later when Eldest Sister suddenly burst into the office. "Something's happened!" she yelled. "I just heard on the radio. The US president has announced that America will recognize the People's Republic of China!"

A shocked silence descended over the room. Although I had predicted the abrogation of diplomatic ties between Washington, DC, and Taipei in a speech the night before, I hadn't expected it to happen so soon. In fact, I had thought it would take place the following February, during the Chinese Lunar New Year.

US President Jimmy Carter, along with his advisers, had announced the intention on December 16 to establish formal diplomatic relations with the People's Republic of China. Because the People's Republic would not permit US diplomatic relations with both China and Taiwan, the Carter administration informed the Chiang government that the US-ROC diplomatic relationship would end the following year. Now that many autobiographies and memoirs of the people involved in the decision-making process have been published, I know that Carter had a fantasyland perspective of China. One of his relatives was a missionary in China, and Jimmy Carter himself had been to China when he was in the navy.

At first the Chinese Communists had been reluctant to settle the matter, because the issue of Taiwanese sovereignty had not been resolved. China claimed sovereignty over Taiwan, and the Nationalist government claimed sovereignty over China, Taiwan, Tibet, and even Mongolia—long an independent country and a member of the United Nations. But starting from November, the People's Republic had decided to speed up negotiations. By mid-December there were rapid developments, which were kept out of the news by government censors.

The timing of the announcement, just prior to the Taiwan elections, led to rampant speculation and the rise of several conflicting explanations. One theory was that the United States felt "sorry" for the Nationalists and did Taipei a favor by making the announcement early in order to give the Nationalists an excuse to cancel the elections. A second theory was that Chiang Ching-kuo had requested the United States to do him a last favor by making the announcement early. A third theory was that the People's Republic had exerted its pressure. Beijing feared the newly organized Dangwai and its pro-independence stance even more than it feared the Nationalist Party, which remained committed to unifying China. A fourth theory was that President Carter was completely ignorant about what was going on in domestic politics in Taiwan. The third theory, pressure from the People's Republic, was perhaps the most accurate.

Following the statement by President Jimmy Carter, the White House issued another announcement for the settlement of the future relationship between the United States and Taiwan. It contained the following four main points: (1) the Mutual Defense Treaty between the Republic of China and the United States would be terminated; (2) all US military personnel would withdraw from Taiwan in four months; (3) the United States would continue to sell defensive weapons to Taiwan as appropriate and necessary; (4) an unofficial liaison office would be established to replace the American embassy. I had analyzed virtually all of these points in campaign speeches. Those who had heard me were astonished when the White House released its announcement. Some even called me a prophet sent from heaven.

My first reaction to the news was to attempt to contact other members of the Dangwai and to avoid panic. Soon it became clear that chaos reigned where optimism had so recently bloomed. I couldn't reach Hsu Hsin-liang. The staff of Dangwai legislative candidate Chang Te-ming phoned to ask me to meet them in Chungli. When I arrived, the place was in total disarray. I tried to calm anyone who would listen and told Chang's staff to take down the more provocative banners.

About an hour later, someone claiming to be an assistant of Kang Ning-hsiang telephoned Chang Te-ming's campaign headquarters, telling everyone to stop all election activities and meet at Kang's Taipei office. When I arrived, Kang's office looked like an empty house that had been caught in the path of a tornado. Campaign literature lay scattered in piles on the floor. He was nowhere in sight. When I finally found Kang at his home hours later, he looked surprised to see me. "Lu Hsiu-lien," he exclaimed, "someone just told us that you were the first one arrested!" He said that he had never given the order for the Dangwai to meet at his office. At this, I became very upset. Clearly we had been the victims of Nationalist foul play. Worse treatment might lie ahead.

When I telephoned Brother back at my campaign headquarters, he sounded like a beleaguered captain weathering a storm. Brother said that as soon as I had left the office, a group of unknown men had arrived and torn down my campaign posters and the banners on the Democracy Wall. An unknown person had painted a sunflower— supposedly the national flower of the People's Republic—where the posters had been. Alongside the sunflower were the green letters *TI*, signifying Taiwan independence. Brother believed the men were Nationalist-paid thugs or secret agents attempting to forge evidence against me.

When my staff had rushed out to stop the men, an argument had ensued, punches had flown, and then the vandals had attacked my office. By the time I called, the hooligans had left, but Brother described the situation as touch and go. He had received a number of phone calls from people threatening to kill the entire family and so had barricaded the office with a heavy metal gate. He advised me to lay low in Taipei until things calmed down.

In Taipei, however, I was disappointed with the group of candidates and political aides gathered at Kang Ning-hsiang's place. They were laughing and talking as if nothing had happened. Later, we learned that President Chiang Ching-kuo had declared a state of national emergency and cancelled all elections. "How could we be so irresponsible?" I wondered aloud. "We aroused the masses with passionate speeches, like heating a pot of water but turning off the gas right after the water boiled." Except, unlike the pot of water that eventually cools, mass sentiment in Taiwan continued to boil. And I, as the first Taiwanese student to return from overseas, was entering the struggle like a moth flying toward flame.

CHAPTER 5

HUMAN RIGHTS RIOT

FEAR OF THE UNKNOWN DARKENED THE DAYS FOLLOWING THE cancellation of elections. Would the government make scapegoats of Dangwai candidates? Would war break out as China, encouraged by its new relationship with the United States, became more belligerent? Would society disintegrate into panic and widespread unrest? The Dangwai candidates issued a statement demanding the government restore elections and allow the Taiwanese people to determine the nation's course. Then all we could do was wait.

Advised against returning to Taoyuan, I decided to stay with my friend Li Ang, a famous woman novelist. Anti-Americanism raged on the streets in Taipei. Listening to the radio, we learned of protests in front of the US embassy and of an attack on the swanky American Officers' Club, where military personnel held dances and parties.

Meanwhile, I holed up in Taipei and worried for the safety of my family in Taoyuan. Death threats continued to pour in, as well as allegations that I was in league with the CIA and the "running dog of the Americans." How else, Nationalist extremists reasoned, could I have known of the impending abrogation of US-Taiwan diplomatic relations? In the middle of the night, Brother's neighborhood rang with cries: "Fire! Fire!" It was a false alarm but a disturbing one. He called the police station, which sent two officers over to guard the house. Brother's children, who were attending junior high school at the time, drew scorn from classmates and teachers for my political activities. During the weekly school assembly, the principal launched into a lengthy diatribe criticizing Dangwai leaders Hsu Hsin-liang, Chang Te-ming, and me—an attempt to humiliate and demoralize our family. Brother also tried to shield Mother from the political storm outside. But he couldn't keep her from hearing the whispers on the streets and in the marketplace, and her anxiety continued to mount, even if she could not grasp the full complexity of the situation.

On January 18, 1979, President Chiang Ching-kuo announced the government would suspend the elections for an indefinite period of time. This forced opposition politicians to search for a new strategy to push Nationalists to reform, and ultimately, to relinquish power. Yet all other alternatives seemed to lie outside the limits allowed under martial law. The choice the Dangwai faced was to challenge the government more directly or retreat. Large public demonstrations and the establishment of independent magazines were manifestations of a new, fundamentally populist challenge to Nationalist rule, which arose on the heels of the government's decision to quash dissent.

My campaign for National Assembly had left me deeply in debt. I had borrowed heavily from the bank at high interest rates and spent a considerable amount on publicity. Eldest Sister helped me pay back some of the debt, in accordance with father's principle, "Never owe anyone anything." But this served to compound my guilt. My political adventurism had jeopardized the safety of my family members, and now they had to bail me out. It was too much. As I cast about for a means of bringing myself out of the red, the idea of publishing a magazine came to mind.

Three days after the cancellation of elections, I approached Dangwai elder Huang Hsin-chieh to propose the formation of a weekly magazine along the lines of *Time* or *Newsweek* in the United States. He was the main financier for many opposition enterprises and quickly became an enthusiastic supporter of the idea. Founding magazines was by no means a new endeavor for opposition politicians. Since the ban imposed on the formation of newspapers in the late 1940s, magazines had been the primary means by which Dangwai politicians could advance an alternative political agenda. Although, once they grew popular, magazines often became targets of government repression and were forced to shut down or continue publishing underground.

In the weeks after my meeting with Huang, I learned that other Dangwai leaders were preparing to publish the new monthly *Formosa Magazine* (Meilidao zazhi), and I toyed briefly with plans to publish my own separate magazine called *Penetration* (Toushi). I had all but written off cooperation with the Dangwai when Huang Hsin-chieh approached me about joining *Formosa Magazine* as deputy publisher and editor. He advised me to sign on for the sake of Dangwai solidarity.

In the absence of real opposition parties and independent media in Taiwan, *Formosa Magazine* was to serve both of these roles. All the key Dangwai leaders, with the exception of Legislator Kang Ning-hsiang, were on the magazine's staff. That meant the same people who had opposed my political campaign now grudgingly included me. A friend, Chang Chun-nan, once drew a cartoon of the decision-making structure of the *Formosa* group. Huang Hsin-chieh was a hat, Hsu Hsin-liang was the face, Yao Chia-wen the neck, Chang Chun-hung the chest, and Shih Ming-teh the legs. The dashing but evasive Shih Ming-teh, who had already served one life sentence in prison for discussing Taiwan independence, was essential for supporting and activating the entire structure. Shih rarely appeared in public. Legislator Huang Hsin-chieh, on the other hand, was the hat that protected and shaded the head. His position as a national legislator gave him symbolic importance. County Chief Executive Hsu Hsin-liang was the famous face that drew attention yet lacked real courage and depth of commitment. Yao Chia-wen was the neck that connected the head with the body. He had a stabilizing and strategic role and could be very stubborn—a bit of a stiff neck. Finally, Chang Chun-hung was the chest and the producer of all the rhetoric and public statements, the source of wind that sounded the horn of the opposition's advance. Never really an insider, I didn't earn the distinction of a body part in the cartoon, although I might have been portrayed as one or both of the hands. My role was primarily that of rally organizer and administrator, a position that seldom made me privy to the secret counsel of the magazine's leadership.

Not surprisingly, in the months that led up to the first issue of *Formosa Magazine*, I spent most of my time engaged in other endeavors. The book I had published during the elections, *Taiwan: Past and Future*, needed revision after the abrogation of US-Taiwan ties and the normalization of the Washington-Beijing relationship. This became the first of three books in a series I published with two other associates. The second book was *Looking Through Hsu Hsin-liang*, primarily a profit-making venture; it sold well because Hsu was the hottest topic in Taiwan politics at the time. The third book in the series, *The Unfinished Campaign*, examined the future of the Dangwai-sponsored reform measures after the cancellation of elections.

In June 1979, an opposition colleague, Chang Chun-nan, and I established an organization called the Dangwai Candidate Association. This association of candidates in the 1978 elections shared many of the same members as the magazine staff, but it operated in a more democratic fashion than Dangwai leadership as a whole. In the Dangwai Candidate Association, we elected board members and voted on procedure and association events. Too often for my comfort, the cartoon "features" of *Formosa Magazine* made important decisions without consulting others or bringing matters to a vote.

By midsummer, the relationship between Dangwai and the Nationalist authorities had become even more tense. Earlier that year, Hsu Hsin-liang and others had led protests against the wrongful imprisonment of one opposition politician, Yu Teng-fa, who the government accused of consorting with Communists in an elaborate frame-up involving allegations of smuggling. The demonstrations held to protest Yu Teng-fa's capture attracted hundreds of people and were the first large-scale demonstrations held under martial law. After the cancellation of the elections, the opposition had taken politics into the streets, a development that the Nationalists viewed with mounting fear and resentment.

Hsu Hsin-liang paid a price for his boldness. Searching for legal loopholes to bring him down, the government found that Hsu had not followed protocol in applying for personal leave as Taoyuan County chief executive before heading to the southern city of Kaohsiung to lead a demonstration. On June 28, the government's watchdog institution, the Control Yuan, suspended Hsu Hsin-liang as Taoyuan County chief executive.

Since I had studied law, Dangwai leaders decided I would go to court to pick up the formal court decision on the day Hsu's suspension was announced. During the subsequent press conference, a provincial assemblyman, Lin Yi-hsiung, walked in wearing rubber flip-flop sandals. These were typically informal Taiwanese footwear, but such events were less formal then. Someone told me that he was sick and couldn't stay long at the press conference, so I invited him to speak first.

"The Nationalist Party (not the Dangwai!) is a rebellious organization," he started. "Internationally, it uses fake democracy to deceive friendly nations. Domestically, it uses the pretext of recovering mainland China to deceive the people." This was vintage Lin Yi-hsiung rhetoric—direct, honest, and provocative. A stunned silence fell over the assembled reporters. In 1979, no one but Lin dared to speak like this.

After the press conference, we went to the home of Huang Hsin-chieh to discuss the most recent political development: the transformation of Kaohsiung City from a provincial city administered under the Taiwan provincial government to a so-called "directly administrated" special municipality. Supposedly, once the population of a city reached one million, its status would be elevated to equal that of a province. In the same way that provincial leaders were appointed by the Executive Yuan, mayors of these directly administrated cities were appointed rather than elected. The change deprived the people of Kaohsiung City of the right to elect their mayor, and reflected the government's latest ploy to retain control of the leadership in Taiwan's largest cities.

I proposed that we hold a rally to protest Hsu's removal. At the time, the political atmosphere was very intense in northern Taiwan and Taoyuan County, where Hsu Hsin-liang had been chief executive. The Nationalists predicted riots in the north and reinforced their military and police presence there. Even Hsu Hsin-liang himself grew reluctant to force the government's hand. But the south of Taiwan was left unguarded. I suggested we make secret preparations for a rally in Kaohsiung.

Yao Chia-wen and others had doubts that we could pull it off in the three days remaining before July 1, the date Kaohsiung would be made a special municipality, and a symbolic day for our demonstration advocating democratic reform. But Chang Chun-nan volunteered to take care of all the arrangements as long as Dangwai leaders agreed to speak. The others agreed to allow Chang Chun-nan and me organize the event. Even Yao Chia-wen seemed curious to see what we could accomplish.

Chang Chun-nan rented a bus with a loud microphone. I had banners made that read, sarcastically: "To 'celebrate' the changing status of Kaohsiung, meet the Dangwai tonight at Rotary Park!" When I arrived at Chang's home on the morning of July 1, I saw the bus parked in front of his house and several men standing about who looked like government secret agents.

Chang handled their surveillance with characteristic wit. He put his family and several of his students on the bus and loudly told a representative from the bus rental company that he was taking workers from his factory on a day trip. The agents overheard this and seemed to buy the story. As I got on the bus, the tour guide gave her usual welcoming speech, as if we were going sightseeing. We tried not to giggle as she introduced tourist attractions.

After we arrived in Kaohsiung, I brought out the banners and hung them on the sides of the bus. The bus driver realized he had been tricked, but he was Taiwanese and didn't seem to mind. Then, at a time and place designated beforehand, the Dangwai leaders all stepped onto the bus, with secret police tailing us in hot pursuit. The bus cruised the streets of Kaohsiung, publicizing our rally over the bus microphone, until the Kaohsiung City police pulled us over. They claimed we were too loud, a convenient excuse to get us off the road. Several Dangwai leaders stood arguing with police, while a crowd of onlookers gathered around and a unit of military police marched over. The police didn't know what to do. The Nationalists had been taken by surprise after focusing their riot-control strategy on Taoyuan and Chungli to the north, expecting protests there following Hsu Hsin-liang's removal. With just an hour of publicity, the word of the Dangwai event spread quickly throughout Kaohsiung, and that evening a crowd of 10,000 attended our rally in Rotary Park, a large turnout for an "illegal" political event.

A crucial turning point in Nationalist tolerance of Dangwai activism occurred later in July, at a monthly meeting held by the Dangwai Candidate Association in Taichung, a city in central Taiwan. The agenda would have been perfectly innocuous in any democratic country—a day of speeches and lectures at a hotel, followed by a rally in the park nearby. But as soon as the bus carrying opposition leaders entered Taichung, it was clear that the Bureau of Investigation had done its homework. Military police stood in pairs at the intersections of nearby streets. At the park, just a hundred yards away, stood a line of fire trucks.

Police stopped us in front of the hotel and demanded that the banners advertising the event be taken off the sides of the bus. The banners read "Dangwai Candidate Association," and I was quite proud of the fact that never before had the word "Dangwai" appeared in print, not even during the 1978 political campaign. A huge argument ensued. Why were our banners prohibited, I demanded, when those of traveling Buddhist monks and foreign dignitaries were not? As the debate grew more heated, a group of youths appeared and started shouting at us, "Kill the Communists! The people of Taichung don't welcome you!" The youths were right-wing extremists to whom our opposition to the party-state made us "Communist" sympathizers.

A large crowd of onlookers gathered to see what was going on. Folksinger Chiu Chue-chen took out his guitar and started singing Taiwanese songs, just as firefighters turned their hoses on the crowd. Agitators and onlookers alike were drenched. Angry people wrestled with the firefighters for control of the hoses in a massive fire-hose squirt-gun fight. The police chief radioed for a unit of riot police armed with shields, masks, and electric "cattle prods." To add a dose of satire to what had become a ludicrous spectacle, the Dangwai started singing "Recover the Chinese Mainland," a song popular within the military. The riot police responded by attacking the crowd with electric cattle prods. Dozens of people fell dizzy and vomiting on the ground. The Dangwai hurriedly boarded the bus. Yao Chia-wen was so angry that he stood in the door of the bus kicking the right-wing agitators as the bus drove away. Chang Chun-hung and Chang Chun-nan got on the bus loudspeaker and denounced the brutality of Nationalist rule. When the bus pulled away from the hotel, it was accompanied by a long line of squad cars that tailed us until we left the city limits.

We spent the night outside town and drove back into the city the next day, intent on holding a press conference in the hotel coffee shop. The place was crawling with secret police. The press had apparently been frightened away. All I could do was read a statement protesting police conduct. "We'll be back for justice in one month's time," I announced, before walking out.

One month later, I had devised our counterattack. The secret police had tapped most of our phone lines, so the Dangwai used several telephone conversations to trick the government into thinking we planned to hold a rally down in Taichung outside the same hotel on August 28.

"Linda," I said, while speaking on the phone to Shih Ming-teh's American wife, "don't forget to bring the microphone!"

"No problem, did the banners come out all right?"

"Perfectly."

On the day of the feigned rally, Chang Chun-nan went to check out the Nationalist response, asking a Dangwai groupie, who we suspected was a Nationalist spy, to go with him. The rest of us stayed home. Chang waited in the hotel coffee shop, while right-wing protestors and agents gathered outside. When no other Dangwai showed up, the agitators knew they had been fooled. This ruse confirmed our suspicions that Dangwai activities were being monitored very closely and that right-wing rabble-rousers in league with the government were Nationalist mercenaries—possibly recruited from mainlander underworld gangs—or were government agents in disguise.

The Dangwai Candidate Association filed charges against the Taichung Police Department for excessive use of force and violation of civil rights in the riot of July 28. We also filed charges with the military court against the Garrison Command, the government organization in charge of the secret police. Both cases proved fruitless but served as precedents for using the judicial system to mount institutional challenges to the Nationalist monopoly in power.

By early September, the Dangwai-sponsored *Formosa Magazine* was ready to promote the release of its first issue. Hsu Hsin-liang assigned me to organize a big media splash by throwing a cocktail party at the Cathay Hotel in Taipei. All the important Dangwai figures would be invited, as well as a number of journalists and most of the prominent Nationalist leaders.

By the late 1970s, moderates within the Nationalist ranks advocated the inclusion of more Taiwanese in governmental positions and negotiation with Dangwai politicians. Hard-liners favored a more iron-fisted approach to silencing the opposition and held greater influence over the military establishment and secret services. As relations with the Dangwai deteriorated further, the hard-liners advocated the use of coercion to crush dissent. We hoped to cultivate a better relationship with Nationalist moderates by inviting them to attend the *Formosa*'s promotional party. The attendance of important Nationalist officials would also lend an air of legitimacy to Dangwai activities.

Experience renting space for activities opposed by the government had taught me, as the event's organizer, to be devious. Too often the hotel or landlord would turn us out as soon as the Nationalists turned up the pressure. Hsu Hsin-liang suggested giving a very large deposit to the Cathay Hotel, complete with a contract stipulating that if the hotel annulled the agreement, it would have to pay compensation twice the amount of the deposit. I reserved a room large enough for five hundred guests, under the false pretense of hosting a wedding banquet.

Sure enough, as soon as secret agents got wind of the event, they leaned on the hotel management to cancel the agreement. The hotel manager, afraid to lose such a large sum of money, pleaded with me to go to the local police precinct and get a permit beforehand. With the Nationalist Kuan Chung negotiating for us, we were granted a permit, after it was pointed out that, with the exception of President Chiang Ching-kuo, almost all major Nationalist officials were invited to the cocktail party.

My plan called for making the event a very formal occasion, in order to give the impression that the Dangwai was a mature and well-organized opposition party. I had grown concerned by the cowboy-style showdown mentality of some of my colleagues and hoped that a more moderate approach might forge new political paths. Invitations were ornate and delicate. Visual aides were erected inside the banquet hall outlining Dangwai policy goals and recent events. I even wore a red-laced Chinese *qipao*, a traditional long, slim dress, for the occasion.

Tactical resistance by Nationalist hard-liners made my moderate approach extremely difficult. Just hours before the party was to start, dozens of Nationalist loyalists gathered outside the Cathay Hotel to protest the event. They had been misinformed that the radical Dangwai independence advocate, Chen Wan-chen, would return from the United States for the occasion. (In fact, she was on the government's blacklist and barred from coming home.) Mostly veterans of the Nationalist civil war in China, the men picketed with banners saying "Indict the National Bandit Chen Wan-chen" and "Is Patriotism a Crime?" and "Beat Hsu Hsin-liang to the ground!"

As the guests began to arrive, the crowd of protesters grew larger and more aggressive. The demonstration blocked the main street in front of the hotel, and riot police were called in to prevent a clash. Several women mistaken for Chen Wan-chen were attacked. The situation outside descended into chaos, prompting the police to bring in two armored buses and to offer to escort magazine employees away.

"Today's cocktail party is legal and nonviolent," I announced from the podium. "The illegal behavior is that of the protestors outside. Anyway, to leave just as the party is getting started would be inappropriate. Therefore, I ask the police to please remove the protestors, and invite everyone here to wait and see how the Nationalists handle the situation."

Applause greeted my remarks and everyone remained in their seats. The protest did not abate. Apparently, members of the Presbyterian Church had arrived outside and distributed to the crowd a declaration demanding democracy and Taiwan independence, with the effect of pouring gasoline on the fire of right-wing passions. Jeers were audible through the walls of the hotel: "We're warning you traitors, if you come out the front door, not even the police can guarantee your safety. Conclude this seditious gathering and walk out the side door with your tails between your legs!"

Guests and employees of *Formosa Magazine* waited inside the banquet room for over three hours, until Shih Ming-teh leaped up to the podium asking the young men present to prepare a "self-defense brigade." He told them to go behind the hotel to a construction site, where they would find sticks to use as clubs. Shih intended to enclose the elderly and the women in a phalanx of armed Dangwai and fight his way out of the hotel. A military man by training, Shih had spent more than half his life in prison for his beliefs and was extremely confrontational when cornered. Standing behind the podium with his thin mustache, dapper clothes, and dark, flashing eyes, he looked like a Taiwanese Errol Flynn. Shih Ming-teh understood life inside prison; years behind bars had estranged his first wife and two daughters. He had nothing more to lose but his life.

The secret service personnel, sitting quietly among the guests until this point, realized a crisis was at hand. A number of them got up and went outside to negotiate. The riot police and the fire trucks moved to push the protesters back, and the party guests poured out of the hotel, jumping into waiting cars.

That same night, the feared public security chief Wang Sheng had invited Hsu Hsin-liang and Chang Chun-hung to dinner. With the riot going on outside the hotel, Hsu and Chang were too afraid to cancel the engagement. But when Wang Sheng's aides drove by the hotel to pick them up in Wang's jeep, the protestors recognized Hsu and Chang but not the security chief's car. Right-wingers pounded the jeep with rocks, shattering its windows and denting its hood.

The media exposure that *Formosa Magazine* received from the standoff at the Cathay Hotel made it an instant hit with readers. Journalists from every major magazine and newspaper had attended the cocktail party and witnessed the spectacle. The first issue of the monthly sold 63,000 copies. By the third issue, *Formosa Magazine*'s circulation crested 100,000 copies—second only to the *Taiwan TV Guide*. Revenue pouring in from the sales allowed the magazine to set up nine offices in major cities and counties throughout Taiwan, facilitating greater ties with local constituencies. The *Formosa Magazine* group had taken on the institutional trappings of an opposition party.

Until this point, our fight against the Nationalists had been like fording a river: There were stones in the river that we had to step on in order to cross; we didn't know how deep the river was, nor did we know how stable the stones were. Each step was a risk, for if we stepped on the wrong rock, we could easily fall and drown. Hardened revolutionaries like Shih Ming-teh had slipped from the rocks before; one more fall wouldn't hurt. But those of us who had never fallen attempted to take precautions with every step.

In the months that followed, tensions heightened enormously. Military personnel started keeping an eye on our rallies, no longer through surveillance, but through the sights of machine guns mounted on rooftops. On two occasions in November and December, young men with crew cut hairstyles attacked *Formosa Magazine* offices in Kaohsiung and Taipei, smashing windows with axes and clubs and wrecking office furniture. No one was seriously injured. But I began to fear our nascent democracy movement would take a tragic turn, if the Dangwai didn't tone down its confrontational rhetoric.

"We need to change our style," I told Huang Hsin-chieh one day. "We should hold fewer rallies and more indoor, formal discussions and workshops." I suggested the Dangwai organize an event of this kind on December 16, exactly one year since Jimmy Carter's abrogation of diplomatic ties and the cancellation of elections. I also proposed using the occasion to state our pro-market economy and anti-Communist position, a distinction in our platform that had become important in the face of accusations that we were pro-Communist. Shih Ming-teh and Yao Chia-wen agreed, and I made plans to host a political symposium in the large Sun Yat-sen Memorial Hall and to invite moderate Nationalist advocates of democracy, such as the mainlanders Hu Fo and Tao Pai-chuan, as speakers.

On the evening of December 8, I noticed a black car full of government agents parked in the alley outside my apartment in Taipei. When I left my apartment in the morning, the car was still there. "Excuse me," I said, walking over to the car, "which department are you from and why have you been here all night?"

"You know why we're here!"

December 9 was Mother's seventy-first birthday. The family planned a big celebration in Taoyuan. Eldest Sister met me in Taipei, and we took a taxi to the bus stop with the black car following closely behind. This was the first time agents had so brazenly tailed me, and like the unwanted advance of a clumsy lover, it made me feel disgust and pity all at once. I assumed the agents would leave when I got to Taoyuan and they saw I wasn't attending any Dangwai activities.

When Eldest Sister and I got onto the bus, two of the agents bought tickets and got on with us. The other two followed behind in the black car. I turned to the two agents, saying, "I'm going home now. Aren't you tired of following me?" Eldest Sister and I took another taxi home from the bus stop, with the black car creeping along behind. The agents parked the car in front of Brother's home.

Little did the agents know that Brother owned two houses connected by a garden passageway. The houses extended between two parallel streets and had two entrances. I left the agents outside watching one door while I did errands, going out through the other. That night the agents telephoned Brother's home repeatedly, claiming to be my friends from various social circles. They wanted to make sure that I was still at home.

When the family all went off to a restaurant the next day to celebrate Mother's birthday, an agent phoned the restaurant, posing as a distant relative and offering to send flowers. Eldest Sister believed him and made me go to the entrance of the lobby to answer the call. Sure enough, one of the agents was waiting outside, snapping photographs of family members arriving at the birthday party. All he wanted was to make sure that I hadn't left, but a grim mood fell over what should have been a festive occasion. I decided to fight fire with fire. "What are you doing here?" I shouted at the agent with the camera.

"I'm waiting for someone," he replied, with a lopsided smile.

"You dirty cockroach! You've been waiting around for hours. Get out of here!"

When he ignored me, I called the police and had my brother-in-law come outside with his camera and retaliate by taking photos of the agent.

Since the National Assembly race, I had become quite famous in Taoyuan. The police chief himself drove over to investigate. When officers approached the agent taking photos, he whispered something to the chief, probably telling him of his "special mission" from the government.

The chief faced a dilemma. Nationalist higher-ups could easily fire him for failing to cooperate, so he tried to extricate himself from the situation with a face-saving white lie: "Ms. Lu, this is a simple misunderstanding. That man is only waiting for a friend. I'll ask him to go next door." The agent took a few steps away from the restaurant door and the police left.

That night, I told my family to inform all callers that I was resting and didn't care to be disturbed. Then, I slipped out the back entrance of Brother's house and caught a bus to Taipei, with the agents watching the front door. The ringing of the telephone greeted me as I walked in the door of my apartment. "Great," I thought, "another cockroach call."

It wasn't. An employee from the Kaohsiung office of *Formosa Magazine* was on the line. Two volunteers at the magazine had been taken to the Kaohsiung Police Station and beaten up. The men were seriously injured. As deputy publisher of the magazine, I was expected to go down and help to sort things out. Urgent phone calls from magazine staff continued to wake me until the early hours of the morning.

The bus ride to Kaohsiung from Taipei takes as long as six hours. Normally it's a pleasant trip as you leave the densely populated north of the island behind and swing south past dark green tropical forests and the orderly rows of rice fields. In southern Taiwan, the pace of life is slower than in the north, and I had always found the transformation, both in scenery and attitude, to be a relaxing one. But when I arrived in Kaohsiung on December 10, I sensed a new tension. Streets were blockaded. Soldiers and police stood at major intersections in nervous clusters.

I got off the bus and walked toward the *Formosa Magazine* office, and from a distance, I heard a voice projected through a sound system, reprimanding the police for the brutal beating of the volunteers. A huge crowd of angry people milled around outside. The inside of the office looked like an armory for a militant demonstration. Hundreds of torches, affixed to long wooden clubs, lay stacked in rows underneath rolls of *dazibao*, big-character posters, bearing political slogans.

The innermost room, where Yao Chia-wen and Shih Ming-teh were seated, had the air of a war council. Yao Chia-wen was studying a map of Kaohsiung with a red felt pen in his hand. I could see from the diagrams that they were planning a march but that riot police had blocked the original route along the main street in front of the Tatung Department store. Yao and Shih were debating an alternative route.

"What's happening?" I cried.

"Nothing that concerns you," Yao barked, "Get out!"

Yao and I had never really seen eye to eye on Dangwai strategy. Yet this time, I didn't challenge him. The tone of his voice and his tense posture told me that he was under a lot of pressure. I quietly left the room with the dizzy feeling that my life was slipping out of control. The moment had arrived, when I had to choose between supporting well-meaning but reckless Dangwai leaders or leaving my comrades to their fate in a dangerous confrontation with the Nationalists. A more pragmatic woman would have washed her hands of the whole affair and left immediately. Hsu Hsin-liang had recently lost his nerve and left Taiwan for the United States, after a fortune-teller predicted disastrous consequences if he remained in the country. I could have done the same.

Outside the office, I bumped into Chang Chun-nan from the Dangwai Candidate Association. Usually a jolly comrade, Chang wore a mournful expression. I could see that Chang, too, had realized that months of friction between Dangwai and the government were coming to a head. We walked next door to grab a quick bite to eat, and over dinner we agreed to hang on as the roller-coaster ride of the democracy movement rounded a new and more dangerous bend.

When we got back to the office, demonstrators were massing like troops going into battle. Tens of thousands of people were gathered and ready to march. Someone passed a lighted torch to me. Never comfortable with militancy, I quickly passed it on to someone else and fell into line with the marchers as the crowd began to move. Taking a look at the faces in the crowd around me, I noted with alarm that not all of the demonstrators appeared to be concerned citizens or even activists. In our midst marched a contingent of young men wearing navy blue jackets with small ROC flag emblems. They all had short, military-style haircuts, and I knew immediately where they were from.

By this time Chang Chun-hung and some other Dangwai leaders had arrived. They stood on a platform above a sound truck armed with a microphone and loudspeakers and covered with political banners. A friend spotted me walking below and invited me to join her on the truck. "It's dangerous down there," she said. It wasn't the masses she feared.

As I got onto the truck, the man next to me was shouting an anti-Nationalist invective over the loudspeakers: "In the struggle to determine Taiwan's future," he said, "fists are mightier than bullets." Someone in the crowd threw an egg at the speaker, but half of it landed on my face. The man that threw the egg had a crew cut and wore a navy blue jacket. The crowd responded with waves of indignation, chanting, "Catch him, beat him, kill him!"

Someone else grabbed the microphone and tried to calm the crowd: "Let him go, don't fall into the government's trap! Let us be careful now."

The demonstration came to an uneasy halt. A line of riot police was marching toward us, and a white mist drifted in the direction of the sound truck. The police had released tear gas toward the crowd.

The microphone was pushed toward me. I pushed it back, refusing to speak. The protest was descending into chaos, and I didn't want to waste my words.

At that point, a man from the *Formosa* office rushed over with word that another 20,000 demonstrators were trapped in front of Tatung Department Store nearby, barricaded and surrounded by military police. He wanted us to force the police to open the blockade and allow that crowd to join us; but with tear gas drifting in our direction, we wanted to evacuate as quickly as possible.

I was unfamiliar with the streets of Kaohsiung, so I asked the Dangwai writer Yang Ching-chu for directions to evacuate the area, because he was a native of the city. The crowd had other ideas, with many people calling out for a march on the Kushan Precinct Police Station, the site of the beating of two *Formosa* volunteers the night before.

Meanwhile, a messenger burst into the police station where Yao Chia-wen and Shih Ming-teh were negotiating with Nationalists. "How can you sit here talking to them?" the man cried. "They're blasting tear gas on us!" With this news, the negotiations over the demonstration broke down. Yao Chia-wen and Shih Ming-teh rushed over to the sound truck, and Yao redirected the crowd onto Ruiyuan Road, a small side street, avoiding police roadblocks and the high likelihood of a violent confrontation at the police station. In this unexpected move, Yao had spun the march around and headed it back toward a circular plaza in front of the *Formosa Magazine* office.

As the crowd moved away from the tear gas cloud, a minister from the Tainan Theological Seminary grabbed the microphone and shouted, "If your vehicles come any closer, the masses will turn them over!" His words pumped courage into the crowd disheartened by retreat.

The side street going toward the *Formosa* office passed through a quiet residential neighborhood. Concerned citizens and curious passersby poured out of their shops and houses; the crowd swelled enormously as newcomers joined our ranks. When the speakers shouted until their voices went hoarse, I stepped forward and took the microphone for the first time that night. Standing on the platform above the truck, I could look into the second- and third-story windows of the homes we passed. I saw people watching television; others were having dinner. On the sidewalk, young couples strolled along hand in hand.

"Citizens of Kaohsiung," I said, "today we must unite against Nationalist oppression. It's not the time for watching your favorite sitcom. It's not the time for romance. It's the time for strength, for solidarity. Please come out! March against Nationalist terrorism! Charge against the Nationalists!"

People within earshot put down their rice bowls and ran out to see what was going on. More and more joined. When we got to the Phoenix Bridge Restaurant, at a cross street, a small group of men clothed entirely in black and armed with clubs poured onto the street, attacking the police and soldiers in front of the demonstrators. "Let Taiwanese not fight Taiwanese!" I shouted, trying to quell the brawl. The marchers pushed on while the fighting spread to the flanks of the column. It was hard to tell who were agents provocateur and who were our supporters. The attackers wearing black fought so effectively that I felt certain they were professionally trained.

At last, the sign announcing the *Formosa Magazine* bobbed in front of me, and the brawl subsided as the march left the narrow street. Other Dangwai leaders took the microphone and announced the end of the rally. "The Nationalists sent massive troops to suppress us, yet we broke through their barricades tonight. We can go home as victors! Let's go home!"

Few heeded the call for pacifism. Cries for the demonstrators to disperse continued with little effect. The crowd grew even larger as stragglers caught up and supporters enthusiastically chanted, "Speech, speech, speech!"

With a serious expression on his young face, Chiu Chue-chen—the unofficial Dangwai bard—mounted the sound truck with his guitar and led the crowd in singing the Taiwanese folk song "Awaiting the Spring Breeze." This calmed some 70,000 demonstrators in front of the *Formosa* office, so when someone asked me to speak again, I took the microphone. Little did I suspect that I was about to give the most costly speech of my life.

My beloved fellow Taiwanese, all of you with a conscience, with compassion, my name is Lu Hsiu-lien. I'm from Taoyuan. Today, December 10, is International Human Rights Day. For hundreds of years, Taiwanese have never had a chance like they have today, a chance to give resounding expression to the appeal of our hearts for justice, to cry out our demand for human rights. Today is a great day. . . . The founder of our nation, Dr. Sun Yat-sen, once said, "People's rights don't fall from heaven, you have to fight for them." Human rights don't come naturally, they don't come by themselves, they have to be achieved with our sweat, with our blood, with the whole strength of our bodies.

Beloved members of the police force, you are also human beings, you are also Taiwanese. You have blood. You have tears. Do you not feel ashamed of what you are doing today? What you are doing today is extremely clear. Today you have already gone against many of President Chiang Ching-kuo's own teachings. . . . You have already put to shame the words of Prime Minister Sun Yun-suan, "In politics learn from Taipei." You've made him lose face. If you continue this disgraceful behavior, you'll make the Chinese laugh until their teeth fall out. You're not counterattacking the mainland, you're giving the Communist bandits good propaganda.

Beloved members of the security force, I know you're wearing helmets, you're wearing uniforms; but if you take off your helmets, if you take off your uniforms, your hearts are the same as our hearts, your blood is the same as ours. Please before you leave, remove your helmets, remove your uniforms.

You are Taiwanese, too. . . . In the nations of the world, countless heads of state have been overthrown, banished, assassinated. This should change the color of the heavens, and fill the grass and trees with sorrow. Many of these rulers were dictators that used force for power and wealth, and lived by this brutal and merciless code. For the passing of these rulers there is no sorrow;

instead the people recite prayers of thankfulness to Buddha.

The Nationalists' many failures have awakened the Taiwanese people. Everyone knows the meaning of democracy, human rights and rule by law. Gradually, the average citizen has become dissatisfied with the ruling party's thirty-year rule, and the Dangwai-led democracy movement has, in the year since the cancellation of elections, progressed like wildfire. So many friends have stood on the side of the Dangwai. But there are others, dissatisfied and unforgiving that the government has allowed the Dangwai to breed and multiply like so many mosquitoes. I want to explain why the Dangwai, this groups of fools, are not afraid to sweat and run up and down the island without thought for themselves, without concern for their families. What's the hurry, anyway?

Some people say the Dangwai are savage and violent. Some say Dangwai are separatists. I ask you, why is the Dangwai savage? Where do they disagree with the government? Today, everyone has seen that the drivers of the riot trucks are Taiwanese and ordinary citizens—these people are the real separatists among us. If the Dangwai are savage or forceful in nature, this is because the Nationalists rule without the permission of the Taiwanese and have yet to return authority to the eighteen million people. In truth, the Dangwai are not savage at all: they're fools. Do you think they lead normal lives?

Two years ago I had a comfortable life in the United States, living each day for myself. But when I heard that China and the United States were to establish diplomatic relations, I knew that Taiwan was soon to sail into very troubled waters. I couldn't eat. I couldn't sleep. I gave up my degree prospects at Harvard and the opportunity for comfort in the United States in order to join the Dangwai struggle.

The danger of Nationalist rule was, of course, that the party had become too enfeebled internationally to protect Taiwan's interests. And due to its dictatorial control of national, provincial, and local government, the regime didn't legitimately represent these interests in the first place.

The crowd had gone silent listening to my speech, but the grinding of huge motors awoke everyone to a new danger. In the distance, massively dark shapes moved toward the crowd. The shapes were of beasts breathing clouds of white smoke into the air and terror into my soul.

"The dinosaurs are coming!" I shouted, as my mind grappled to explain the appearance of the glowing headlights on ghastly antiriot trucks spewing tear gas.

As the shapes grew larger, the crowd erupted into howls of anger. People scrambled for clubs and other weapons to defend themselves. Kang Ning-hsiang, a respected legislator, was dragged in front of microphones, where he appealed for calm and passive resistance. Instead of following his lead, the crowd chanted antigovernment slogans: "Protest police brutality! Return our freedom of speech! Release political prisoners! Long live the Taiwanese people!"

I got off the truck and watched in horror as demonstrators, who had no plans of rioting when they arrived earlier that evening, moved one by one to pick up sticks, rocks, torches and held their ground in the face of police calls of "Withdraw! Disperse!"

Suddenly, the wind shifted back in the direction of the ranks of police and soldiers, blowing the white clouds of tear gas backward. A great wave of laughter rolled across the crowd as dozens of riot police fell staggering under the white cloud. Then, the protesters launched a counterattack, hurling missiles of every sort, swinging clubs, even tearing a telephone booth from the sidewalk to heave at the approaching trucks. Riot police reeled under this onslaught, and then pushed forward in tight ranks of silver shields, their steel batons swinging. The demonstrators fought back, fell swooning from wounds or tear gas, or turned to flee police encirclement.

In the midst of the clash, the Dangwai leaders quickly assembled in a nearby coffee shop. Everything had happened so suddenly, and the sheer terror and immensity of the riot had caught us off guard. Some in our midst suffered from tear gas inhalation, including Chen Chu, who was taken to the hospital. Chiu Mao-nan, a provincial assemblyman who had organized a contingent of protestors, was almost shaking. "Will they arrest us now?" he asked. No one answered. We realized that we were surrounded by secret agents in the coffee shop and couldn't discuss anything. "Let's meet up in Tainan City" was the whispered consensus. To avoid attention, we slipped away in small groups.

The city of Tainan, an old Dutch seaport, lies just to the north of Kaohsiung. That night the trip to Tainan seemed to last forever. The night air was cool. Distances loomed large and intimidating after the tight city streets. I had lost all sense of proportion and direction. "Are we going the right way?" I asked the driver impulsively. "Usually it takes only forty minutes to reach Tainan. Why does it seem like we've been on the road for two hours?"

Sitting next to me, Legislator Kang Ning-hsiang just chuckled, "The road is always long when one's heart is heavy."

At the Tainan Hotel, Kang Ning-hsiang rented two rooms, one for the men and another for the women. Shih Ming-teh and Yao Chia-wen arrived shortly thereafter. I went in to wash up and take a nap while the others held a meeting. Some were optimistic, some pessimistic about the likely outcomes of the clash.

In the early hours of the morning, I got up and rejoined the others, who had accomplished very little, since the "dragon's head," Huang Hsin-chieh, was nowhere to be found. It was agreed that a statement should be released explaining the Dangwai side of the story and that $5,000 should be donated to the police injured in the conflict. Several attempts were made to contact Huang in Taipei. He was not home. Using mutual recollections of the night before, we attempted to piece together the whereabouts of the magazine's first in command. Sadly, it became clear that misunderstandings between Huang and Commander Chang Chi-hsiu of the Taiwan Garrison Command, the city's top law enforcement official, had exacerbated tensions between protesters and military police.

On the evening of December 10, long before the action started, Huang Hsin-chieh had been summoned to Kaohsiung because negotiations between *Formosa* leaders and the police had failed to yield results. Commander Chang had made a personal request for Legislator Huang to go down to Kaohsiung to resume negotiations. When Huang had arrived at the Kaohsiung railway station at around 6:00

P.M. that evening, he had been greeted in person by the commander and invited into the VIP lounge. This had prompted the first misunderstanding of the evening, because the aide accompanying Huang on his trip thought that Huang had been arrested. After waiting for a long time in the railway station, the aide had rushed to the *Formosa* office, announcing that Huang had been detained by the police.

Meanwhile, Huang and Commander Chang had been able to strike a bargain on proceedings for the evening. The compromise was that there could be speeches but no march, and that the rally could be held only at the "original location." Unfortunately, neither side had clarified what "original location" meant. Huang thought it meant the Tatung Department Store. Unfortunately, by the time Huang left the negotiations, the march he had promised to halt was already in progress. He had tried in vain to stop the demonstration, shouting, "The march is over now, everyone please go to Tatung Department Store to hear speeches!"

Apparently, the commander had had something else in mind by the "original location." When Huang saw that military police had barricaded the entire area around the department store, he felt Commander Chang had deceived him. The commander, for his part, was incensed that the march had taken place.

With Shih Ming-teh and Yao Chia-wen in tow, Huang had charged back to the police headquarters, screaming, "You cheated me!"

"You cheated us!" the police had responded.

In the middle of this shouting match, a messenger had run in with the word that riot police had used tear gas on the marchers, prompting Shih and Yao to race back and redirect the march toward the *Formosa* office.

Dazed by the escalation of events and plagued by hunger, Huang had gone off for a bite to eat. It was a long dinner, and by the time he got back to the site of the march, the crowd had already returned to the office. We heard later that Huang had even asked some military police, "Where did the crowd go?" By the time Huang had caught up with the action at the *Formosa* office, I was making a speech. "Lu Hsiu-lien's crazy!" he had told Shih Ming-teh.

When it was Huang's turn to take over the microphone, he had shouted, "I warn you, police! Do not come any closer! If anything happens tonight, you must take responsibility." The police had ignored his words. "The rally is over now!" Huang had cried. "Everyone, please go home and get a good night's sleep!" He had missed too much of the conflict that night to understand the mood of the crowd, or to earn its respect. Someone had poked Huang with a stick from behind, which made him realize that the stage wasn't the place for him. He had hurriedly left the scene to catch a bus back to Taipei. Huang was probably still on the road when we tried to telephone him.

An air of sobriety fell over the Dangwai leaders. Clearly, misunderstandings had precipitated the conflict, as well as a government plot to infiltrate the demonstration and wreak havoc. When we bought the Kaohsiung morning newspaper, there was half a page of reports on the incident, none containing particularly vociferous criticism. This provided some sense of relief. Yet there was no consensus on a future course of action. Kang Ning-hsiang wanted to go back to Taipei to better observe the Nationalist response, as the party was in the middle of the Fourth Central Committee Plenum. Yao Chia-wen went to the prosecutor's office in Yunlin County to the north to prepare a legal defense. Shih Ming-teh assigned me to write the memorandum on the incident.

As it turned out, the Nationalist propaganda machine was slow to move but powerful once in motion. The Garrison Command, the branch of the military in charge of the secret police, held a press conference on December 11, accusing us of seditious behavior. The military spokesman linked the Kaohsiung Incident to the meeting I had planned for December 16, which they called an "anti-America conference." This was a transparent attempt to weaken foreign support for the Dangwai by making the United States think the protest was anti-American. Nationalist officials at the Fourth Central Committee Plenum released damning statements. Other government officials, including all the mayors and county chief executives in Taiwan, released a joint statement condemning us as "violent rebels." Even the non-Nationalist mayors of Tainan and Taichung drew a clear line separating themselves from *Formosa Magazine*. Their joint statement read: "We deeply resent the violent and irrational behavior of *Formosa* employees. The government must sternly punish these elements, who have no respect for the law and intentionally cause trouble, in order to stabilize society and satisfy the people." Soon, the mainstream press echoed these condemnations. Editorials across the island called for punishing *Formosa*'s violent behavior at the Human Rights Day demonstration that quickly earned the moniker "Kaohsiung Incident."

On Tuesday, December 12, two days after the demonstration, the Dangwai held a meeting at the home of Huang Hsin-chieh. We were all very depressed, and when I got there at around 10:00 A.M., people were talking about the threatening phone calls and other harassment they had been subjected to over the past two days. Chen Chu had received so many threatening telephone calls that she had notified the police.

Huang Hsin-chieh wanted me to check out some hotels to see if we could book a space to hold a press conference that weekend. "Are you kidding?" I shot back, "We don't have time to wait until Saturday! The Garrison Command has already held a press conference. We need to clear our name as soon as we can!" Without looking around the room, I glanced at my watch. "Today, at 5:00 P.M., we'll hold a press conference at the *Formosa* office in Taipei. That will allow reporters to attend before they go to the office at 7:00 P.M."

The meeting had stretched into the noon hour when a friend telephoned with word that a member of my staff at Pioneer Publishing had been gassed on the night of the Kaohsiung Incident. "Ms. Yang" had gone down to Kaohsiung to help me sell cassette tapes of Taiwanese folk music on which the government had imposed a ban. She had ended up in emergency care. I had been so preoccupied with other concerns that I hadn't noticed she had disappeared. Apparently, Ms. Yang had fainted in Kaohsiung and then fainted again after returning to Taipei. She was, at the moment, in the emergency room of Jenai Hospital.

I didn't have any money with me to cover Ms. Yang's medical expenses, so Huang Hsin-chieh's wife gave me some cash, and a

Dangwai friend agreed to take me to the hospital on the back of his motorcycle. As soon as we stepped outside and got on the motorbike, a black government car pulled out behind us. The more powerful car kept up with us on the wide thoroughfares, so my friend darted into alleyways too narrow for the car to follow. The car stopped, and one man and one woman jumped out and chased after us on foot.

The agents had received special physical training, and it was difficult even for the motorcycle to negotiate the narrow lanes. When we arrived at the hospital, the agents were still with us, and they followed us inside. "Say, can you tell me where the emergency room is?" I asked one of the agents.

"I don't know!" she snapped back.

In the emergency room, I found Ms. Yang lying in bed with an intravenous needle stuck in her arm. Her face was pale. Ms. Yang's mother stood beside her in a state of panic. "Little sister Yang," I said, "can you hear me?" Her glazed eyes looked off into the distance and she did not respond. My stomach twisted with guilt and regret. If only she hadn't accompanied me down to Kaohsiung! It suddenly occurred to me that she had perhaps encountered something more than gas poisoning. Later, I learned that Ms. Yang had fainted and been raped. Afraid that staying by her side too long would bring more hardship, with the government agents watching my every move, I handed Ms. Yang's mother money to pay for the medical expenses and left.

At 5:00 P.M., I was at the *Formosa* office in Taipei for the press conference. The large number of journalists that showed up was surprising, considering the extent of the Nationalist vilification of the Dangwai. Huang Hsin-chieh was the first to speak, followed by Yao Chia-wen and Shih Ming-teh. The three men outlined the *Formosa* view on the Kaohsiung Incident contained in the documents "Memorandum of International Human Rights Day" and "Message to Our Compatriots." The central thrust was as follows:

> This magazine expresses the deepest concern and regret to injured riot police and frightened citizens. . . . We ask the cooperation of the secret service establishment in seeking a peaceful and ratio-

nal solution to the people's demands for democracy and human rights. We hope the administration will not belittle the intelligence of the citizenry through the continuation of idiotic policy. We believe that in the aftermath of this unfortunate incident, the government should avoid missteps that will lead to political turmoil playing into the hands of the People's Republic, or use the Kaohsiung Incident as an excuse to prolong its military rule.

The next speaker was Lin Yi-hsiung, who had clear distaste for the apologetic line taken by the magazine's leadership. "You reporters only listen to the Nationalists," he said. "You've never reported the truth; I despise you!"

Shouts of resentment greeted his outburst. Some reporters walked out. It took the joint effort of Huang and Yao to calm the journalists down and convince Lin Yi-hsiung to apologize. Yet at some level, we all shared Lin's frustration, if not an appreciation for his tactics. For three days and nights, we had shuttled back and forth from the north of the island to the south. None of us had slept or eaten well. Every newspaper we opened and television report we saw attacked the Dangwai. The Kaohsiung and Taipei *Formosa* offices had suffered from repeated violent attacks and disturbances. Needless to say, exhaustion and frustration weakened our response to the Nationalist-controlled media's unilateral attack. As far as influencing the domestic media, the press conference appeared to be a failure.

As the journalists began to file out of the room, Diane Yin from the *New York Times* stayed behind to interview me about the "Kaohsiung Incident," the name given to the clash by the news media.

"All of this is an elaborate trap the Dangwai descends into one step at a time," I said. "What's terrible is that even now, we don't know who's moving our hands and feet." Images flashed through my mind of the young men with crew cut hairstyles and matching jackets who had thrown eggs on the night of the demonstration, and of the numerous other attackers. "Taiwanese society is divided into two extreme camps, and I worry that a third party will occupy the center during the struggle between the Nationalists and the Dangwai."

Why had I planned an "anti-American" demonstration for December 16, she wondered, referring to remarks made at the Garrison Command's press conference.

"We never planned an anti-American demonstration. We made plans for an anti-Communist conference. That's all." I asked the office secretary to bring out a copy of the application for a permit to corroborate my remarks. "See here," I said, pointing to the event title on the document, "anti-Communist conference."

My eyes continued down the page, and to my surprise I saw that the permit called for a march on the presidential palace by 30,000 people to "pay respects" to the president! No wonder the secret police had been so nervous and had made me the target of their surveillance. They feared Dangwai planned a rebellion. My heart became heavy with panic; there was the sick feeling of betrayal. Dangwai colleagues had exposed me to untold dangers by leaving me in the dark while they hatched a secret plan to hold a demonstration in Kaohsiung.

That night, I invited a group of *Formosa* employees to dinner at a Chinese hotpot restaurant near National Taiwan University. Usually I didn't host dinners, because of the large expense, but I had just received a dividend from the magazine. Taking the money myself didn't seem right; I didn't go into the office regularly or take part in many strategy meetings. Perhaps I had a premonition of the tumult to follow, but I was reminded of Jesus and his farewell dinner with the Twelve Apostles. "You never know," I said jokingly, "this could be our Last Supper."

When we left the restaurant, I saw the secret service men who had followed me all day waiting outside. Chen Chu's nerves were so frazzled by constant harassment, not to mention tear gas inhalation, that she suggested we spend the night together for safety. I agreed, and we decided to stay in the spare room of the editorial offices of the magazine. In retrospect, we could not have chosen a more controversial location. Shih Ming-teh and his American wife Linda Arrigo shared a room in the same complex. Provincial assemblyman Lin Yi-hsiung had an apartment on the ground floor of the building. From the standpoint of the secret service agents, we had returned to the site of "crouching tigers and hidden dragons."

Shortly after we returned from the restaurant, Yao Chia-wen called us to a meeting at his place. Shih Ming-teh, Chen Chu, and I shared a cab, with three black government cars following behind. Two cars had been tailing Shih Ming-teh, and one had been following me. "Are they secretive enough?" Shih asked, waving to the cars behind us. He sensed a new tension between us after my discovery that he had concealed plans for a march on the presidential palace, so he tried to lighten the mood. I played along. At the moment, solidarity seemed more important than strife.

"We should catch a ride with them rather than waste money on cab fare!" I said.

When we arrived, several more black cars were parked outside Yao's residence. It looked more like a secret service convention than a stakeout. Dozens of men and women walked around clutching walkie-talkies. Yao chaired the meeting and assigned everyone duties for the following day. He asked me to take charge of the office in case anything happened. Shih Ming-teh had been to prison twice before. We were certain that Shih couldn't escape going back very soon. The rest of us had no idea what to expect.

Back at the *Formosa Magazine* office, Shih Ming-teh and Linda rushed to make several overseas phone calls, in an attempt to garner foreign assistance if something should happen. Shih was visibly preparing himself for the worst. He wrote a statement of divorce for Linda, so that she could have freedom during his incarceration. I overheard Linda shouting that she had torn up the statement; then the two retired to their bedroom.

Exhausted from fear and stress, Chen Chu and I fell asleep in the guest room. Meanwhile, Linda stayed awake to keep close watch on the situation outside. Just as dawn began to lighten the sky, she heard a pounding on the main gate below. Linda ran to the telephone only to find that the telephone line had been cut. From the front balcony, she saw a crowd of men in front of the building's ground-floor courtyard. Linda shouted for Shih Ming-teh, then went to the living room and barricaded the front door, using the couch, chairs, the table—anything she could move.

"Don't come in," Shih yelled, coming out of the bedroom. "I have planted a bomb in the doorway. If you open the door, it will explode." It was a ruse to gain more time.

"Get up! Get up!" Shih shouted in the direction of our room. "They've come to arrest us!"

I rolled over in bed, feeling like I had just gotten to sleep. As soon as I could open my eyes, my first thought was to get dressed as quickly as possible. If I was to die and stand face to face with my ancestors, I wanted a modicum of respectability. I ran to the bathroom to wash and to brush my hair. When I came out of the bathroom, everyone had disappeared.

As soon as Chen Chu had heard Shih's warning, she had run onto the rear balcony to warn Lin Yi-hsiung in the apartment below, thinking the Kaohsiung Incident had little to do with him and that he could help handle Dangwai affairs after we were imprisoned. Still wearing her nightgown and bedroom slippers, Chen Chu jumped from the office balcony down to the ground, screaming, "Lin Yi-hsiung! Lin Yi-hsiung!" and twisting her ankle in the process. Chen Chu was on the ground writhing in pain when secret agents found her and placed her in handcuffs.

In the apartment below, the secret police broke a window to gain entry, and Lin's wife was the first to awaken, as several police rushed into their apartment. In front of his wife and three frightened daughters, Lin was handcuffed, led barefoot across a floor covered with broken glass, and stuffed into a waiting squad car.

Upstairs, the pounding on the door outside had given way to the incessant ringing of the doorbell. No matter what happens, I told myself, the situation has to be dealt with bravely and responsibly. I had done nothing more than give a speech on the night of the Kaohsiung Incident. Certainly this was not a punishable crime. I walked calmly into the living room, moved away Linda's barricade, and prepared to open the front door.

"Lu Hsiu-lien!" The cry came from behind me. I turned to see four or five large men coming through the kitchen. They had climbed into the office from the rear balcony.

The man shouting my name was none other than the young agent who had followed me around the clock for five days—the very one who had harassed me at Mother's birthday party. Even more shocking was that when I looked over the men's shoulders, I could see the lithe shape of Shih Ming-teh, snaking along a fire escape four houses away and preparing to leap to the ground.

Holding up my hands, I surrendered silently and lowered my eyes so that no one would turn to see the outline of Shih's figure on the fire escape. I plopped down into a chair while more agents crowded into the living room; I realized that some of them had been tailing me for days. Two men held my arms, while two women searched me, ordering me to turn over the office key.

"This is a search permit from the prosecutor's office," said one agent, producing a piece of paper. "You are a lawyer and we want to handle everything according to the letter of the law." My eyes skimming the paper, I read, "Suspected of sedition." Treason? My heavens! Shock and disbelief rendered my mind completely blank. Treason was punishable by death.

Suddenly, a woman's piercing scream came from the back balcony. Several agents had caught Linda, and her cries were like those of a chicken in the talons of an eagle. She had climbed onto a neighbor's balcony to borrow a telephone and seen the agents below her. The agents had grabbed Linda as she knocked on the neighbor's back door to be let in. I watched quietly as she was searched. Her eyes met mine for an instant as I was led out the door. That was the last time Linda and I would see one another for seven years.

The agents took my keys away as I sat inside the black government car. Agents were sent to the Pioneer Press, where I kept one room as a residence. A thorough search was conducted for evidence linking me to an alleged plot to overthrow the government. When the agents found nothing, they confiscated all the books stored at Pioneer Press. The press lost approximately 30,000 volumes, and I went bankrupt overnight.

CHAPTER 6

PATRIOTISM IMPRISONED

AS SOON AS I ENTERED THE JINGMEI DETENTION CENTER, located in a suburb of Taipei, I could feel my self-confidence slip away. Guards took my watch, wallet, and jewelry—small symbols of individuality that linked me with the outside world. Even my eyeglasses were taken, without which I was nearly blind. I was left wearing a black sweater under a brown jacket, black skirt, and high-heeled shoes that looked incongruous in my stark surroundings. To my myopic eyes, the cold gray walls of the prison cell took on a foggy, dreamy quality. Then, I heard the clicking approach of a guard, the hard soles of her shoes ringing out in the corridor. The sound stopped in front of my cell, followed by the rattling of keys.

"Ms. Lu," the guard announced crisply, "you will come with us."

They led me into a larger room where four government agents awaited. "Sit down!" an agent barked. "You have been arrested for plotting to violently overthrow the government. This crime carries a mandatory death penalty. Only full cooperation can save you and protect the welfare of your friends and loved ones. This case is a political one that will be solved through political means. Understand? Tell us everything that happened on the night of December 10. Do not attempt to hide your guilt or your participation in the Dangwai conspiracy."

"I am not guilty of sedition and there was no conspiracy."

"No conspiracy? Ms. Lu, we have independent sources of information that clearly document your participation in numerous schemes to topple the government. You will confess your guilt. Now, what was your role in the violent attack on government forces on the night of December 10?"

I tried to outline the events leading up the Kaohsiung Incident as clearly as possible. My explanations were constantly interrupted as agents shouted down my remarks. This was the opening salvo of interrogation that lasted around the clock for more than fifty days. Agents rotated in shifts, taking breaks for meals. Everything I said was greeted with cold sarcasm or heated disagreement. The agents insisted I write a "confession." I was to write down everything that I knew about the Dangwai, describe everything I had done on the night of the Kaohsiung Incident, and sign the paper at the bottom. My refusal to sign a confession brought on a tirade of verbal abuse, punishment, and humiliation. Never satisfied with my portrayal of events, they forced me to write and rewrite the confession countless times.

After the first few days of no sleep and nonstop interrogation, I was already exhausted and numb from the lashing verbal attacks. In the interrogation rooms, black window covers blocked out the sunlight, and I could no longer distinguish day from night. There was no contact whatsoever with the outside. No phone calls, newspapers, or consultation with defense lawyers. When I returned to my cell, there was no darkness that might allow deep sleep. Four bright TV monitors lit the corners of the room, and fluorescent lights glared down from the ceiling day and night. There was no bath or shower, only a half-gallon bucket of hot water that was refilled each day. I never saw other prisoners and only heard the clicking footsteps of guards in the hallway. When the clicking stopped in front of my cell, I knew another round of interrogation was about to begin.

My interrogators were intent upon demonstrating that I had ties to the overseas Taiwan Independence Movement. They insisted that I was a member of the movement and that I divulge everything I knew about pro-independence organizations overseas. Although I had attended conferences and meetings in Europe and the United States, I actually knew very little about the pro-independence groups beyond their demands to end Nationalist rule, establish democratic government, and declare Taiwan's independence from China.

During one interrogation, I stood facing several agents seated at a table. I had only the high-heeled shoes that I wore on the day of my arrest, so standing for hours and answering their tedious questions proved an exhausting task. The agents began by discussing the fate of a purported spy named Wu Tai-an, who the government claimed to have executed.

"Many people don't believe Wu Tai-an was really executed," one agent said, speaking in a low voice, "and as a result they have continued to defy the government."

"Many people don't believe Wu Tai-an ever lived," I countered, "because no one ever met him."

Another young agent walked forward and produced a photograph. The photo showed the blood-spattered figure of a bare-chested man executed by firing squad. "Traitors like you deserve to die!" he shouted. "In two days, your family will collect your corpse!"

A third agent presented me with a funeral home notice addressed to Wu Tai-an's wife that asked her to pick up his remains. "Read it out loud," he demanded. I began to read it. "Louder!" he shouted. By the time I had finished reading, tears of humiliation burned my cheeks. I was nearing the limits of my strength.

"Start composing the inscription for *your* gravestone!"

I numbly complied: "Lu Hsiu-lien, thirty-six years old, author and feminist. . . ."

"Executed for treason!" the man screamed, finishing the sentence and slapping the table with both hands. "Military regulations mandate that all prisoners are executed naked from the waist up. How do you feel about that?"

"She should make out a will," suggested a female agent, sympathetically. "Miss Lu, would you like to write your will?"

"No!" I sobbed, "Wu Tai-an never existed. He was a Nationalist creation intended to frighten the Dangwai." The allusion to my barebreasted execution struck a deep chord. It was a very personal attack on me as a woman, and the closest the interrogators had come to sexual harassment.

"Only cooperation will save you! Cooperation. Understand? Now, tell us the truth about your involvement in the Taiwan Independence Movement. Tell us more about your conversations with Chang Wei-chia in Switzerland!"

Chang Wei-chia was the friend who had first introduced me to the independence cause. While in Switzerland, Chang had asked me to find out if a friend of his had returned safely to Taiwan. I was given a code and told to write him a postcard when I returned to Taipei. The Bureau of Investigation had intercepted this postcard, claiming that it was evidence that I supported groups attempting to overthrow the government.

"I don't know anything beyond what I have already told you," I protested.

"'I don't know?' Ms. Lu, 'I don't know' is no longer a phrase you are allowed to use. Remember this: in front of us, you don't have the right to say 'I don't know!' We'll give you another try. How does one become initiated into the Taiwan Independence Movement?"

"I don't know," I said softly.

"Your life is at stake, yet you oppose our efforts to help you!"

One of the agents motioned for me to approach the table. "Here is pen and paper. Write 'I don't know' on every line."

I scrawled out "I don't know" repeatedly. The agent carefully tore the paper, line by line, and handed me the pieces.

"Now, eat your words. Every one."

I took the pieces and slowly put them into my mouth.

"Every piece! Now open your mouth. Show us that you've swallowed them. That's good, real good."

I felt sick, humiliated, unbelievably exhausted. Death seemed better than continuing to live in this manner. Death was my one sure escape. The agents left me standing in the interrogation room for six hours in high-heeled shoes, legs quivering, and weeping uncontrollably. I was not allowed to rest, eat, or even go to the restroom.

When I returned to my cell, I took out a small notebook that I had managed to keep hidden since the night of my capture. Its pages provided my only solace by allowing me to record my experiences. I wrote that I had not eaten and that I was made to stand for several hours.

The following day, the guards searched while I was away and confiscated the notebook. The interrogators read it and asked if I planned to take revenge, saying that henceforth they would stuff me to the gills. Writing, in any fashion, had been my way of escaping the horror of my circumstances. Not only did I lose an important account of my early imprisonment, I lost my only means of processing, emotionally, those endless days.

For three or four days thereafter, my food tray was overflowing with rice, vegetables, and meat. It was easily enough food for two people. One agent watched to make sure I finished everything—every last piece of vegetable and grain of rice. Once, they cut the rectum out of a chicken and made me eat that, too. Worse than this humiliation resulting from their discovery of my notebook, its confiscation made me fear that continuing to write could worsen my hardship.

One day soon after, the clicking of boots stopped in front of my cell. Keys rattled and the iron door clanged open. "Ms. Lu, you'll come with us," the military policeman said. I was already dreading the threats and abuse I would have to endure.

"Ms. Lu," one of the agents said, "we are fully aware of your intimate connections with the United States Central Intelligence Agency. Today you will tell us all you know about the CIA."

"I don't know anything about the CIA," I said.

"What did you say?"

"I am unaware of anything but the name."

"Is that so? Then, I'll tell you about the CIA." I was made to listen while the man lectured me for hours about the activities and organization of the CIA. At first I thought the arrangement was pretty good, an interrogation session free of harassment.

Two days later, the same agent ordered that I be given pen and paper. "Write down everything you know about the CIA."

"I don't know anything about it."

"How can you say that? I spent hours explaining what the CIA is and what it does. Write what you know about the CIA!"

I took the pen and paper and wrote several of the points the agent had mentioned, and was forced to sign the paper at the bottom. This was another tactic that, with careful manipulation of the evidence, created a false "confession."

At other times, my interrogators were conciliatory, the flip side of the strategy known in Chinese as *heilian bailian*—black face, white face—which implies that coercion should be mixed with incentive, the proverbial carrot to go with the stick. The lure of a quick release in exchange for compliance was the favorite carrot of the interrogators. One day an agent told me, "According to article nine concerning punishment for treason, all that is required is for you to 'act in complete honesty and fully cooperate' and you will be allowed to go home without punishment."

When I asked to see the actual text of the regulation, my request was denied. Later, I learned this was a bald-faced lie. The actual regulation stated that cooperative conduct had to include surrender or providing evidence that led to the capture of other "conspirators." This could not apply to anyone arrested from the *Formosa Magazine*: surrender was irrelevant, and all conspirators, with the exception of Shih Ming-teh, had been captured after the first wave of arrests on December 13.

One day, shortly before the Chinese New Year, my interrogation session was interrupted by the arrival of a man who the other agents addressed simply as "senior officer." I could tell by the way they treated him that his rank must be very high. The man was short, somewhat portly, and wearing gold-rimmed glasses. Flashing me a warm smile, he motioned for the other agents to leave the room and sat down beside me.

"Ms. Lu," he sighed, "we know how intelligent you are, how well educated, and in your own way, how patriotic you can be. I am a very kind man. As a devout Buddhist, I know that all people commit wrongs sometime in their life, and that if you make amends, then everything will be all right. I've helped many people in the past. All that you have to do is to tell us the truth and cooperate fully; then you won't have a problem. I can arrange your release, and you can go home for the New Year holiday. Sign the confession so that we can all go home. I swear by the name of Buddha that if you sign the confession, I will send you home."

I didn't believe him. But I couldn't show the "senior officer" that I didn't believe him without inviting his wrath. I knew the man would continue to lecture and plead until I signed the confession. I signed it so that he would leave.

Shortly thereafter, in an act of staged benevolence, the agents informed me that I could write a letter of two hundred Chinese characters each week. I used that precious allowance to write to Mother. Agents also told my family they could write me once a week. None of our letters were ever delivered. They told my family that I refused to reply to their letters and told me that my family had no interest in writing to me. Meanwhile, the Bureau of Investigation collected our correspondence to use as evidence in court.

In letters to Mother, I repeatedly asked about her health. The agents, reading letters from Eldest Sister and Brother, knew that her condition was grave. One day, the agents asked if I wanted to know about Mother's health, implying that she was on the verge of death. "Be more cooperative," they said. "Maybe we'll allow you to see her before it's too late." I feared this was another ruse, but the thought of Mother suffering caused me to break down. I began to cry, and the female agent, who I secretly named Goblin, sat down next to me and dried my tears.

"Let's go to the restroom and wash your face," she said. "We really share your feelings. Just do as they say and you'll be allowed to go home."

Another time, an agent with a beefy-looking face came up, peered at me, and asked, "Did you have cosmetic surgery on your eyes to create double eyelids?" In Mandarin Chinese, there are words for "single eyelid" and "double eyelid," to distinguish between eyelids common in the West and the single eyelids common among East Asians. Some Asians seeking to look more "Western" have had cosmetic surgery for double eyelids. Surprised by the question, I said, "No, why do you ask?"

"Your brother, Lu Chuan-sheng, has single eyelids."

Unless these guys were watching Brother very carefully, they would not have detected the difference. I feared that Brother, too, was in custody, and the thought of his arrest made my heart ache.

"Would you like to see your brother? He's in the next room!"

I was thunderstruck. The thought of Brother in prison and the agony this would cause his wife and children, not to mention Mother, was more than I could bear. I began to cooperate with the agents in hopes of protecting Brother and the rest of the family from harm. I acknowledged my guilt in the alleged conspiracy to overthrow the government. I wrote and rewrote new confessions according to the government's wishes, adopting the interrogators' accusations verbatim. My capitulation could result in a death sentence, but I felt I had no other choice.

In spite of the horror of my interrogation and the devious schemes to elicit false confessions, I was spared the agony of physical torture that other Dangwai comrades endured in prison. Men were treated more harshly than either Chen Chu or me, especially those who resisted. Lin Yi-hsiung, the tough son of a logger, with the reputation for being a no-nonsense, straight-talking politician, paid a horrible price for refusing to sign false confessions. Lin was forced to go for days without sleep and was beaten repeatedly—his arms wrenched behind his back in the infamous "airplane" position, a form of torture commonly used during mob rallies in the Cultural Revolution in China. His liver and spine were permanently damaged as a result. When Lin fainted from the pain, agents called in a doctor to revive him with an injection. In a form of torture called "Mongolian barbecue," Ping-Pong balls were jammed into his mouth, cigarettes were used to burn his cheeks, and hot pepper juice was squirted up his nose. Lin lost twenty-seven pounds in the first two months of confinement. Although Lin Yi-hsiung didn't even give a speech on the night of the Kaohsiung Incident, he was tortured until he signed confessions saying that he had exhorted the crowd to attack the riot police.

Another opposition comrade, the writer Yang Ching-chu, who endured similar beatings, has said, "They take what you don't know, make it what you know, and then turn it into your confession." A tragedy was narrowly avoided when agents told Chiu Yi-ping, another Dangwai, that his wife had committed suicide. Chiu Yi-ping tried to kill himself by slashing his throat with a ballpoint pen. Luckily, he didn't succeed. The story of his wife's suicide turned out to be a plot by government agents that succeeded in eliciting his confession.

The only Dangwai leader not in custody was Shih Ming-teh. On the morning of our arrest, Shih had slipped away during the distraction caused by Chen Chu's fall to the ground. As the agents rushed in her direction, Shih sprang onto the roof of a single-story Japanese-style house. From there, he clambered onto the fire escape of another apartment building—where I last saw him—before leaping safely to the ground. Shih walked to a large intersection in search of a cab. There were none around because it was still early, so he walked into the heart of the city. He made it almost to the presidential palace, an area of heavy police surveillance, before a taxi picked him up and took him to the home of an old cell mate. At Shih Ming-teh's behest, the friend called a member of the Presbyterian Church. The church had a reputation for supporting the Taiwan Independence Movement.

Representatives of the church arranged for Shih to hide in a house in northern Taipei. Later, he was taken to meet the head of the church, Pastor Kao Chun-ming. Shih had three requests: that the church provide a place for him to hide, at least temporarily; that church officials use international connections to press for the release of the *Formosa* staff; and that foreigners help to work out a plan to spirit Shih Ming-teh out of Taiwan. For three weeks, members of the church hid him in their homes in various neighborhoods around Taipei. An intern in dental school gave Shih false teeth and operated on his face to change his appearance. The plastic surgery, performed with crude implements, shortened his sharp jawbones and gave him plump, rounded cheeks.

Meanwhile, the government offered a large cash reward for information leading to Shih's arrest. A special police task force led an island-wide manhunt for him, using troops from the army, navy, and air force. All *Formosa Magazine* offices were searched and closed down. In the end, one of Shih's old cell mates sold him out for the reward money and skipped off to Thailand. On January 8, the police caught up with Shih Ming-teh after twenty-six days on the run. Those who had protected him, including the head of the Presbyterian Church, went to jail for sheltering a fugitive.

Once Shih was in prison, his interrogators told him that my cancer had reemerged with a vengeance, that another comrade had serious heart trouble, and that if he confessed to plotting the violent overthrow of the Nationalist government, we would be sent to the hospital. If not, we would suffer without medical attention, and he would feel responsible if we died. Shih knew that it was probably a lie but his sense of honor would not allow him to put our lives at risk. For him, the consequences of confessing would be the most severe. He had already served jail sentences twice for advocating independence. If convicted again, it might cost him his life. Reluctantly, Shih Ming-teh agreed to comply with his interrogators' demands.

By the sixth week of incarceration, I noticed the interrogators' attitude begin to change. The questions they asked were milder and less political in nature. Lectures replaced shouting sessions. I wondered whether the international community had pressured the Nationalists for leniency. I was asked to rewrite some earlier confessions in order to moderate their tone. In one instance, I had written at my interrogator's insistence that I hated President Chiang Ching-kuo for his cancellation of national elections a year earlier. I was asked to change the wording to say that I hated the president because I was concerned about the future of Taiwan. The agents probably thought that with Shih Ming-teh in prison and with confessions in hand from the eight major defendants in the *Formosa* case, the military court would have little trouble winning convictions, and that different drafts of confessions could be manipulated to serve various purposes in court.

On February 27, the day before we were to go to court, I was allowed to meet with Brother and learned that he had not been arrested. Our first conversation was an awkward one. We had been denied communication for weeks, and an agent stood next to Brother recording our every word. Still, Brother delighted me by saying that he would serve as my defense attorney at the trial. He had already read the text of the confessions and feared that I had been tortured or coerced into making the damning statements.

"Did you suffer?" he asked, making the motion of a punch with his hand.

I shook my head no. Brother swallowed uncomfortably, realizing he must speak more plainly. "You studied law," he said, "and know that if a person's confession is not made voluntarily, then it is invalid. Illegal means are not permissible when extracting confessions. The judges you will have in the court tomorrow are the best in Taiwan. If you suffered anything of this sort, then you must speak out in court. Everyone must speak out! Remember, it's not necessary to voice any political demands. Addressing the confessions will be enough."

When I asked about Mother's health, Brother dismissed my questions, saying that she was fine, that there was nothing to worry about. Brother didn't want to burden me with Mother's agony at such a difficult time. Indeed, if I had known of Mother's illness, I might not have had the strength to go on.

On the way back to my cell, I saw another of the *Formosa* defendants, the writer Yang Ching-chu. It was impossible for us to do more than acknowledge each other with our eyes. Yet seeing him reminded me that I was not alone.

That night I dreamed that Professor Jerome Cohen, my mentor at Harvard, had come to Taiwan. He walked off the plane carrying a snake, its head pinched between his fingers. In Chinese mythology, snakes are symbolic of bad emperors. Subconsciously I was hoping Professor Cohen would come to my rescue. Later, I learned that Professor Cohen had tried to come to Taiwan for the trial. He got as far as Hong Kong, but the Nationalists had refused to grant him a visa to enter the country.

On February 28, or "2-28" as the day has been called since the tragic 1947 anti-Nationalist uprising, I went to court with several other Dangwai to receive the official indictment. Each of us was flanked by a military police officer, or a female agent in the case of Chen Chu and myself.

"Why have reporters and the defendants' families not been allowed in?" one defense attorney asked.

"What business is it of ours if no one chooses to attend?" the presiding judge replied.

"Is this an open trial or not?"

"It is an open trial."

After a quick consultation, the entire defense team walked out of the courtroom in protest. The military officials had denied entry for journalists and defendants' family members. The judges acted to make amends: dozens of people, as well as journalists from Taiwan, Hong Kong, the United States, and Europe, poured into the courtroom. For five minutes the presiding judge permitted jostling photographers and TV cameramen to record the scene. Court secretaries recorded the name, age, address, and ethnicity of each of us—we were all Taiwanese. Then, with the exception of Huang Hsin-chieh, who was scheduled to testify, the rest of us were led back to our cells.

At lunchtime, we were brought out again to meet with our family members in the cafeteria. Eldest Sister was there and I gave her some information about my imprisonment to pass on to Brother. She had some advice for me from Brother as well.

"Ah Lien," she said, using my Taiwanese nickname, Water Lily, "the most knowledgeable military judge in the nation will preside over the trial. Everyone is very concerned about you and the other defendants. You must speak out during the trial and let the judge know how you've been treated. Remember, you must speak out!"

I was so excited to see so many dear faces that I didn't notice the absence of Lin Yi-hsiung's wife. Brother noticed, however, and asked my sister-in-law to telephone her. Lin's wife came immediately.

"Someone called this morning and said there would be no trial today," she explained, upon arriving.

Later, Lin's wife called home to check on her three daughters. There was no answer, so she asked one of Lin Yi-hsiung's aides to go to the house and make sure everything was all right. The aide entered the Lin home to find the family's eldest daughter, Huan-jun, who had been stabbed repeatedly, writhing in blood on her bed. Immediately, the aide phoned the police and two editors at an opposition magazine. The two editors rushed over and found Lin Yi-hsiung's mother lying dead in the basement stairway, her throat slashed. An hour later, the police found the bodies of Lin's two twin seven-year-old daughters,

Ting-jun and Liang-jun, in the basement storage room, their spines severed by knife wounds. Lin Yi-hsiung's wife rushed home. Her friends intercepted her and told her not to go inside. Instead, she went to Jenai Hospital, where her eldest daughter, Huan-jun, was undergoing emergency surgery. One of the stab wounds had pierced the girl's lung. Friends told Lin's wife of her mother-in-law's death. Afraid the shock would be too great, they said the twins were safe.

The horror of the Lin family murders shook Taiwanese society to the core. Suspicion was immediately cast upon the government and extremist factions of the Nationalist Party. Lin's house had been under twenty-four-hour surveillance by secret agents. The murders had occurred in broad daylight, with the killers walking in and out the front door.

Many people speculated that the Nationalists sought to teach the Dangwai a lesson for leaking information about their treatment during incarceration. Just one day before her death, Lin's mother and Lin's younger sister had been given permission to visit him in prison. His younger sister had asked him if rumors of his torture were true.

"What do you think?" he said.

"My boy has been wronged!" his mother wailed, grasping his meaning. "My boy is innocent!" She shouted so loudly that I could hear her cries from my cell on the second floor of the detention center. Afterward, Lin's mother told others of her son's torture, including a representative from a human rights organization in Japan. No one imagined that because of this, Lin's mother would be silenced forever.

After Huan-jun had undergone seven hours of emergency surgery, the deputy secretary-general of the Nationalist Party arrived at the hospital with an announcement: the government would permit Lin Yi-hsiung to return home to deal with the tragedy. Secret service operatives would mobilize to protect the family members of the defendants in the *Formosa* trial; a reward would be offered to anyone providing information about the killers' identities or whereabouts.

Taiwanese culture places great importance on giving family members sufficient time to deal with the grief of departed loved ones. It is best to have time for *xinli zhunbei*, or psychological preparation, for a sudden tragedy. In contrast to this, at 10 o'clock that night, Lin Yi-hsiung was taken from his cell without being informed of the reason for his release. Met at the prison gate by friends and family, Lin emerged pale but jubilant. No one said a word about the killings. Escorted first to the hospital for a medical checkup, Lin was laughing and joking with friends, even as doctors discovered his body was covered with scars from weeks of torture. Lin Yi-hsiung insisted that everyone go out to celebrate his release. His friends agreed and left, drinking until their sorrow became impossible to conceal. It was a Dangwai colleague who told Lin that Huan-jun was in the hospital and that his mother had been killed. The following day, another friend informed Lin of the twins' deaths and of his eldest daughter's now stabilized condition.

When Lin's wife came to see him in the hospital, his grief was too great for words. He sat quietly weeping before he wrapped his arms around his wife saying, "Now there are only three of us. You, me and Huan-jun."

"You are lying to me! You lie!" she wailed. "Liang-jun, Ting-jun, where are you? Mama wants to go with you."

Later that afternoon, Lin Yi-hsiung and his wife went to the Taipei Municipal Mortuary to stroke the faces of their loved ones for the last time.

Suspicion of government involvement in the murders was heightened when it was learned that Taiwan scholar Bruce Jacobs had telephoned the house and spoken to the eldest daughter and to the twins moments before they were slain, and that the police offered him a large sum of money for a testimony "corresponding to their suspicions"—in other words, as a payoff for false testimony.

When we defendants heard the news of the murders, we struggled to regain our dignity and strength. The trial in which we were soon to take part would require an all-out effort. At long last, the Dangwai would have the chance to voice its views in a public forum.

Trial proceedings began in earnest on March 18. The military courtroom was about thirty feet by sixty feet in size, decorated only by a large portrait of Chiang Kai-shek. Flags stood on either side of a raised platform, behind which sat five judges wearing shiny blue robes with long black sleeves. Two secretaries sat to the side, wearing black robes. The two prosecutors wore similar robes in black and red. Eight defense lawyers wore white robes with black sleeves. A wooden barrier separated the defense from the prosecution. In front of the barrier, the so-called material evidence from the riot was piled high— wooden clubs, metal bars, torches, battered police helmets, and broken riot shields.

The back half of the courtroom was allocated to journalists, who came from Taiwan, the United States, and Europe. Seats were provided for two members of each defendant's family and for ranking government or Nationalist officials who wished to view the proceedings. With the surge of media interest following the Lin murders, the trial had become the place to be for all aspiring politicians and the focus of the nation.

The government's selection of prosecutors and judges revealed a careful calculation of ethnic interests. In general, mainlanders were more likely to protect the party-state. The presiding judge was a mainlander, but the four other judges, who seldom spoke or raised questions, were Taiwanese. Their role was symbolic and intended to deflect criticism from the island's Taiwanese majority that the court was ethnically biased. The lead prosecutor was Taiwanese, but the other prosecutor was a mainlander. In contrast, the entire fifteen-man defense team was Taiwanese.

According to the prosecutors, Shih Ming-teh had acted as the mastermind behind the *Formosa Magazine* plot to overthrow the government. He was portrayed as a veteran advocate of independence since his organization of the Taiwan United Battlefront, while serving in the military in 1959. Although that organization was just a group of youngsters who discussed independence, the fact that the members were in the military caused the government to view it as a serious threat. Legislator Huang Hsin-chieh was portrayed as the primary financial backer of the *Formosa* group. The prosecution linked Huang to illegal contacts with Chinese officials and an investment scheme to smuggle eel fry into Taiwan from China in order to fund opposition activities. At that time, contact with China was banned, and contact with Chinese officials was seen as treasonous, especially for members of the political opposition.

A five-person task force within the *Formosa* group, including Yao Chia-wen, Hsu Hsin-liang, and Chang Chun-hung, was accused of planning to violently overthrow the Nationalists through a two-pronged strategy. Short-term strategy involved meetings and demonstrations leading to a gradually escalating pattern of violence against government troops, with the goal of fomenting revolution to topple the government. Long-term plans allegedly centered around the *Formosa Magazine*, a legal means of achieving illegal ends. Unsanctioned political parties, after all, were illegal at the time. Opposition demands, such as human rights and democracy, were portrayed as a means of cloaking violent intentions. The prosecution depicted Chen Chu, head of the Kaohsiung branch of *Formosa Magazine*, Lin Hung-hsuan, and me as the agents of the overseas Taiwan Independence Movement, who had the express purpose of participating in the plot to overthrow the Nationalists.

The prosecution's accusations were not without some strands of truth. Huang had made contact with Chinese officials, albeit without compromising state interests, and he had bankrolled many Dangwai activities. A five-person task force did exist to formulate strategy designed to bring about the end of Nationalist rule. That Chen Chu, Lin Hung-hsuan, and I had returned from abroad around the same time could be explained by the growing vitality of the Dangwai movement and our desire to improve the lot of our fellow citizens. The key component of the prosecution's case that was false was its portrayal of the opposition's intent to overthrow the Nationalist regime violently. At no time was this our strategy. Until Chiang Ching-kuo cancelled elections, we had hoped to work within the existing political system. Subsequently, we sought to bring about political reform through peaceful demonstrations and increased grassroots organization. The popular appeal of our cause was the main source of our confidence that ultimately we would be judged innocent by the people of Taiwan, if not by the military court.

In order to corroborate accusations of violence, the prosecution produced witnesses who testified about the beatings they had received on the night of the Kaohsiung Incident. "The mob yelled orders for four or five protestors to attack individual riot police," said one military policeman. "They said it doesn't matter if you beat them to death. They hit me in the head with clubs and torches, broke my nose, and continued to beat me after I had fallen to the ground. Afterward, I was sent to the hospital and received eighteen stitches."

According to the testimony of a shopkeeper in downtown Kaohsiung, "Two MPs were chased inside the store, and the mob outside broke down the shop's metal gate, shouting, 'If you don't open the door, we'll break in!'"

The wife of a doctor said that one battered military policeman accompanied by a police officer stumbled into her house on the night of the demonstration. She claimed the protestors stood outside yelling for her to send out the MP, and shattered the glass front door of her home.

Other material evidence consisted of pictures of wounded military police, tapes of shouted slogans, torches recovered from the scene of the demonstration, rocks, clubs, metal bars, and ribbons of red, yellow, and green signifying independence. The prosecutors, and in fact the government, staunchly refused to consider testimony of citizens injured by military police, ridiculously insisting that no such injuries had occurred.

The real reasons for the clash between protestors and riot police were never raised. The prosecution did not mention the riot police encirclement of the demonstration or the use of tear gas, or consider the role of secret service agitators and the agents provocateurs in black who attacked police and soldiers outside the Phoenix Bridge Restaurant. The prosecution placed great emphasis on the words *charge* and *hit* as they appeared in speeches on the night of the riot, the latter of which, in the Taiwanese expression *pa piang*, simply means to go all out, break through obstacles to progress, or struggle for survival, not to physically attack people. But in Chinese characters, *pa* means "to hit" and *piang* means "to work hard." Prosecutors interpreted the meaning of *pa piang* word by word and concluded that its use reflected my intention of inciting violence—their only evidence of my "violent sedition." In its attempt to portray the Kaohsiung clash as a violent revolutionary act, the prosecution could not account for the absence of attacks on other Nationalist officials or for the lack of guns and other armaments.

On the first day of the trial, Chen Shui-bian, a young defense attorney representing Huang Hsin-chieh, revealed the central theme of the defense's legal strategy. Chen was a short, wiry man of dark complexion who spoke Mandarin with a strong Taiwanese accent. He knew that without the confessions, the government did not have enough evidence for conviction. The prosecution's case, he argued, relied entirely upon the confessions given during incarceration, and any deception or torture by interrogators rendered the confessions invalid as evidence. While few might have guessed it at the time, the trial marked the political debut of Chen Shui-bian, the man who would later serve with me as the two-term president of Taiwan.

The prosecutors rebutted Chen's argument by calling him a liar: "The prosecution is shocked at the defense's implication that his client, Legislator Huang Hsin-chieh, may have been tortured. In investigating this case, prosecutors made certain Huang was never subjected to torture. To raise this now reveals nothing but deviousness on the part of the defense. Huang is well educated, a senior legislator, and knows that he spoke the truth in the confessions that he signed. The only penalty in this case is death. Therefore, if there is no truth in the claims against him, he has no reason to acknowledge them."

Huang Hsin-chieh testified that he had confessed to sedition at the prosecution's prompting, with the understanding that it would mitigate his sentence. "The interrogation sessions lasted for fifty to sixty hours at a time. They began very early and lasted until very late," Huang said. "I was so miserable at the time that I welcomed death. In order to reduce the sentence, I wrote several confessions, which I never thought would become evidence against me."

Wan and sickly from weeks of incarceration, I was taken to the prison clinic and given an injection to pep me up on the morning of my first court appearance. When I took the stand to testify, the challenge to the legality of the confessions continued. Presiding Judge Liu Yue-ping asked several general questions concerning my involvement in the case before granting Brother, acting as my defense attorney, permission to speak on my behalf.

"There are two points I would like the court to consider," Brother said. "First, that the defendant endured more than fifty days of constant interrogation. Her mind was troubled; she was frightened—a psychological handicap. Please ask her what sort of handicap. Second, the defendant has said that she was forced to stand for two whole days as punishment for failing to accede to her interrogators' demands. The prosecutors told her what to write in her confessions. When she didn't comply, they showed her terrifying photographs and said if she didn't confess, then they would imprison her family members. I ask the court to investigate this matter, as the transcripts of the interrogations and the so-called self-confessions clearly reveal that the defendant's testimony on the first day of her incarceration varies considerably from testimony given two months later."

"The court will consider this matter and conduct the necessary investigation," the judge said. Clearly he was hoping to sidestep the issue.

"As this concerns my rights, would it please the court if I spoke a little concerning this matter?" I asked.

"The court will allow you to speak in due course," the judge replied.

Strangely, the prosecutor appeared displeased with the judge's response. "After hearing from Huang Hsin-chieh," he said, "the defense has continuously attacked the integrity of the prosecution in an effort to redirect blame for wrongdoing. Quite to the contrary, prosecutors conducted this investigation in full cooperation with the Bureau of Investigation. I assure you that there was no torture whatsoever. In the interests of the truth, I ask the judge to use his power to determine whether confessions were lawfully obtained or not."

The judge shifted in his seat nervously. He turned toward me slowly, "Ms. Lu, you may address the court."

Remembering the advice of Brother and Eldest Sister to retract my confession, I had prepared myself for this moment. "I would clarify two points," I said. "First, investigators never tortured me physically. But according to article 98 of the regulation on interrogation, the subject of interrogation. . . ."

"Speak plainly," the judge interrupted. "There is no need to recite the law verbatim in this court."

"There are other means besides torture to extract confessions, more sophisticated means . . . ," I continued, choosing my words cautiously.

This time, the prosecutor interrupted, "Prosecutors investigating this case have the obligation and responsibility to determine whether torture or other improper means were used. The defendant continues to hem and haw over this. Force her to speak clearly on this matter!"

"Please ask the defendant to explain the meaning of 'more sophisticated means,'" Brother interjected.

The courtroom had gone silent as tears of frustration appeared in my eyes. With a nod from the judge, I continued, "Thank you, your honor. I was not tortured. After I wrote the confessions, the agents were very polite, even bringing me hot tea to drink. But I have thought carefully about the fifty days of interrogation and four hundred hours of questioning. The agents had four different means of obtaining confessions through interrogation. The first was destroying your identity and self-esteem. . . ."

"Lu Hsiu-lien," the judge interrupted, "this is a military courtroom. Desist with this abstract testimony. Saying what you know will be sufficient, and speak slowly."

All I could do was give a clear example:

The agents infused each interrogation session with their assumptions. For instance, portraying me as an advocate of independence or as a spy for the CIA. Their questions made me address these topics. I was not allowed to say "I don't know" or "I don't remember." They would say to me, "Here there is nothing that can't be remembered clearly." When I said that I really didn't know, they forced me to literally eat my words written out on paper. They also told me that coming to the Bureau of Investigation was the same as taking off all my clothes. "We see you very, very clearly," they said.

Agents showed me pictures of Wu Tai-an, lying half naked and bloody, and said that if I didn't write a self-confession, then I would be the next Wu Tai-an. They had me read the notice from the mortuary to Wu's family and asked me if I wanted my family to carve "Lu Hsiu-lien, thirty-six years old" on my headstone. I thought that my death had already been decided and feared for the safety of my family.

I am a person that has been very ill before. During the more than fifty days that I spent in prison, I was sick more than forty days. Sometimes I couldn't eat. One day, I had watery rice at 6:00 A.M. and didn't eat again until 9 o'clock at night. Several times they forced me to stand in punishment for hours on end wearing high-heeled shoes. During interrogation, the agents said my activities were violent, and their allegations of violence became allegations of treason. The self-confession was written by them, not me.

The prosecutor leapt to his feet. "Your honor must determine if the defendant is really speaking the truth!"

The judge asked me if I wanted to take a moment to compose myself, and told a female guard to bring me a glass of water. The defense attorney representing Lin Yi-hsiung shot his hand into the air, shouting for permission to speak. The other defense lawyers glared at him to be silent, but he didn't seem to notice.

"Let the defendant continue to speak," Brother urged. "Your honor, this is a matter of life and death, and also a matter concerning the reputation of the state."

The judge saw his opportunity to change the subject and recognized Lin's attorney. However, the prosecutor brought the proceedings back to my testimony:

Your honor, this matter has implications for the reputation of the state. I suggest that the accused be allowed to continue her statement. The prosecution requests that the judge question the defendant more carefully concerning her questioning during incarceration. The interrogation was observed twenty-four hours a day by prosecutors and conducted in accordance with due process. The defendant was fed three meals a day and allowed to take naps after lunch. She went to sleep before 10:00 P.M. every night. The defendant was never kept from eating or sleeping. When Lu Hsiu-lien arrived at prison, she had a cold and was given medication and medical attention. Everyone is aware of the defendant's advanced education and legal training, but her testimony is absolutely untrue.

The judge sighed. "Will the defendant please continue?"

As I gave more damning examples of my treatment during interrogation, a strange metamorphosis took place among Taiwanese reporters, who were shocked and troubled by what they heard. My testimony so radically departed from government propaganda that had vilified the *Formosa* group during the weeks of our imprisonment, and my suffering appeared so real and human, that reporters returned to their newspaper offices and insisted on printing my testimony. It even made the front page of the nation's largest newspaper, the *United Daily News*. Moreover, according to former newspaper editor Yang Sen-hong, an overconfident President Chiang Ching-kuo had directly ordered all media to report on the trial proceedings verbatim. Chiang's assumption was that Dangwai would confess their crimes in court and that, regardless of what the defendants said, his government had sufficient popular support to weather this political storm.

For the first time since the 2-28 Uprising, the media—especially mainstream newspapers—began to publish the truth concerning the opposition. Years of censorship were temporarily suspended, as revelations about how confessions had been obtained exploded in daily news reports. Equally important, the Dangwai's political message (including the advocacy of Taiwan independence) was broadcast to the international community via the mainstream media for the first time.

Reports by members of the foreign press brought international pressure to bear on the Nationalists for leniency. The Associated Press (AP) ran the following paragraph in the report based on my testimony:

Sitting before a five-judge panel, Ms. Lu testified that investigators used obscene words during her interrogation and threatened to make her strip so they could embarrass her enough to tell the truth. The threat was never carried out, she said. Ms. Lu also testified that she was forced to stand for two days and not given any food on another day. Otherwise, she said she was not tortured during her one hundred days of detention.

Apparently, the woman who wrote this dispatch, a journalist based in Hong Kong, didn't understand Chinese very well and relied on secondhand accounts of trial proceedings. The result was a slight exaggeration of the situation, serving to further ignite international concern. That day, investigators tracked down the journalist, and the Government Information Office director, James Soong, held a televised press conference demanding the AP run a correction. The woman was barred from attending further trial sessions. Columbia University scholar James Seymour has said that other foreign media, including *Newsweek*, the *International Herald Tribune*, and *Time Magazine*, were subject to government censorship and their publications were confiscated in Taiwan.

I was the first defendant to retract my confession; I had complete trust in Brother, who served as my defense attorney. However, not all defendants were equally confident in their lawyers, some of whom had been unknown to them before the trial, and not all defendants were present to hear my testimony. The following day, defense lawyers repeated in court that I had declared my confession to be invalid for reasons of duress and coercion, dropping the hint for other defendants to do likewise. As more defendants took the stand, nearly every one cited the abusive interrogation he or she had suffered in prison. Lin Yi-hsiung retracted his confession in a written statement. Still rocked by the murder of his mother and twin daughters and understandably cautious, Lin said that he preferred to submit his statement in written form because its contents had repercussions for the reputation of the state.

By addressing the court, we had the opportunity to clarify Dangwai objectives and to open a debate on such issues as democratization and independence. We did not deny a relationship with radical overseas advocates of independence. Instead, we portrayed ourselves as a more moderate opposition group, seeking democratization and increased participation in national politics for the native Taiwanese majority. At that time, mainlanders dominated nearly every ministry and influential government post. Aging National Assembly members and legislators elected to office on the Chinese mainland in 1947 still held the vast majority of seats in parliament. As Shih explained during his testimony before the court, the real purpose of the *Formosa Magazine* was to "promote an opposition party without a name."

The government's decision to hold an open trial marked a real departure for judicial process. Earlier trials of political dissidents by military courts had seldom taken more than one day, and had never been open to the public or the media. The decision to open this trial has been attributed to President Chiang Ching-kuo's displeasure with the handling of the investigation, rising foreign pressure of legal transparency, and Chiang's confidence that the defendants would admit fault and beg for clemency. Domestic and international commentators hailed the "*Formosa* trial" as a step forward in liberalization of the Nationalist-dominated court system.

The flush of freedom experienced by journalists faded quickly. Yet, as censors moved to regain control, pushback by journalists did not completely disappear. The fact that newspaper readership had shot up astronomically during the trial indicated to would-be media moguls the lucrative possibilities that went with printing the truth. The door to freedom of the press, once opened, proved difficult for the Nationalists to close again.

In May, the court announced our sentences. Huang Hsin-chieh was sentenced to fourteen years in prison, after which his "public rights"—the right to vote and run for office—would be suspended for ten years. Shih Ming-teh was sentenced to life in prison without parole, and permanent suspension of his public rights. Lin Yi-hsiung, Yao Chia-wen, Chang Chun-hung, Lin Hung-hsuan, Chen Chu, and I were given twelve-year sentences, and our public rights were suspended for ten years after release. Our defense team appealed the conviction, but it was upheld by the court of appeals on June 10.

The military court ruled the confessions obtained during interrogation were reliable evidence. The court ruling declared, "It is indisputable that those who sought 'Taiwan independence' have committed a seditious crime." Nevertheless, citizens who followed the trial remained unconvinced of our intent to violently overthrow the government. Had the *Formosa Magazine* staff simply been held accountable for the disturbance in Kaohsiung, this might have been an acceptable, even if an unjust, outcome in the eyes of many. Yet, sedition was too much. In the prescient words of Chang Chun-hung, "On trial [were] not only the eight of us but the nation's democratic future."

The cause of democracy had received a tremendous setback, but widespread dissatisfaction with the court's decision led to a surge in popularity of opposition political candidates who were in any way associated with the trial, including members of the defense team and wives of the imprisoned. When national elections resumed in the fall of 1980, the success of these candidates demonstrated the public's ruling of "not guilty."

On June 10, 1980, I was in my cell when I was handed the statement from the court of appeals: "Original sentence sustained." I read the statement carefully and tossed it on the floor. In a way, the verdict was a relief compared with the weeks of doubt after the trial. At least now my release, however distant, could be conceptualized in finite terms.

The prison guard who handed me the notice stood quietly watching my reaction before informing me that Chen Chu and I would be cell mates. At the time, I was occupying cell 61 and Chen Chu was in cell 59. She had also received the notice. Our cell doors opened simultaneously. We rushed into the hallway to embrace one another, glad that our isolation had ended and that we could vent our grievances and share our thoughts. For the next week, Chen Chu and I talked nonstop about the Kaohsiung Incident, the trial, our incarceration, and plans for the future.

The guards also gave me permission to use a faucet in a small room at the corner of the floor. For six months, I had washed with only a washcloth and a half-gallon pail of water. In June, the tropical heat of summer penetrated the concrete walls of the prison, making the splashing of cold water a luxurious experience.

I soon found that Chen Chu could not sleep well. She muttered strange sounds in the night, garbled sleep talk, and sometimes cried. We slept very near to one another in our small cell, and she woke me several times when she flung her leg across my arm.

Even though I wept for hours or sometimes days on end, I felt Chen Chu's grief had deeper, far more troubled implications that were rooted in the trauma she had experienced during interrogation. Occasionally, I mentioned my interrogation, but Chen Chu never wanted to speak of hers. There had been a great deal of evidence connecting her with the overseas independence movement. Only once did she mention that the interrogators possessed taped recordings of her conversations with people in the independence movement, and that she had almost fainted the first time they played them back for her.

Whenever I thought of Mother, I wept. In the final days of the trial, Eldest Sister made an appeal for leniency on my behalf. She told how since my operation, my thyroid had never fully recovered. Even more terrifying for me, Eldest Sister said that upon hearing of my arrest, Mother had been hospitalized and Mother's life "was in constant danger."

While I had feared for Mother's health, her condition was far more serious than I could have imagined. Diabetes had sapped Mother's strength for nearly a decade before my imprisonment. Just two days before the Kaohsiung Incident, at her seventy-first birthday party, she had appeared more frail than ever. When Eldest Sister learned of my arrest, she and Brother agreed they should keep the news from Mother as long as possible. This was not to be. Mother was watching television when the news of my arrest flashed across the television screen. When friends came over to comfort her, she collapsed and broke her left leg. Mother's leg never mended. Lying in bed, she would burst into tears at the mention of my name. (Anxiety over Mother's health caused Brother to develop an ulcer.) Later, when Mother's condition worsened, she would drift in and out of consciousness, murmuring my name.

In October 1980, the prison authorities moved Chen Chu and me into a small blockhouse located in the compound of the ironically named "Benevolence Rehabilitation Institute." High walls covered with razor wire surrounded the structure's small courtyard. There were cameras and recording devices in the bedroom and in the small living room, monitoring our every move. In spite of the intrusive surveillance, the blockhouse was relatively comfortable. We had a television and a refrigerator, and for the first time in nearly a year of imprisonment, we were allowed to eat with chopsticks, rather than plastic spoons. Although Chen Chu and I were completely isolated from other inmates, on one afternoon per week we were allowed to enter the prison yard to play badminton for one hour. On Tuesdays, one family member could visit for thirty minutes, during which our conversations were recorded and a guard was present to take notes.

In an apparent attempt to rehabilitate us politically, the Nationalists sent scholars to give us lectures. The first professor was a Nationalist "liberal," who had been my classmate at the University of Illinois at Urbana-Champaign. I had introduced him to my cousin, who eventually became his wife. Lecturing us sternly during two-hour study sessions, he didn't seem anything like the charming, carefree graduate student I had known. "You have taken the wrong road," he said. "Hopefully, you will change your views from this point on."

Apparently my former classmate entertained hopes of advancing his career within the Nationalist Party by drawing a clear line between us, or at least by convincing me to see the merit of the ruling party's policies.

"Don't think that talking to me like this will do you any good!" I told him.

Fortunately he only came twice. An elderly general in the army, a devout Catholic and University of Illinois graduate, took his place. General Chao Ben-li always brought gifts, news, and encouragement and enjoyed reading aloud passages from the Bible.

Our primary information about the outside world came from these lectures, watching government-controlled television news, and reading the Nationalist-controlled newspaper *Central Daily News* and the right-wing magazine *Dragon's Flag*. Every night at 10 o'clock, the lights went out and the television was turned off. The only place we could turn on the light, and the sole place without cameras, was the bathroom. This was where I retreated to write. Writing fiction was at once a diversion from the tedium of prison life and a means of escaping the barred windows and cement walls.

Prison administrators insisted that I return to them every piece of paper that they gave me, so I wrote on the only type of paper that no one monitors: toilet paper! Using the bottom of an overturned bucket as my desk and the toilet seat as my chair, I wrote for hours each night in ant-size Chinese characters. When finished, I carefully rolled up the manuscripts and tucked them into the lining of my comforter. My technique became so refined that a prison guard searching my comforter ran her hands across its worn surface but didn't discover anything, although my heart almost stopped when I saw her. I quickly turned away, fearing that she would see my face green with fright. By summer, rolls of tissue swelled the lining of my bedding, and I had the excuse to spirit the comforter out of prison.

"Eldest Sister," I said during the weekly visiting period, "can you take my comforter home and wash it? It's far too hot to use in this weather, and there's no extra space in the blockhouse."

"Why don't you just throw it out? I will bring you a new one."

"It is a little shabby," I said, "but I have had it since my first year in prison. It has special sentimental value. Please take good care of it."

Eldest Sister always understood me. Once safely home, she took out the rolls of tissue and gave them to a good friend, who deciphered the tiny characters and carefully recopied everything I had written.

Eldest Sister's own life was undergoing radical changes. She had married a man who worked for the national railway, and had been living relatively quietly in a suburb of Taipei as a housewife. Three days after my arrest, Eldest Sister told her husband, "I'm going to get my little sister back. I'll be busy working with the relatives of the other imprisoned Dangwai, and I may not be around to cook you dinner. You're going to have to get used to cooking yourself or eating in restaurants. If you can't do that, I'll get a divorce!" Her husband reluctantly agreed.

The day after the murder of Lin Yi-hsiung's mother and twin daughters on February 28, the government had stationed two guards in Eldest Sister's home; they were there twenty-four hours a day for six months. The pretext was to protect her. She knew they were watching her every move. Whenever Eldest Sister left the house, a plainclothes officer accompanied her, even when she went to the market to buy vegetables.

Every Tuesday, Eldest Sister came to visit me in prison, and every Wednesday she went to see Mother. One afternoon after visiting me in prison, Eldest Sister received a phone call from overseas. A woman spoke to her kindly in English for several minutes. Eldest Sister didn't understand a word. A few minutes later she received another phone call. This time it was a man who spoke Taiwanese. "Hsiu-rong, I'm with a human rights organization in the United States. Did you go to visit your sister today? How is she? Like you, we hope she will be released soon."

Eldest Sister told him that my health had deteriorated in prison, and that the food I ate was unsanitary. They talked for several minutes. "What's your name?" she asked.

"I can't tell you that," he replied.

The man called every Tuesday afternoon at 1 o'clock for years. She never met him or asked his name again. But the knowledge that he would call and that he represented an international organization fighting for my release was invaluable encouragement.

At first, Eldest Sister refused to speak of Mother's health during our Tuesday visits. She wanted to protect me from grief and guilt. But I knew Mother's condition must be extremely serious; otherwise she would have come to see me. Consequently, much of my internal energy was spent worrying about Mother's health. I made countless appeals to prison administrators to allow me to visit her, all to no avail. My emotions were volatile: just the thought of Mother brought me to tears. Mother's Day was particularly heart-wrenching when Chen Chu, who knew many songs, sang an old Taiwanese tune, "Mother, Please Take Care of Yourself."

Early one morning in the spring of 1981, I had a dream in which I saw a ball of soft white light. As the ball floated nearer to me, I saw that it contained the shape of a woman who looked much like Guanyin, the goddess of mercy, sitting in the lotus position next to my bed. Her hands were clasped together and her fingertips pointed toward me, blessing me. As I studied the figure more closely, I saw that it was Mother. Her face wore a faint smile, and her eyes were warm and free of pain. When our eyes met, I felt the enormous strength of her love. Then, Mother gradually ascended to heaven on billowing white clouds. I awoke to a clap of thunder outside the blockhouse, followed by heavy, driving rain.

"She's saying good bye!" I cried. "Chen Chu, wake up, wake up!" I needed someone to serve as a witness to what I had experienced. After I breathlessly related the dream to her, Chen Chu agreed with me that according to Buddhist thought, my dream meant that Mother's spirit was already departing to heaven.

Fearing that I would never see Mother alive again, I submitted another request to visit her in the hospital. When I received no response, I launched a hunger strike. I recalled that a hunger striker in Northern Ireland had died after fourteen days, but I had no idea how many days I could survive without food. Weakened since my thyroid carcinoma in 1975, my health had deteriorated in prison. My metabolism was abnormal. I had gained twenty-five pounds of bloated water weight. A strangling sensation in my throat sometimes left me gasping for breath. When these fits passed, I vomited blood. Heart palpitations and incontinence plagued me. By refusing to eat, I knew that I risked my life, but I had no alternative. Mother had given me life. If she should die, why should I mind dying?

The first few days of fasting were uncomfortable. I suffered sharp hunger pangs and dizzy spells and had difficulty sleeping. At meal times, Chen Chu gobbled up her meal to spare me the agony of smelling food. Gradually I lost my appetite as my stomach contracted and my body weakened. On the fifth day of my fast, I met with the deputy director of the Benevolence Rehabilitation Institute. Pretending to be kind and considerate, he presented me with a statement signed by the president of Chang Gung Hospital indicating that Mother's health had improved.

"You will feel better, Ms. Lu, and resume eating now," the deputy director said. Taking a piece of paper from his pocket, he said, "You really are a devoted daughter. This application for permission to see your mother was so well written that each one of us who read it was deeply moved. Ms. Lu, as learned and famous as you are, your strong devotion to your mother is quite a virtue."

He read my petition out loud and tears rolled down his cheeks. "Ms. Lu, I am going to make a copy of this petition for my children to read and memorize so they will grow up with your traditional values. I have been telling people how wise you are."

The report from the well-respected president of Chang Gung Hospital, and the deputy director's surprising empathy, gave me hope that Mother would survive until I could see her. I agreed to end my hunger strike.

Two weeks later, the kindly old general giving us classes offered to go to Taoyuan to check on Mother and bring me word at our next session.

"How is she? How is she?" I wanted to know, when General Chao returned. Instead of replying, the general sat down and, placing his hands on his knees, began to cry.

"Lu Hsiu-lien, I arrived too late." The prison authorities had kept news of Mother's death from me for ten days!

According to the regulations, prisoners should be allowed a twenty-four-hour leave to return home for the death of immediate family members. Prison authorities informed me they would give me two hours on the day of Mother's funeral procession, from 11:00 P.M. to 1:00 A.M. The Bureau of Investigation, they said, had received reports that former Taoyuan County chief executive Hsu Hsin-liang, then exiled in America, had sent a group of Taiwanese nationalists to assassinate me. Special precautions were necessary, but they would send a large team of secret service agents to protect me.

I knew the alleged plot against my life was a lie. Hsu Hsin-liang had been my colleague. He had even hoped that I would succeed him as the Taoyuan County chief executive. The flimsy Nationalist excuse was rooted in the fear that I would make damning statements to the press. I had the sickening feeling the statement from Chang Gung Hospital certifying Mother's good health had been a fake, and that the deputy director's tears had been those of a crocodile.

Arriving at Mother's funeral with a host of government agents and police cars in tow, cloaked in darkness like a thief, would be an injustice to the woman who had suffered far too much on my account. Mother had always been proper and upright in her dealings with everyone. I didn't want to dishonor her ghost.

"I strongly protest the inhumanity of the Garrison Command's denial of my rights as a grieving family member," I said. "I will not return home under these conditions."

At 2:00 A.M., Brother received a phone call from the Garrison Command. "Come to the Benevolence Rehabilitation Institute at once. Something has happened to your sister."

With tears in his eyes, Brother turned to Eldest Sister, busy with preparations for Mother's funeral, and said, "Lu Hsiu-lien has heard the news and committed suicide!" Brother had not told me of Mother's death because he had feared my reaction, intending to invite me home on the seventh day after her passing, traditionally when the spirit of the departed returns, or on the hundredth day, the final day of mourning. Weeping and preparing themselves to retrieve a corpse, Brother and Eldest Sister hurried to the Institute only to find me alive, but in a standoff with prison authorities.

"Lu Hsiu-lien says she will not return home for the funeral procession. She is renouncing her rights. We have papers for you to sign."

Relieved beyond words, Brother signed the papers and the three of us huddled together for a moment of grief. Brother and Eldest Sister returned to prepare for the funeral, and that night, alone and in the dark, I apologized to Mother for the agony I had caused her and for not comforting her during her illness. In the ultimate violation of the Chinese value of filial piety, duty to one's parents, I had not said farewell to her while she still lived, nor would I attend the ceremony marking her death. While reporters and friends went to the funeral services for Mother, hoping to see me, I knelt on the ground in the prison yard, my face wet with tears, worshipping Mother who was ascending to heaven.

For the next year, my own life meant nothing to me. Depression became a permanent mental state. Then, a new lecturer replaced General Chao. Wu Kun-ju, of the philosophy department at National Taiwan University, had received his doctorate in theology in Germany and had little interest in politics. I found that I enjoyed his purely academic discussions. Under Wu's tutelage, I read widely from Buddhist texts, the Bible, and books on science and astronomy. The theological understanding of life and death that I developed eased the pain of Mother's passing. Using the simple metaphor of riding on a train, I saw human beings as passengers traveling to different stops in the universe. When our spirits pause at one station, it's called life; when they continue on, it's called death. When humans complete their tasks on Earth, their spirits move to different planets and to different levels of existence. Father's body died, I told myself, but his spirit must be somewhere else in the universe. Mother must have missed him very much, so she went to seek him elsewhere. It was a philosophy that I created for myself, a perspective without permanent life or death, and one that provided comfort during the darkest days of my life. I was required to write an essay for Professor Wu just as if his lectures had been part of a university course. He liked my paper so much that he suggested the prison authorities publish it.

Perhaps Professor Wu's greatest gift to me was interceding with prison authorities to allow me to write openly, and on proper paper. He got the Benevolence Rehabilitation Institute to agree not to confiscate my manuscripts. He also negotiated for the return of the notebook in which I had written each night after interrogation by government agents. The contents of that notebook were later entitled "Sleepless Nights" and published in a Taipei newspaper.

One year after Mother's death, the Nationalists agreed to release me for a brief visit to Mother's grave site on Tomb Sweeping Day. My former lecturer, General Chao, had pulled strings and urged President Chiang Ching-kuo to allow the visit. Early in the morning of April 5, Brother arrived at the Benevolence Rehabilitation Institute and drove me to a cemetery in the town of Linkou. There I saw Mother's name written on a shiny new tombstone amid the rows of other tombstones stretching toward the horizon. With tears streaming down my cheeks, I knelt, lit incense, and prayed for her spirit. Mother had known little but work, worry, and self-sacrifice in her lifetime. With no education, she had never had the opportunity to rise above the barriers that women of her generation faced. She had derived meaning from life, not through her own accomplishments, but through the accomplishments of her children.

If human existence was a train ride, mine had been a haphazard one. Kneeling there, life flowed before me like a series of dreams. Some were beautiful, like blossoms shivering in the winds of early spring. Some were nightmares, full of horrible ghosts. Some were sweet, like the touch of a loving hand. Some were bitter, like Taiwan's struggle for freedom. I stood up, looked at the rows of tombstones and the expanse of the sky, and swore to myself that I would make Mother proud, and in my own way give significance to her life.

From that day forth, I redoubled my efforts to make the most of my days in prison. I wrote essays on philosophy and law, two novellas, and the first draft of a full-length novel entitled *Empathy*. Each night after lights-out, I crouched next to the window to make use of the light shining in from the courtyard, and I also wrote sitting on the toilet where I was invisible to the cameras. Although the prison authorities promised not to confiscate my writings, the less they knew about how much I wrote, the better. In the summer months, when the heat became unbearable, I pressed myself against cool cement walls until I could bear to write again.

At the time of the Kaohsiung Incident, the Nationalists held a dim view of the principles of international human rights, believing Taiwan's most prominent dissidents could be jailed with impunity.

Since the 1947 crackdown that killed tens of thousands of Taiwanese, the Nationalists had effectively silenced political opposition with the threat of violence and imprisonment. The *Formosa* trial was different. Word of our arrest spread quickly to Taiwanese communities around the world. Protest rallies were held in New York and Los Angeles. Overseas Taiwanese groups joined forces with international human rights organizations to push for our release. Persistent lobbying by overseas Taiwanese and a letter-writing campaign by Amnesty International won the support of influential members of the US Congress, including congressmen Stephen Solarz, Jim Leach, and Fortney Stark and senators Edward Kennedy, Claiborne Pell, and Charles Percy. These politicians urged President Chiang Ching-kuo to end martial law, pardon the "Kaohsiung Eight," and resume elections.

The efforts of one Taiwanese in particular, known to human rights colleagues only by his pseudonym, Bruce Lee, had a major impact on my case. He used the moniker of the kung fu star out of fear that the Nationalists might have him killed for supporting me and the other imprisoned dissidents. A member of Amnesty International Chapter 101 in Albuquerque, New Mexico, Bruce Lee (whose real name was Chang Hsi-tian) broke down in tears at a chapter meeting as he explained that nearly all of Taiwan's key opposition leaders had been jailed following the Kaohsiung Incident. He noted that I had founded the Taiwanese feminist movement and attended Harvard Law School. This connection to America and feminism made the group feel closer to me. On the spot, Amnesty International Chapter 101 adopted my case, even before receiving formal approval from the Amnesty International Secretariat in London.

On December 16, Chapter 101 sent a petition of signatures collected in Albuquerque supermarkets to pressure the US Congress to take action. Meanwhile, Government Information Office director James Soong was using the full power of his office to convince the international community that the Kaohsiung Eight were violent revolutionaries. Congress wavered on whether to support our cause until it received the first petition signed by 350 people from Albuquerque. Chapter 101 sent thousands of postcards advocating my release to

President Chiang Ching-kuo, Premier Sun Yun-hsuan, other cabinet members, top Nationalist officials, legislators, and members of the US Congress. The kung fu human rights fighter even sponsored the printing of some of these cards himself. The postcards pictured me wearing dark glasses and a pink mini skirt while cutting a birthday cake with Chiang Ching-kuo—a chance photo taken during my days at the Executive Yuan. In March 1980, the Amnesty International (AI) headquarters sent out a fact-finding team to attend the *Formosa* trial, which led to AI's decision to formally adopt the Kaohsiung Eight as prisoners of conscience after confirming the nonviolent nature of our case.

In prison, I had no idea that Amnesty International was lobbying for my release. The first hint of Chapter 101's involvement came during a visit by Eldest Sister. The jailers, as usual, sat nearby taking notes when she said, somewhat nervously, "A professor from New Mexico sends her regards."

"I don't know anyone from New Mexico," I replied, surprised.

During a visit a month later, Eldest Sister said, "The mayor of New Mexico came to Taiwan. I met with him at the Grand Hotel in Taipei, and he gave me a gift for you. He said in New Mexico you have many friends concerned about you."

To my astonishment, Eldest Sister handed me a small painting of blown sand portraying a Native American. I was speechless. Nothing could have seemed more distant and foreign to my surroundings. In prison with only Chen Chu for company, I felt forgotten by the world. I had no way of knowing that Amnesty International had fought for my release since my incarceration in 1979. Prison officials never delivered the hundreds of letters and dozens of parcels sent by Amnesty volunteers all over the world.

"Eldest Sister, the man who gave you this painting must be the mayor of a city in New Mexico. New Mexico is a state and American states have governors."

"Oh," she paused, considering. Eldest Sister hadn't heard of New Mexico before meeting the mayor.

"A human rights organization," she continued, "Amnesty International, told the mayor about your imprisonment, and he had asked to see you after arriving in Taipei. This request embarrassed the Nationalists, but the government allowed him to meet with me."

All of a sudden, I felt as if I were enjoying a sunbath in early spring. I saw blossoms everywhere. Blossoms of human love and the green grass of justice. We had not been forgotten. I could tell that support from overseas had boosted Eldest Sister's morale as well. Although she was a tireless source of love and assistance, Eldest Sister had been deeply affected by Mother's death and my imprisonment. She worried constantly about my physical condition. After her meeting with Mayor John Kinney of Albuquerque, she took up correspondence with members of Amnesty International in the United States in hopes that more foreign pressure might help to secure my early release. Eldest Sister's letters in Chinese were translated by a senior researcher at Columbia University's East Asian Institute, James Seymour, and forwarded to Chapter 101 in Albuquerque and to other members of Amnesty International in the United States and Europe.

Eldest Sister's letters helped to alleviate the frustration of the human rights volunteers. Chapter 101, in particular, had sent hundreds of letters and lobbied extensively on my behalf, but they had received no response from Taiwan. Through Eldest Sister's letters, the human rights volunteers gradually formed a better picture of my living conditions and health problems and obtained information that aided their efforts to free me. In February 1982, Eldest Sister sent the following letter to James Seymour, who relayed its contents to Chapter 101:

I only recently received your letter because I have moved. Deeply appreciated your concern regarding my sister's condition. She only has visits on Tuesdays for a total of thirty minutes. If three people visit, each one is only granted ten minutes. She has not received any of the letters that you have sent and so hasn't responded. Please forgive her. She and Chen Chu live in adjacent small rooms and are constantly monitored on closed-circuit TV, and there are also tape recorders that apparently monitor every conversation. A visitor must pass through three doors to get inside. Lu Hsiu-lien and Chen Chu eat together every day, but not with other prisoners. They both have a prison guard with them twenty-four hours a day. The food is very poor but two kilograms of food can be delivered by the family. Because Chen's family lives some distance away, I usually prepare food for both of them, as well as clothes and other daily necessities. I am worried that it might be hard for the women to pass the time, so I send them some arts and crafts materials, such as for knitting and embroidering supplies. . . . Only one hour of exercise is permitted per week. Although Lu Hsiu-lien weighs about sixty kilograms now, she looks bloated from water retention. (She used to weigh fifty-one or fifty-two kilograms.) I received a postcard from Lu Hsiu-lien on January 25 saying that she has discomfort in her eyes and throat. I am very worried that her thyroid cancer might be recurring. We are not allowed to send her medicine, and it would be miserable if she gets sick in prison.

In March, Eldest Sister wrote again to relay my need for immediate medical assistance. After receiving the translation of the letter detailing my symptoms—shortness of breath, choking sensation, vomiting blood, heart palpitations, incontinence—Chapter 101 asked an Albuquerque doctor to review my case, and the preliminary medical opinion was that I might be suffering from a recurrence of thyroid cancer. If untreated, the AI volunteers worried, the cancer might kill me. Chapter 101 quickly made preparations for an international "Urgent Action" campaign that appealed to Amnesty members around the world to act immediately by intensifying pressure on the Taiwanese government.

During a medical checkup, the doctor responsible for my health in prison simply felt my neck and concluded that the symptoms had nothing to do with my old thyroid cancer. Members of Chapter 101 remained skeptical of this diagnosis, despite assurances by the Government Information Office and even the US State Department that I continued to "enjoy good health." The Nationalist-affiliated Chinese Association for Human Rights, in response to Chapter 101's queries, even went so far as to say that I was allowed daily exercise outdoors and was taking a yoga class.

Chapter 101 telephoned Eldest Sister every Tuesday evening after she returned from her prison visit. AI learned that the Nationalists were clearly stonewalling and that the US State Department had been given incorrect information. My health problems remained serious.

With the Amnesty-sponsored Urgent Action prompting renewed concern, on May 20, 1982, columnist Jack Anderson decided to make my imprisonment the focus of his syndicated column. "Documents obtained by my associate . . . give a harrowing picture of Lu's physical torment," he wrote. "She is in almost constant pain; she has trouble breathing and feels a strangling sensation in her throat. Lately she has reportedly been vomiting blood, and her weight has increased alarmingly, making her face and body puffy."

It was impossible for me to know the extent of the activity occurring abroad on my behalf. I wasn't aware that Amnesty International had launched a worldwide letter-writing campaign, or that I had been adopted as a prisoner of conscience by AI Chapter 70 in Erlangen, West Germany. I had no idea that dozens of magazines and newspapers had written of my plight, including *Ms. Magazine*. Nor did I know that Amnesty's requests that I be allowed to take a correspondence class with a foreign university had prompted the Nationalists to allow Chen Chu and me to take classes with Professor Wu Kun-ju. I did, however, begin to hope that if foreigners knew about our situation, then the average Taiwanese did as well. Clues appeared that gave me reason for optimism.

Three times a year, a hair stylist at the Benevolence Rehabilitation Institute gave the inmates permanents. I didn't like the way the woman did my hair, so I protested. The administrators realized that since I had visitors so often, it would look better if I appeared more presentable. They allowed a young stylist from the outside to come in and fix my hair. I didn't know the young woman's background, so I didn't say much to her, but when the guard stepped out for minute, the stylist whispered to me, "Ms. Lu, I feel so sorry for you. We all feel bad for you."

"How do you know me?" I asked.

"I've read all of your books," she replied. When the woman finished, she wouldn't take my money. "It was my pleasure to perm your hair, Ms. Lu," she said. The stylist came back two or three times and never accepted payment.

Living in near isolation led to a mind-numbing routine, disrupted occasionally by talks with the Benevolence Rehabilitation Institute workers in charge of our so-called rehabilitation. One of them was a short, dumpy woman surnamed Chang. "I will not be antagonistic toward you," I told Chang. "I know that you are only doing your job, and if you didn't do it, someone else would." I insisted that she handle her work professionally and in full accordance with prison regulations. Chang agreed that would be best.

With this understanding, we got along well at first. Eldest Sister had given me a how-to book on knitting, and Chang gave me some tips on knitting a sweater. Chang claimed she knew where to get yarn for a low price, and I gave her money to buy some. She also said her father was an expert at fortune-telling and offered to have him give me a reading using the Chinese zodiac. Among all the fortune-telling methods, I think the Chinese zodiac formula is one of the more interesting. Out of curiosity, I agreed. The results were interesting. I was fated to go to prison. The reading of my relationship with different family members and the description of my personality were quite accurate. Chang saw that I was satisfied and demanded payment. I gave her the money, but the fact that she hadn't mentioned payment earlier irritated me.

I knew that the authorities intercepted all of my letters, so I used my correspondence as a way to express dissatisfaction. I wrote a letter to Eldest Sister, attaching sample pieces of the yarn Chang sold me, and asked her to find out the going rate. Eldest Sister asked at several stores and wrote back that Chang was grossly overcharging me. I asked about the cost of fortune-telling in a similar manner, with identical results: Chang had cheated me.

In order to provide myself with more ammunition to combat prison authorities, I asked for a copy of the "Benevolence Rehabilitation Institute Management Rules." A careful reading revealed that some regulations went beyond legal bounds. For example, policy mandated that we speak in Mandarin Chinese and not in Taiwanese, Hakka, or aboriginal languages. Prison law, by comparison, only says that one cannot speak "foreign languages," such as English.

Approaching the head warden, I said, "Since Taiwanese is not a foreign language, you cannot legally prevent us from speaking it." My concern was for Eldest Sister, who had grown up during the Japanese Occupation and didn't speak standard Chinese well. She felt nervous every time she came to see me, because she was not permitted to speak in our native tongue.

"The guards," who were mainlanders, "do not understand Taiwanese, so speaking Taiwanese makes it difficult for them to file reports on your conversations," the head warden replied.

"Well, that's your problem, not mine," I responded. "Unless, of course, you are suggesting that Taiwanese is a foreign language, and that Taiwan is not part of China?" With this, Benevolence Rehabilitation Institute authorities had nothing more to say, and enforcement of the language code was relaxed.

I also used the recording devices that monitored my conversations during each family visiting session for airing grievances. For example, when Brother came, I would ask him seemingly innocuous questions about Chang's actions. "Prison authorities are supposed to teach me knowledge. If they are not knowledgeable, they should at least provide moral inspiration. If they are neither knowledgeable nor moral, how can they provide guidance?" I filled him in on the details of Chang's petty corruption before continuing. "Given these circumstances and evidence, is this behavior illegal?" I asked.

"Sure," Brother replied.

My concern was not financial, but ethical. Regardless of our status as prisoners, I wanted the authorities to deal with us fairly and treat us with respect. Naturally, my conversation with Brother was reported to higher authorities. When the time felt right, I submitted a formal report.

Two weeks later, a prosecutor was sent to investigate. He interrogated me, but this time Chang, and not I, was the defendant. The head of the Garrison Command, Taiwan's military police force, even came to the Benevolence Rehabilitation Institute to give the counselors a lecture, using the very argument that had I stated in my report—the importance of reforming political prisoners in the interests of the state. Chang was eventually replaced.

Whenever possible, I attempted to make friends with our guards, sharing food that Eldest Sister brought or engaging in idle chat. This was difficult at first because the Dangwai had been depicted by state-controlled media as cruel, unpatriotic, and even violent.

"I hope you don't mind my telling you this," said one of the guards, "but we were so afraid of you at the beginning. We worried that the two of you might attack us at night. The authorities have accused you of being dangerous, you know!"

"Of course, I know that but do you still believe it?" I asked, laughing.

"No, not any more. Otherwise I wouldn't be talking to you like this," she said blushing. "You are kind and generous."

Slowly Chen Chu and I developed a friendly relationship with our jailers, two housewives who had been hired to watch us for the duration of our prison sentence. Regulations such as turning out the lights in the blockhouse became more lax, and our guards sometimes joined us in watching television late into the night. On one occasion, during the national elections of 1983, the four of us sat crouched around the TV waiting for the election results. The jailers were staunch supporters of the Nationalists and had taken to heart news reports that opposition candidates would make a poor showing.

"You people are so mean and militant that you will fail," one of them said with a smile. Since she seemed in good spirits, I decided the time had come to give her a political education. Picking up a copy of the *Central Daily News*, the Nationalist mouthpiece, I pointed to an article about the election and said, "Look at how the newspaper criticizes these Dangwai candidates. I bet you that the ones attacked most strongly are the ones most likely to win." With that I took a red pen and underlined several names of Dangwai politicians, some of them the wives or relatives of the codefendants at our trial.

The counting of the ballots took longer than we had expected. We were awake through the night. It was a breach of regulations. If the prison authorities had caught us, our guards would have been punished. When the results were announced, my predictions proved surprisingly accurate. All of the candidates I had underlined were elected, and a couple of them received the highest number of votes in their multiple-member electoral districts.

On another occasion, while watching the news on television, I turned to the jailers and said, "As soon as one leaves the country, there is no such thing as the Republic of China."

"What nonsense are you babbling?"

"When you leave the country, the Republic of China does not exist. Just listen to this report about the visiting delegation of American governors. Every one of the Americans interviewed uses the word 'Taiwan.' None of them says 'Republic of China.' The subtitles in Chinese say 'Republic of China,' but no one else uses the word."

The jailers looked at me with something akin to awe. After that, when they read something in the newspaper that they questioned or found interesting, they would discuss it with me. One day, one of them came to me with a newspaper in hand. "Didn't you say that you went to Harvard University?" she asked, passing me the newspaper.

My hands shook with excitement as I read the article that she had circled. My old mentor at Harvard, Jerome Cohen, was in Taipei. I knew nothing of the international events that had brought him to Taiwan, nor could I guess that the Nationalists would allow us to meet.

A few days later, the jailers woke me early to say my request for medical treatment of my swollen thyroid gland had been granted. I quickly changed my clothes and was taken by car to the Tri-Service General Hospital in Taipei. Before the doctor could inquire about my condition, an agent came over and whispered in my ear, "A professor from the United States is here and would like to see you. Is that all right?"

"Of course, I'd love to see him!"

Guards escorted me to the luxuriously carpeted hospital VIP

room, where Chiang Ching-kuo's personal secretary, Ma Ying-jeou, was waiting with Professor Jerome Cohen and Yao Chia-wen's wife. Handing me a bouquet of flowers, Professor Cohen gave me a huge hug. Tears rolled down my cheeks. Neither time nor adversity had changed the warmth of Professor Cohen's friendship. Both of us wept as we recalled the optimism of our last conversation six years earlier in his Harvard office, when he had encouraged me to come back to Taiwan to run for the National Assembly.

"You are nobody here in the States, but you might become somebody at home. Why not go home and work for your people?" he had said.

"You know the situation in Taiwan," I had replied. "I might be jailed if I go into politics."

A smile had creased his cheeks. "Then I will wave a flag for you in Taipei!"

It had taken him six years to fulfill his promise to wave that flag. The government had denied him a visa to enter the country during our trial, and on his subsequent visits, it had refused to let him visit me in prison. So Professor Cohen had written a lengthy opinion piece in the *Asian Wall Street Journal* explaining the injustice of my treatment and had encouraged the faculty and staff from Harvard Law School to write to President Chiang Ching-kuo urging clemency.

"Just last night, I hesitated before asking him," he said, referring to Ma Ying-jeou, "if I could see you, because I doubted that it could be arranged. According to ROC regulations, foreigners cannot visit friends serving prison sentences, but Ma Ying-jeou consulted with President Chiang Ching-kuo. Early this morning he called to say you were in the hospital—not in prison—so he could take me to see you!"

In hushed tones, Professor Cohen explained how he had agreed to serve as a lawyer representing the survivors of Henry Liu, a Chinese writer murdered in Daly City, California. Henry Liu had written a critical biography of President Chiang Ching-kuo, something few had dared to do in the past. But Liu had run into serious trouble when he started to write a book about Madame Chiang Kai-shek. It was rumored that Chiang Ching-kuo's son, Chiang Hsiao-wu, had arranged for assassins from the Bamboo Union gang to kill the writer.

In the United States, the Liu murder had generated a wrath of criticism from the media and the Congress. The *New York Times* published a scathing editorial in February 1985: "Taiwan is a republic only in name. One family, one party and one cause permeate its politics." The reaction on Capitol Hill was to pass legislation threatening to bar arms sales to any country found guilty of harassing people in the United States. For Taiwan, long dependent on arms sales from the United States, the situation had become very precarious. US support for the Chiang family's rule had become more tenuous than ever.

When the Taiwanese media caught wind of these developments, public opinion forced the Nationalists to hold the murder trial in Taipei. The widow of Henry Liu hired two criminal lawyers from the United States to represent her. One of these lawyers was Professor Cohen, chosen for his expert knowledge of Taiwan and US law.

Although he hadn't served as a trial lawyer in years, Professor Cohen eagerly accepted the position in the hope that serving as a lawyer in the Liu murder trial would also place him in a strong position to pressure the Nationalists for my release. His instincts proved accurate. The Nationalist government treated him with far greater respect than ever before. Jerome Cohen's influence, and the threat of further embarrassment to the Chiang family, prompted President Chiang Ching-kuo to allow the two of us to meet.

After Professor Cohen and I parted, I returned to the blockhouse. His visit was a sign that sooner or later the government would free me. Six days after my meeting with Professor Cohen, my guards came to say goodbye.

"Good luck in all that you do," they said. "We'll miss you."

"I guess this means that I'll be leaving?" I asked.

They just smiled and left. I began packing my possessions. Early in the morning on March 28, exactly one week after my meeting with Jerome Cohen, the head warden at the Benevolence Rehabilitation Institute summoned me to his office. "Congratulations!" he said with a smile. "The authorities have decided to set you free today. You've been granted medical parole." As the weight of his words sank in, a feeling of detachment and numbness swept over me.

"Please remember you are a medical patient and should behave accordingly," he continued. "Your conduct will affect the fate of your cell mate, Chen Chu, and your other comrades."

The terms of medical parole stipulated that my release was for medical attention only. If I recovered, I would return to the Benevolence Rehabilitation Institute to complete my twelve-year sentence. The warden made it very clear that I must also refrain from any anti-government activities.

Ironically, on the eve of my release, prison authorities could not immediately contact Brother, who they wanted to serve as a guarantor of my good conduct, so they arranged for Eldest Sister to come stay with me in the meantime. A busy trial lawyer, Brother was tied up in court all day. Eldest Sister and I spent my first day of "liberty" in the blockhouse!

By early evening, the warden had been unable to contact Brother, so he agreed to allow Brother to sign the prison documents after my release. A sad but optimistic mood pervaded the room as I said farewell to Chen Chu, my cell mate of five years. We had experienced so much together.

"On the outside I will do my best to set you free," I told her.

Night had fallen by the time I left the Benevolence Rehabilitation Institute compound on the last of 1,933 days in prison. Balmy spring air and a light mist wrapped around us as Eldest Sister and I waited at the prison gates for a government car to take us to Brother's home. An hour later, the familiar lights of downtown Taoyuan came into view. The car pulled to the curbside at Brother's three-story house. I was home.

In Taiwanese society, body contact with others is rare. Hugging, kissing, and handshakes are uncommon, even among family members. But the moment of my return was so emotional that Brother and I embraced with tears in our eyes. "Sorry I made you wait so long," Brother said. Sobs choked my response. Aunts, cousins, nephews, and nieces surrounded me, delighted by my return. Several journalists were waiting as well. When the conversation turned to the circumstances of my release, one reporter from the *China Times* said, "We were originally told you would be released a week earlier. What happened?" I had been released on March 28. I counted back seven days to the date of professor Cohen's visit on March 21.

"I don't really know," I replied. "Perhaps the Nationalists wanted to save face by not releasing me on the same day I met Professor Cohen. They couldn't be seen as caving in to pressure from the Americans!" That was in truth what had happened, thanks to the valiant efforts of Jerome Cohen, Amnesty International, and other overseas Taiwanese and foreign friends. I was grateful beyond words for the unexpected turn of events that led to the restoration of my liberty, almost as suddenly as it had been taken from me 1,933 days before.

CHAPTER 7

IN SEARCH OF DESTINY

ACCORDING TO TAIWANESE CUSTOM, I SHOULD HAVE STAYED IN Brother's home. He is the family's only son and I am an unmarried woman. But after more than five years in prison, I found it difficult to feel comfortable anywhere. I was unaccustomed to the noise of traffic on the streets of downtown Taoyuan, and I worried that the large number of visitors coming to see me, mostly friends and journalists, not to mention the intrusive surveillance of government agents, would affect Brother's work. It would be quieter, I thought, in Eldest Sister's apartment in a suburb of Taipei, and more convenient for meeting opposition colleagues.

My promise to Mother as well as isolation from society had left me itching to reexperience the world outside. Much to Eldest Sister's consternation, I insisted on taking daily walks to exercise and have a look around.

"Don't go out, please don't," she said. "One prisoner who spent fifteen years in prison got killed three days after his release because he didn't know how to handle traffic." As if she were afraid that I would disappear again, Eldest Sister insisted on accompanying me everywhere I went. One week passed like this before I told her that I had to go out by myself.

"Don't go!" Eldest Sister protested, "You can't even walk properly."

Unfortunately she was right. After more than five years in prison, I struggled with the discomfort of cramming my feet into leather shoes. I had worn only slippers for years. High-heeled shoes made me dizzy, and my legs shook when I walked up stairs. There hadn't been stairs in prison either. Bereft of exercise for too long, I felt unsteady just crossing the street. At times, speaking proved difficult, too. I had become accustomed to silence during my years in prison and had trouble summoning words to express my thoughts. My knowledge of English, for example, was nearly lost.

Solitude and years of reflection had taught me that wisdom is gained through personal experience. I might succeed or fail, but I had to at least try to regain my physical and mental capacities. In spite of Eldest Sister's warnings, I walked to the nearest bus stop one morning and randomly selected a bus bound for Taipei. I got on and found my heart pounding. Would people recognize me? Would I ever fit in again? As the bus drove slowly past people and places in the city I had not seen for nearly six years, a deep regret swept over me. The world outside didn't appear any different. The sun shone brightly, people smiled and shopped in traditional marketplaces, flirting boys and girls waited by the bus stop just as they had before. My sacrifice seemed trivial, even silly. I pressed my face to the window, and tears poured down my cheeks.

Spending time with friends in the opposition helped to stave off depression. Old friends and colleagues threw party after party in my honor. As I listened to younger members of the opposition boldly criticize the Nationalists, I realized some things had changed. They didn't fear the same kind of retribution the Kaohsiung Eight had endured.

Ten months later, when Chen Chu got out of prison, she got her turn to be guest of honor at all the parties. On one such occasion she whispered to me, "Our sacrifice was really too much wasn't it?"

"Why?" I asked.

"Look at these young freedom fighters. They criticize so much and don't even have to serve jail time."

"That was the purpose of our struggle," I said. "Our sacrifice paid the price of their freedom."

Yet compared to that of others, my own suffering appeared slight at times. Once, some months after my release, an old friend came to see me along with another man I had not met before. "Ms. Lu, I think the sentence handed down to you by the courts was too harsh," the friend said.

"Most people think so," I replied.

"I don't know about that," said the other man, his lips cracking a bitter smile. "I served a fifteen-year sentence for an essay that I wrote in college. The government released me in time for the Kaohsiung Incident, where I heard you speak to the people at the rally. You said everything I've wanted to say my entire life and you only did five and a half years in prison. You deserved a longer prison sentence than mine!"

"Then I should thank you," I said. "Perhaps without your sacrifice the government would have sentenced me to death!"

Shortly after I joined Eldest Sister and her husband at their home in Yungho, a government agent moved into the apartment above us. My presence had become a burden, and Eldest Sister had already suffered too much on my behalf. Her husband was harassed at work. His superiors denied him promotions, as punishment for his wife's kinship with a "traitor." I decided to accept a friend's offer to move into his apartment nearby. Liu Feng-sung had been sentenced to prison for a minor role in the Kaohsiung Incident and had been released before me. His wife, Wong Chin-chu, was a music teacher who was later elected as a national legislator and county chief executive. We had the same circle of friends, and I felt that staying at his apartment would make it easier to meet with opposition activists.

People dropped in from all corners of the island and our conversations lasted deep into the night, inevitably returning to the complexities of the Kaohsiung Incident. It was during these chats that I discovered that few people understood the dynamics of the demonstration on December 10, 1980, or the interrogation and imprisonment of the Kaohsiung Eight. The second of the eight to be released, after Lin Yi-hsiung, I felt a responsibility to put all the pieces together by writing the book *Re-Trying the Formosa Case*.

As my tentative research progressed, I became convinced of a right-wing conspiracy to wipe out the opposition. The growth of popular support for the Dangwai in the months preceding the Human Rights

Day march had put fear into the hearts of the more conservative arm of the Nationalist Party. Secret service groups, anticipating escalating confrontation, hatched a plot providing the pretext for the arrest of opposition leaders on charges of sedition, a crime punishable by death. Agents were planted among the marchers to provoke an incident. Riot police encircled the peaceful demonstrators and launched tear gas attacks, inciting the jittery crowd to violence. Afterward, the Nationalist-run media laid sole blame for the violence on the marchers and on the leaders of the rally, and the higher-ups in government jumped on the bandwagon with harsh condemnations.

The *Formosa* trial marked the culmination of the conspiracy and a turning point for the fortunes of both the Dangwai and right-wing conspirators. President Chiang Ching-kuo, who had been left in the dark about the conspiracy, became suspicious. Conflicting statements by the secret service and by eyewitnesses left Chiang smelling a rat. Sources within the Garrison Command told me the president even went on a secret fact-finding trip to Kaohsiung, where he saw the duplicity of his advisors. Chiang arranged for an open court martial of the Kaohsiung Eight, instead of one behind closed doors. While not exonerating the *Formosa* group, President Chiang broke with tradition in giving us a chance to explain our position to a free press.

Even after my release, researching the *Formosa* case remained taboo. Perhaps realizing my intent, secret police tapped my phone line and shadowed me wherever I went. When friends or organizations telephoned to invite me to attend a conference or public event, the Garrison Command engaged in pressure tactics to discourage my attendance, threatening Brother and my cousin, the two people who, as my guarantors after my release, could legally be held accountable for my actions. "If Ms. Lu's activities continue, we will find fault with you!" the Garrison Command told Brother.

Realizing that I would have more freedom to write about the Kaohsiung Incident overseas, I applied for permission to leave the country as soon as possible. Once again the assistance of my influential friend, Professor Jerome Cohen, proved invaluable. I asked him to negotiate with the Nationalists on my behalf so that I could return to

Harvard as a graduate student, while receiving medical treatment. He appealed to Fred Chien, then the Taiwan representative in Washington, DC, making countless phone calls on my behalf. It took one year to win permission for me to leave Taiwan and to make arrangements for me to study at Harvard University as a research fellow in the international law and human rights program.

As soon as word came that I could leave Taiwan, Amnesty International and overseas Taiwanese put together an itinerary for my visit. I knew only that Eldest Sister would accompany me and that our first stop was San Francisco and our last stop Harvard University in Cambridge, Massachusetts. In May 1986, we boarded a direct flight for San Francisco, where my old friend and Harvard classmate Chang Fu-mei and other overseas Taiwanese waited to meet us.

Chang Fu-mei briefed us on the arrangements for a tour of the United States: "This year is the twenty-fifth anniversary of Amnesty International, and you have been invited to participate in the AI national celebration in Washington, DC." Other speaking engagements with Taiwanese communities, Chang Fu-mei said, would take Eldest Sister and me all over the country for the next four months. We went sightseeing, too, including a visit to the Grand Canyon and to the gambling casinos in Las Vegas. Eldest Sister loved every bit!

In Los Angeles I was interviewed in a Hollywood studio, along with several celebrities drumming up publicity for Amnesty International. The next major venue was the twenty-fifth anniversary celebration in Washington, DC. Roughly 1,000 people were in attendance when I took the podium as a keynote speaker at Georgetown University and told the crowd of my capture and imprisonment. By coincidence, the AI celebration had fallen on June 7, my birthday, and on my mind was the tragic demise of Mother, who had brought me into this world forty-four years before:

> As for my poor mother, she fainted and broke her leg over the shock of my arrest. She lay in bed weeping and murmuring my name for one and a half years until her final moment of life.
> I had made every effort to gain permission to see my mother

before she died in vain. As a last resort, I started a hunger strike. In order to stop the hunger strike, the authorities gave me a false medical report that showed that my mother's health was improving. She passed away within a month. . . . It has given me a lifelong regret that I was never able to see her after her seventy-first birthday celebration, which was two days before the Kaohsiung Incident. Life played a cruel joke, didn't it?

However, life seems to be a merciful joke to me today. Today is my birthday and here in front of you, members of the honorable and humane Amnesty International, I am mourning the misery of the one who gave birth to me. Amnesty International calls itself a conspiracy of hope. Indeed, I am here today to share with you the hope that one person's sacrifice shall be rewarded by another's benefit; that the darkness of jail shall be enlightened by the sparkling gleam of human dignity; and that the dictator's viciousness shall be overcome by massive, popular support for human rights. . . .

In front of you stands, with dignity and vigor, a feminist who has suffered 1,933 days of confinement, along with twelve years suffering from thyroid carcinoma. Her dignity relies on the belief that the limits of humanity are only defined by the individual, not by outside repression. Her vigor springs from the commitment that where there is injustice, there must be struggle. Fortunately, although she has lost her liberty, her youth, and her health, she has not lost her will or dignity. . . . Special thanks for your impartial concern toward human rights, regardless of race, nation, fame, or gender. Human rights is in itself worthy of respect. People of all colors deserve the same dignity. . . . It is only when the protection of human rights can be assured on a nondiscriminatory basis that the value of human rights can be truly realized.

After the banquet that evening, the former French justice minister was slated to discuss abolition of the death penalty. Instead, the Amnesty International chairman came out carrying a birthday cake and the entire assembly joined in wishing me a happy birthday. Overflowing with surprise and gratitude, I acknowledged the kindness with tears of joy. Later, I learned that Congressman Stephen Solarz, attending the celebration, had enjoyed my speech so much that he posted a copy of it in the *Congressional Record*.

Not long after the meeting in Washington, DC, Amnesty International invited me to attend a special AI benefit concert at Giants Stadium in New Jersey with seventeen other former prisoners of conscience. Musicians including Miles Davis, Joan Baez, the Police, and U2 performed before a crowd of 55,000. That night, I fielded questions from American television networks NBC, CBS, and ABC in my first contact with America's television media.

In Washington, the leader of the Albuquerque Chapter of Amnesty International, Mary Kay Dunphy, invited Eldest Sister and me to fly out to New Mexico to meet the entire group that had labored for my release. We happily accepted her invitation. Our hosts in Albuquerque told us many touching stories. Mary Kay Dunphy had written me postcards and letters in prison nearly every other day for two years. I never received them. But someone at the Garrison Command or the Bureau of Investigation read them, and that is more important. I will never forget her determination and faithful correspondence. One letter, written during the second year of my imprisonment, shows her strong sense of personal involvement in my case:

"Sometimes when I think about you being in prison for the last year and a half (when I first became aware of your situation) I feel as though I am there with you—and I wish there were more ways that I could help you. Please write and let me know how you are doing. Remember: 'If all the world hated you and believed you wicked while your own conscience approved you, and absolved you from guilt, you would not be without friends.' From *Jane Eyre*. Love, Mary Kay Dunphy."

Mary Kay's interest in fighting for my release was piqued, in part, by a class she was taking at the University of New Mexico called the Philosophy of Liberation, which required an internship. Mary Kay didn't even know where Taiwan was when she took up my cause by working with Amnesty International. As part of her internship, she pledged to send 5,000 letters to the Taiwanese government on my behalf. This figure eventually trebled, and a total of 15,000 postcards were mailed to President Chiang Ching-kuo advocating my release.

When we arrived in Albuquerque, Eldest Sister looked out at the red rocky bluff of the Sandia Mountains and cried, "How could it have been possible that you had a savior in such a strange and remote desert!"

"It's like the saying, 'within the four seas, we are all sisters and brothers,'" I replied. That was indeed how I saw the Amnesty International volunteers who labored so tirelessly to free me, a stranger and a foreigner, except that I shared their beliefs in the value of freedom, democracy, gender equality, and the fundamental dignity of humanity.

It turned out that even in a city as removed from Taiwan as Albuquerque, New Mexico, Chapter 101 had encountered Nationalist harassment. On December 10, 1981, Human Rights Day, two years after the Kaohsiung Incident, Chapter 101 hosted an event open to the public at the University of New Mexico. The main speaker for the evening was Linda Arrigo, the American wife of Dangwai leader Shih Ming-teh whom I had last seen on the morning of my arrest. Several days before Linda was scheduled to speak, the posters advertising the event at the University of New Mexico campus were torn down. Even the replacement posters were torn down. Before the event, a man described as Asian told a Chapter 101 member that he had called the campus police and the Albuquerque police because he was genuinely concerned for the safety of those attending the meeting. The man said he knew that Linda traveled with armed bodyguards who were thugs and that he feared violence. This concerned the University of New Mexico staff and the members of Chapter 101. They knew that Linda didn't travel with bodyguards. Although no violence occurred on the evening of the event, Chapter 101's coordinator saw an Asian man crouched outside in the bushes, apparently watching those attending the event.

During our Albuquerque visit, Eldest Sister and I had the opportunity to meet Mayor John Kinney, who had given me the portrait of the Native American, and the kung fu freedom fighter Bruce Lee, actually named Chang Hsi-tian, who had alerted Chapter 101 to the plight of the Kaohsiung Eight the day after our arrest. Albuquerque television, radio, and print media all sought interviews; I happily obliged.

Eldest Sister and I continued traveling to speaking engagements with Taiwanese communities across the country, including summer camps for overseas Taiwanese students in Ithaca, New York, and in Houston, Texas. Everywhere people were eager to hear my perspective on events in Taiwan. Crisp breezes scattered the red autumn leaves by the time I arrived in Cambridge, Massachusetts, to resume my studies at Harvard.

Originally, I had planned to pursue a PhD, but on my return I became a research fellow studying international human rights programs and devoting most of my time to writing the book *Re-trying the Formosa Case*. Many friends at home and abroad had kept careful records of events related to the Kaohsiung Incident and willingly provided research materials. I completely reexamined the case—reviewing falsehoods admitted as evidence, the use of interrogation to extract confessions, evidence of government conspiracy, and political conditions leading up to the confrontation. The research required was daunting and the book more comprehensive than any other written on the subject.

The summer after my first year back at Harvard, I received a number of invitations to visit Europe, including from Amnesty International chapters in Germany and the Netherlands. I invited my friend Chiu Chue-chen, the Dangwai musician, to come over from Taiwan to meet me. Chiu had served four years in prison just for singing the Taiwanese folk song "Awaiting the Spring Breeze" on the night of the Kaohsiung Incident. Together Chiu and I traveled to East Berlin to get an impression of the Communist world, from Vienna to Geneva alongside the beautiful Alps, and to The Hague, Amsterdam, and Munich, where the German branch of Amnesty International hosted its national conference.

Early on, I had discovered Chiu's talent for music and encouraged him to work on recording Taiwanese folk songs for popular distribution. In the late 1970s, records and cassettes in the island's native languages were all but unavailable because of government restrictions on any language but Mandarin Chinese. For three decades, the Nationalists had suppressed Taiwanese art and culture, making people feel like barbarians without a culture of their own. In 1979, Chiu and I had recorded the first album of Taiwanese folk songs together, with Chiu singing and playing the guitar and me explaining the meaning of each song in the context of Taiwanese history.

It had been difficult to find a studio that would allow us to record tracks in Taiwanese. Several refused. Others kicked us out once they realized our intentions. I felt like a smuggler of contraband when, on the day of the Kaohsiung Incident, I received the first hundred copies of the album and went down to Kaohsiung to sell the tapes at the demonstration. During the chaos and rioting, all the copies disappeared. Fortunately, the album earned a measure of popularity in spite of its first unorthodox debut. After my release, I heard bootleg copies of the album playing all over Taiwan and even abroad.

Chiu Chue-chen and I had a marvelous time traveling in Europe. At an Amnesty conference at The Hague, Chiu warmed up the crowd by performing an old Taiwanese folk song; I translated the lyrics to the delight of thousands. The song, a romantic tune about a Dutch doctor saying farewell to his Taiwanese sweetheart, captured the hearts of the audience. Almost no one present knew that the Dutch were Taiwan's first colonial rulers, occupying the island from 1624 to 1662, or that this was one of the cruelest chapters in the island's history. When we finished, people exclaimed, "We shouldn't have done that! We never should have occupied Taiwan!"

Dynamic political change in Taiwan in the late 1980s prompted my decision to return home. On September 28, 1986, the Dangwai defied a government ban on political parties and founded the pro-independence Democratic Progressive Party (DPP). The following year, President Chiang Ching-kuo surrendered in the face of overwhelming popular pressure, lifting martial law and restoring a number of civic and economic freedoms that had been denied. Thirty-eight years of martial law, the longest in modern history, had come to an end.

It is said that history means little to a child, but everything to an old man. Chiang Ching-kuo, in his seventies and nearly blind with diabetes, had begun to worry about his legacy and assented to Taiwan's gradual transition to democracy. Chiang made Lee Teng-hui, a

Taiwanese educated under Japanese colonial rule, his successor. And, in the final two years of his life, Chiang frequently said, "I am Chinese and I'm also Taiwanese." This sweeping recognition of Taiwanese identity paved the way for reconciliation between mainlanders and Taiwanese after his death.

The cessation of martial law removed a host of restrictions governing Taiwan's society, including the ban on founding newspapers. By 1989, Kang Ning-hsiang, the only major opposition leader to have emerged unscathed from the Kaohsiung Incident, was working on a plan to start the first major opposition newspaper, the *Capital Morning Post*. In spite of Kang's status as a senior Dangwai politician, he had only a minor association with the *Formosa Magazine* and therefore had not been imprisoned with the Kaohsiung Eight. Kang telephoned me at Harvard to invite me to join him in Taipei as the chief editorial writer at the newspaper. After considering the offer, I decided to join Kang with the caveat that I would have the opportunity to approve other editorial personnel. I moved out of my Boston apartment and made plans to return to Taiwan.

On the way home, I made brief stopovers in South Korea and Japan. In South Korea, I met with Kim Yung-sam and Kim Dae-jung, both of whom were active opposition leaders at the time and both of whom later became presidents of South Korea. In 1988, Kim Dae-jung didn't seem to enjoy the popularity of Kim Yung-sam, who later bowed out as president after a succession of scandals. Kim Dae-jung, who had a small but fanatical following based in southwestern Korea, lived in a large Korean-style house in Seoul. He struck me as a very gentle and sincere man. Both Kims said that they totally understood Taiwan's situation and heartily expressed their wishes for Taiwan independence—a position they later reversed.

I also had a chance to get a firsthand look at a Korean political rally when hundreds of students protested in front of the Seoul hotel, where I was staying during the four-day trip. Kim Dae-jung's English secretary, a Harvard Law School graduate, was on hand to explain Korean protest culture. "It has become a convention that Korean student demonstrations take sides on major national issues," he said.

"Were you among the student demonstrators in your youth?"

"Of course!" he said. "The younger generation always protests the policies of the older generation, just as the current members of the older generation protested when they were young."

"So what do you think of these student protesters?"

"They're kids having fun!"

My next stop was Japan, where I had a short meeting with Diet member Takako Doi, the first woman to head the Japan Socialist Party and serve as speaker of the Diet. Painfully pro-China, she and I had little in common. After paying courtesy calls on other Japanese politicians, I flew on to Taipei. I was gaining valuable experience in high-level diplomacy, and the visits to Korea and Tokyo were good training for future work in international affairs.

At home in Taiwan, my former Dangwai colleagues organized rallies to give me an opportunity to speak in Taipei, Taichung, and Kaohsiung. Political rallies, illegal during martial law, had become the popular means for opposition politicians to have direct contact with the Taiwanese people. Thousands gathered in parks, school yards, and temples to listen to fiery speeches criticizing the Nationalists. With food stands and stalls selling souvenirs, explosions of firecrackers, and cheers announcing my arrival, these early rallies had the air of a carnival and the intensity of a religious service.

On one hand, I wanted to get to know the country again after my years of incarceration and my stint in America. On the other hand, I wanted to contribute to a debate on Taiwan's role in international affairs and explore possibilities for returning to politics. While traveling in Europe, I had concluded that if the land of my birth became more vocal in international affairs, it could win a measure of protection against Chinese territorial expansionism. In addition, Taiwan's isolation from international organizations and lack of official channels of communication with other nations bred misunderstanding and vulnerability. Only China benefited from Taiwan's silence.

Back in Taipei, serious problems arose at Kang Ning-hsiang's *Capital Morning Post*. Kang had invited the famous opposition journalist Antonio Chiang (Si ma wen wu) to serve as editor in chief. The two had cooperated closely in the past, but over the years a rift had grown. Chiang declined Kang's offer. Without consulting me, Kang hired another editor in chief, a man formerly with the conservative newspaper the *United Daily*. Fearing the editorial slant would be biased toward the Nationalists, I declined the position at the *Capital Morning Post*.

For a time, I wondered if I had made a mistake returning to Taiwan. The opportunity I had hoped would allow me to reenter the Taiwanese political debate had fallen through. But I had shipped my belongings home and could not justify immediately shipping them back to the United States. As I mulled over my next course of action, I considered a simple credo that has served me well at the crossroads in life:

> At the time you are needed most,
> go to the place you're most needed,
> and do what is most necessary for you to do.

In the campaign for national legislature in autumn of 1989, vote buying and violent coercion of voters were typical Nationalist strategies for winning political office. These practices were a serious obstacle to further democratization. My return was well timed: I was most needed in Taiwan, and fighting election fraud was the most necessary task.

"You're crazy!" my friends said. "How can you stop it?"

"We have to," I replied. "Vote buying is a cancer attacking the vital organs of Taiwan's democracy. We must kill that cancer." This metaphor had personal significance. I had been immensely relieved not to experience a reoccurrence of cancer since my surgery.

With a small staff of volunteers, I founded the Clean Election Coalition (CEC). My intention was not simply to stop Nationalist candidates from buying votes, and thereby to help the DPP, which had been increasingly popular since it first participated in elections in 1986. I also sought to lay the foundation for genuine democracy with a two-pronged strategy: boosting awareness of the problem of vote buying, and investigating election fraud and corruption.

Taiwan's "culture of corruption" stems from the legacy of Chinese rule over the island. During the Japanese Occupation, Taiwanese could at least count on the honesty of government officials. This changed under the Nationalists. I can still remember Father criticizing the greed and nepotism of Nationalist leaders, who took through regulation what military carpetbaggers didn't take by force. Nationalist corruption worsened during the transition from authoritarian rule, as the ruling party sought to retain power by rigging elections. Vote buying was rife and vote fraud rampant. The more money candidates spent campaigning, the more they sought to earn through corruption after getting elected. This was especially true for legislators and National Assembly members, who (at the time) had three-year terms during which they had to recoup campaign expenses and raise funds for reelection. Corruption was the easiest way to meet these rigorous financial demands.

To my knowledge, no election in Taiwan has ever been truly clean. In early elections, voters saw candidates' payment for votes as an act of kindness, rather than as a perversion of democratic ideals. Prior to the introduction of opposition parties, most candidates had ties to the Nationalists. For some voters, it didn't matter who was elected: nearly everyone toed the party line. The "old thieves," or mainlanders elected in China in the 1940s, held the majority in parliament. Independents could do little to change national policy. Why not, some people reasoned, sell your vote to the highest bidder? The practice of vote buying and selling gave way to habit and then to expectation. Voters could be heard saying, "If I vote, you must pay my taxi fare. Otherwise I won't vote."

In Taiwanese culture, we are taught to return favors and reciprocate generosity. Refusing gifts or money, in the case of vote buying, can strain interpersonal relationships, especially if the vote buyer feels he or she has lost face. Vote buying preys on greed, the obligation to reciprocate kindness, and fear.

Voters would ask me, "What should I do when I am offered money for my vote? Can I accept the money and vote for someone else?"

"Morally, you should refuse the money," I would say. "But if you accept payment from someone to vote for him or her, it really is a crime. If you cannot refuse the money, don't vote for the candidate!"

The Clean Election Coalition explained to voters that the candidate buying the vote is the true guilty party. The more money the candidates spend buying votes, the more money they intend to pocket through corruption after winning the election. It was difficult, at first, to make people understand the need to maintain the integrity of free choice in a democratic system. Without having the Democratic Progressive Party as an alternative to the Nationalists, this might have been impossible to do.

In hopes of learning basic tips on safeguarding democracy, I made a trip to Washington, DC, where I visited institutes and congressional offices and spoke with congressional aides experienced in studying elections in the developing world. Experts shared their experiences of cultivating responsibility among voters and mobilizing citizens to monitor elections. Yet the big election pundits had few strategies that were practicable back home. Taiwan differed from many countries in that it was a relatively wealthy autocracy. (Social scientists, such as Seymour Martin Lipset, have argued that rising wealth should lead to democracy.) Taiwan also possessed the contradictory mix of a highly educated populace and deeply entrenched corruption. In terms of culture, Taiwan shares similarities with China and Japan, while embracing Western ideas in a manner truly distinctively Taiwanese.

One idea I did glean from the trip to Washington came from the "No Smoking" signs in public buildings—red circle signs with a line through the middle of a burning cigarette. I adapted the same concept for anticorruption brochures and bumper stickers. Our graphics had the same circle design, but instead of a cigarette, we inserted a NT$1,000 note bearing the image of Chiang Kai-shek and the caption "My family doesn't sell votes!"

We also hosted wacky public relations activities to get people's attention, such as renting small, flatbed trucks that we converted into "Democratic Garbage" trucks. These "sound trucks," with loudspeakers attached to the cab and candidates shouting slogans, were a common sight in 1989. Instead of festooning our trucks with campaign posters, we attached brooms and dustpans. Volunteers announced via loudspeaker the goal of sweeping away vote buying by collecting dirty evidence—gifts of cash, watches, porcelain pots, and spice holders that voters received in exchange for promises of support. The scene was so humorous that passersby would listen to our anticorruption message.

Our trucks did actually pick up a number of political gifts. We kept these on display in a showroom at the CEC's Taipei headquarters on Renai Road. Many of the items bore the names of the candidates who gave them. Reporters and ordinary citizens were always crowding around the showroom window to admire the catch of the day, until one morning I came into the office to find the items stolen. The office computer and fax machine had also disappeared. The display window of the office had not been broken, so I surmised that an individual who had office keys but no sense of humor had infiltrated our team and committed the theft.

As word of the Clean Election Coalition spread, we received many reports of so-called "ghost" voters. Unlike in the United States where voters register prior to elections, in Taiwan voters are registered by households and receive government notices informing them of their polling sites on election day. Each voter gets one notice. Some households, however, receive notifications for deceased voters, for prior residents, or for family members living out of town. Informed locals, however, knew which people were actually capable of voting and used "ghost" ballots to support Nationalist candidates. The CEC's team of lawyers investigated a number of such discrepancies, exposing some that could have been honest mistakes and others that were election fraud.

Tips from concerned citizens also prompted an investigation into a land scandal involving the mayor of Taichung. Residents of Taichung, Taiwan's third largest city, had long suspected Mayor Chang Tse-yuan of helping business partners purchase agricultural land and reclassify the property as fit for urban development. Mayor Chang's collaborators reaped windfall profits by reselling the land. The Nationalists had nominated Chang for another term in office when our team of lawyers interviewed local residents and held press conferences denouncing the mayor's actions; public pressure forced the Nationalists to rescind his nomination.

It took some time before the idea of corruption-free elections gained widespread recognition and cleaner elections became a reality. But by the end of 1989, the impact of the campaign was visible in the city of Taipei when voters refused to support candidates caught buying votes. This was not the case in other cities. Still, our campaign planted the seed of voter responsibility, which has since sprouted and taken root elsewhere. Electoral procedures have become more equitable, although illegal campaign practices, such as inviting people to free dinners or even direct bribery, persist in rural areas. The full significance of the Clean Election Coalition didn't become clear until numerous other politicians and citizen groups adopted the same cause, and the concept of clean elections became part of the public consciousness.

There were no elections for national office in 1990. Instead, a fierce debate raged over the retirement of the *laozei*, or "old thieves," from their permanent posts in the national legislature. Citizens, who paid 100 percent of the country's taxes, were demanding greater representation in national government. The aging parliamentarians, elected in China in 1947, were reluctant to step down. Some of them clung to their posts in support of the idea that Taiwan's government was the legitimate government of China. Some believed that the election of the entire parliament would lead to formal Taiwan independence. Still others refused to relinquish lucrative salaries and benefits without securing additional financial compensation.

Fearing that the Nationalist Party would turn a deaf ear to public opinion, I reorganized the Clean Election Coalition into a new organization lobbying for constitutional reform. The Coalition for Democracy advocated the removal of the *laozei* and the passage of constitutional amendments to further democratize Taiwan's political system. The Coalition for Democracy brought together a team of lawyers and scholars to research and discuss these issues.

The Constitution of the Republic of China was promulgated on the mainland on December 25, 1936. Designed to serve China's large population and vast territory, the constitution was entirely unsuitable for use in Taiwan. When the constitution was drafted in China, there were thirty-five provinces—including Mongolia and Tibet—and hundreds of millions of people. The constitution provided for a central government, provincial governments, and county and local governments—all of which were transplanted to Taiwan when the Nationalists lost the Chinese Civil War. In 1990, I compared using the Chinese constitution in Taiwan to putting a grandmother's old dilapidated nightgown on a newborn baby—it was just too large, too old, and too worn out to fit.

For decades, the Nationalists under Chiang Kai-shek and Chiang Ching-kuo had claimed to represent all of China to bolster regime legitimacy. Having national legislators who were elected in China supported this claim. Of course the facade was ridiculous, especially after Beijing took Taipei's spot on the UN Security Council in 1971 and the United States established formal diplomatic ties with the People's Republic on January 1, 1979.

We founded the Coalition for Democracy on May 20, the date of Lee Teng-hui's election as the Republic of China's president by the National Assembly. I wanted to remind President Lee that Taiwan was becoming a democratic society, so he had better listen to the voice of the people and allow popular elections for the office of president.

In front page advertisements in four daily newspapers, I reminded President Lee of the Hans Christian Andersen folktale called "The Emperor's New Clothes," concerning the vain ruler who loved compliments and enjoyed exquisite clothing. The king's court knew he loved flattery, so they never told him the truth.

As the story goes, one day a tailor approaches the emperor saying, "Sire, please allow me the honor of making you a wonderful set of new clothes. The sheerest, the finest, the most beautifully translucent in all the land!"

The emperor happily agrees, and when the tailor finishes his work, the king marches out into the court to show off his new look.

"Marvelous clothes," shouts one courtier. "Long live the emperor," warbles another.

Pleased, the emperor steps out into the street to let his subjects admire his attire. Gasps and shocks are the reaction, until one small boy bursts out laughing, "Look! The emperor isn't wearing any clothes!"

The tailor had only pretended to make them.

The advertisement made it clear that President Lee Teng-hui would not be allowed to become a monarch deaf to criticism and popular support of democratization. Ignoring the voice of the people would make him an emperor without clothes.

On the same day, May 20, 1990, Lee Teng-hui announced the appointment of anti-Taiwan-independence military strongman Hau Puo-tsun to serve as his premier, as well as granting presidential pardons for me and twenty-six other political dissidents. This contradictory proclamation created a huge stir among university students in Taipei. Most supported the amnesty for political dissidents, but prominent intellectuals feared the appointment of Hau Puo-tsun would strengthen the military and secret police at the expense of civil liberties.

Taiwanese university students, echoing the Tiananmen Square demonstration in China one year earlier, took to the streets, demanding constitutional reforms to hasten Taiwan's democratization. Thousands of students encamped outside the Chiang Kai-shek Memorial Hall in central Taipei, engaging in sit-ins and hunger strikes. Unlike the Tiananmen demonstration, the actions of the Taiwanese students were not seen as a threat to the government, but as a source of support for President Lee against attacks from hard-liners within the Nationalist Party. Instead of cracking down, Lee agreed to hold a National Affairs Conference on constitutional reform. The students promptly dispersed.

Earlier that month, the national legislature had passed a resolution requesting a ruling from Taiwan's highest court on the constitutionality of the *laozei*, referring to them with the euphemism "senior statesmen." Yet it was far from clear what position the Nationalist-controlled Council of Grand Justices (similar in function to the US Supreme Court) would take. The Coalition for Democracy's first major activity was a signature drive for a petition urging the Council of Grand Justices to overturn the current law allowing *laozei* to hold office. When I took a group of supporters to deliver the petition, the

Council of Grand Justices refused to receive it. So my colleagues and I launched a sit-in protest on the steps outside the judicial headquarters of the government, until one grand justice, formerly my professor at National Taiwan University, agreed to come out and accept the petition. In June, the Council of Grand Justices ruled that granting the senior statesmen permanent positions in the Legislative Yuan and National Assembly was unconstitutional.

With this ruling on the status of *laozei*, the constitutional reform agenda broadened. Intellectuals debated whether the government should enact a totally new constitution or revise the old one to meet Taiwan's needs. I proposed a two-stage plan: revising the existing constitution in the first stage, and in the second stage enacting an entirely new one.

To avoid a dispute over which country name—the Republic of China or the Republic of Taiwan—would be used on the constitution, I proposed calling the constitution Magna Carta (Minzhu da xian zhang), meaning the "Great Charter for Democracy," after the first British constitution in the thirteenth century. "The Republic of China" is the name of the state that previously ruled mainland China, Tibet, and Mongolia. Its retention is seen as symbolic of commitment to Taiwan's eventual reunification with China. "The Republic of Taiwan" is a name more suitable to Taiwan's actual status as an independent nation-state. Eventually, the DPP adopted my strategy, and with a group of DPP politicians and legal scholars, I assisted in writing the draft of the new DPP-sponsored constitution.

To reward my efforts in drafting a new constitution, DPP chairman Huang Hsin-chieh, former publisher of *Formosa Magazine*, nominated me to stand as alternate for the National Affairs Conference. For DPP politicians seeking recognition and legitimacy, attending President Lee's conference was quite an honor. It was not only members of the opposition who sought to attend; most leading Nationalist politicians and other celebrities did as well. Shortly before the conference, Wu Nai-ren, of the Democratic Progressive Party's New Tide faction, decided to withdraw, and the DPP party leaders nominated me in his stead. I was the last delegate announced.

By the summer of 1990, DPP politicians had gained prestige and greater influence. President Lee met with DPP chairman Huang Hsin-chieh in a lengthy private meeting. The Nationalist Party, under Lee's leadership, was keen to adopt many of the DPP's reform proposals. While DPP legislators would attack the right-wing Premier Hau Puo-tsun, their statements were openly supportive of Lee, Taiwan's first native president.

After attending the first day of the National Affairs Conference, I realized that the Nationalists were using the conference to win support from the DPP for the Nationalist reform plan that ran contrary to my own proposals. DPP leaders stood glowing with pride alongside important Nationalist figures, drinking wine together, and patting each other's backs like brothers. I could stomach neither the radical switch of the Nationalist Party from foe to friend, nor the DPP leadership's lack of resolution to advance its own policy agenda. Achieving my goals appeared futile, so I announced my decision to walk out of the conference. Several members of the policy discussion group to which I had been assigned—almost entirely Nationalist officials— begged me to come back, saying, "We respect you! Please return to the conference. We would love to get along with you!"

The conference was disappointing because the nation had such high expectations. By leaving, I hoped to convey a very clear message: no substantial reform would emerge from the conference. As it turned out, I was right. In my absence, the participants endorsed the Nationalist blueprint for reform, including granting the National Assembly new powers to amend the constitution and approve the appointment of Grand Justices. Many people, myself included, had favored abolishing the National Assembly and retaining the national legislature (Legislative Yuan). The overhauled system would thus have a single legislative body. Nationalist moderates and the DPP did agree to hold direct elections for president and provincial governor, although the implementation of this agreement would not occur for six years.

Prior to the National Affairs Conference, I had received a curious invitation through the assistance of my *Formosa Magazine* comrade Chang Chun-nan. Chang had defected to the People's Republic on the mainland after his release from prison and had been banned from returning to Taiwan. Ostensibly, I was invited to speak at a convention held by the "Taiwanese Association in China."

The upcoming election for the Legislative Yuan in 1992 made me very aware of the fact that if I ran for office and became an elected politician, a class of citizen barred from visiting China at the time, I would no longer be able to travel to China. I chose to accept the invitation to visit China, even though my views on Taiwanese sovereignty and democracy differed considerably from those of the group inviting me. As I later learned, the Chinese leadership in Beijing had taken a special interest in meeting with me after I walked out of the National Affairs Conference. They hoped to use my discontent with the Nationalists as a means of winning my support for China.

Beijing organized a comprehensive tour of Chinese cities and scenic spots on my behalf for one whole month. A car, driver, and escort took me everywhere, and a prominent feminist, Huang Qichao, served as my guide. The itinerary included daily conversations with high-ranking military officials, politicians, and China's scholars of Taiwan affairs. I was somewhat surprised because they had all heard of me, even though I had no official title.

Most of the meetings with Chinese officials began at 10:00 A.M. and continued through the noon hour and into the afternoon. Each time we met, secretaries sat off to one side vigorously scribbling notes. I spent time preparing for these conversations and answered questions as candidly as I could.

"Welcome back!" said the head of the United Front Work Department as I walked into his office. "We understand that the people in Taiwan are all dying to return to their motherland!"

I smiled. "Do you want to hear the truth?"

"Sure, sure."

"Taiwan was ruled by Japan for fifty years and then controlled by the Nationalists for another four decades. During this time very little contact with China was possible. How could you expect the Taiwanese to be enthusiastic about 'returning' to the motherland under a Communist government of which they have heard only troubling rumors?"

The woman who served as my escort in Beijing was second-generation Taiwanese born in China. "Are you anxious to be reunified under Taiwanese rule?" I asked her.

"You must be dreaming!"

I was the first advocate of Taiwan independence with the opportunity to express my views directly to high-ranking Chinese officials. By speaking to them in a diplomatic but honest fashion, I revealed the good will of the Taiwanese as well as our determination not to be ruled by China. Previously, they had had contact only with Taiwanese in favor of reunification, giving rise to the misperception that all Taiwanese shared a similar view. I brought along documents corroborating my points, including one survey of Taiwanese who had recently returned from visits to China. The survey asked whether, after the visit, people preferred to identify themselves as Chinese or Taiwanese and whether they preferred reunification or independence. Responses proved very much in favor of the DPP's platform supporting a Taiwanese identity for the island. I might not have changed the views of the Chinese cadres I met, but at least I educated them and explained why taking Taiwan militarily would not be easy.

In Beijing, I articulated for Chinese officials my belief in the importance of three principles for guiding government policy. I call the three principles *humanity*, *rationality*, and *benevolence*. The first, humanity, is that human needs and human nature must guide policy, the sole purpose of which is to better the quality of life; the second principle, rationality, concerns the implementation of policy, which must be logical and deliberate; the third principle, benevolence, corresponds to the result of any policy or political action and depends upon the two prior necessary conditions. If a policy possesses humanity and is rationally implemented, the result will be benevolent to the society. If the first two conditions do not exist, the policy outcome could be a disaster. The Chinese officials were so amused by my three principles that they took fastidious notes. Later, I heard my remarks were quoted in Chinese Communist Party internal publications.

Several of my appointments introduced me to the scholars in charge of researching Taiwan, China's so-called "Taiwan experts."

After I had spent a couple of days conversing with Li Jiatong, director of the Taiwan Studies Institute in Beijing, he whispered to me, "Ms. Lu, the more I understand Taiwan, the more I believe Taiwan is like a serpent and China like an elephant. If Taiwan attempted to retake China, it would be like a serpent trying to swallow an elephant— absolutely impossible. An elephant, on the other hand, could swallow the serpent, but it would suffer from a permanent ulcer."

The Taiwanese Students' Association in America invited me to speak at a convention held in Xiangshan, a summer resort and the final resting place of China's first president, Sun Yat-sen. Nearly a hundred participants, including scholars from the top universities in Beijing and the United States, were in attendance. My speech on Taiwan's democratization coined a new phrase: I noted that "leaders are just like the collar and sleeves of a shirt: they become dirty easily, so we have to wash them all the time." In Chinese, the expression meaning "leader" is *lingxiu*, or collar and sleeves. Elections, I argued, provide occasions for washing society's *lingxiu*. Even my Communist hosts loved that remark.

After the convention, I flew to Xian and Luoyang to visit some Chinese historical sites and then went to Chongqing, taking a riverboat down the Yangtze River. Eventually, I made my way to Fujian, the home of my ancestors who lived in China nearly four centuries ago. For many Taiwanese, visiting the birthplace of their distant ancestors in China is an eye-opening experience. My ancestors came from the poor mountain village of Zhangzhou in Fujian. In typical Communist fashion, the government had notified the villagers of my visit ahead of time. So when my driver pulled up the dusty road into the village, the entire village turned out for my arrival, dressed in the clothing that they usually only wore for festivals.

Smiling faces crowded around me, speaking the Fujian dialect, the language from which Taiwanese evolved over centuries. After a moment of exchanged pleasantries, a towering big-boned woman pushed her way through the curious villagers. "Auntie Hsiu-lien," she said, "you have come from far away but we have all heard of your wonderful successes in Taiwan."

The woman took my arm and guided me through the crowd in the direction of a newly built home nearby. Inside the building's only bedroom, she quickly shut the door and asked me if I needed to "wash my hands," the Chinese way of asking if I needed to use a toilet. I replied that I did, except I didn't see a toilet anywhere in the room. She stepped out for a second and returned with two wooden *niaotong*, or bedpans, and lined them up side by side. Flashing a smile, she dropped her pants and indicated for me to squat next to her, just like two sisters. She knew that I had traveled all day, and this was her idea of making me feel comfortable!

In 1987, the first year Taiwanese could travel to China since the 1940s, Brother had come to the village of Zhangzhou. His stories of the abject poverty in the birthplace of our ancestors should have prepared me for the living conditions, but I was shocked by the skinny, barefoot children, the illiteracy, dirt-floored houses, poor food, and outhouses instead of modern plumbing. Zhangzhou evinced the absence of comforts associated with modern society.

The government had paid the villagers to host a banquet in my honor, an event to which they clearly looked forward, as it provided them with a far better meal than they would normally have. In Chinese culture, food is the central focus of important social gatherings, and the villagers served the best dishes they could offer. Still, I couldn't help comparing the bland fare to the delicious and richly aromatic banquets common in Taiwan.

Most of the villagers, many of whom share the surname "Lü," made their living farming small rice fields and had very hard lives. As we passed by the village well, they asked me if I had ever brought water from a well by bucket.

"Yes," I replied, "but only during childhood."

So with much huffing and puffing, I lowered the bucket into the dark hole and splashed around until I brought out half a bucket's worth. They got a good laugh out of my amateurish efforts, and I got a reminder of the inconveniences that Chinese villagers put up with and the conveniences that Taiwanese take for granted.

I felt an ethnic and linguistic linkage with the people of Zhangzhou that I do not feel with Americans or Europeans, but not a close enough rapport to merit the use of the word *compatriot*. When the villagers took me to visit the Lu Community Quarter (Longtanlou), the name and location of which Father and Mother had made me memorize from childhood, I stood inside the Quarter and gave a silent prayer of thanks to my ancestors who had had the wisdom and courage to leave Zhangzhou and seek their fortune in Taiwan.

In China, I kept a low profile, avoiding the media and conflict with my hosts. But when I returned to Taiwan, I held a press conference in an attempt to articulate my feelings upon returning home. "Before Taiwan becomes independent," I said, "Taiwan needs to be united." Unity depends upon ethnic harmony, grounded in forgiveness and mutual respect. Decades of dictatorial rule by mainlanders had left a deep ethnic rift in Taiwanese society and political scars that would take time to heal. The trip to China had impressed upon me the need for Taiwanese unity, to withstand the threat of a Chinese invasion.

My thoughts returned to my campaign slogan of 1978: "I love Taiwan!" Love, after all, is the healthiest source of unity. Changing the focus of the Coalition for Democracy from constitutional reform to social reform, I organized the "I love Taiwan! Movement" that held workshops on resolving ethnic differences, where I encouraged Taiwanese to "tear down the Berlin Wall" of ethnic discrimination in our society.

Language barriers were the primary obstacles to improving relations between ethnic groups. For decades, the Nationalist regime discouraged speaking Taiwanese, Hakka, or aboriginal languages. Two generations of Taiwanese children grew up in schools where they were humiliated or forced to pay fines for speaking Taiwanese. School principals, usually mainlanders, made children wear signs around their necks bearing such slogans as "Don't speak dialects!" or "Please speak Mandarin." History and geography classes in schools focused on China, ignoring Taiwan's own history and cultural legacy. Years of fear bred resentment of mainlanders among the wider public, and most mainlanders remained unable to speak Taiwanese, the mother tongue of more than 80 percent of the population.

Nationalist-sponsored denigration of Taiwanese culture was often subtle. For example, Taiwan's most famous museum, the National Palace Museum, focuses on artwork from the collection of Qing dynasty emperor Qian Long and other ancient Chinese dynasties. This art was removed from the Forbidden City and other sites by the Nationalists and shipped to Taiwan in the 1940s. Although the Chinese artwork is superb, the near total absence of Taiwanese art implies the inferiority of the island's own culture.

With Lee Teng-hui's succession as president, Hoklo, or ethnic Taiwanese, leaders gained opportunities denied them by the Chiang regime. By the early 1990s, mainlanders had lost their monopoly on privileged positions in the government and in the Nationalist Party. Their sense of superiority fueled feelings of disenfranchisement, as ethnic Taiwanese began to dominate national politics.

This dissatisfaction among mainlanders eventually led to a split in the Nationalist Party. A splinter group of legislators and high-ranking bureaucrats formed the New Party in 1993. Drawing support primarily from disgruntled middle-class mainlanders, the New Party promoted itself as a morally responsible alternative to the Nationalists and the DPP, and as a strong proponent of reunification with China. Most New Party leaders had enjoyed positions of authority during the Chiang Ching-kuo administration, although other, young politicians joined the party because it was relatively easy to obtain the New Party's nomination for public office.

Accompanying the decline of mainlander dominance was a gradual rollback of Nationalist control over social and political organizations. During the martial law era, in typical Leninist fashion, the party and state had parallel lines of authority. Schools, for example, employed people responsible for reporting on employee conduct to party and secret service organizations. The leadership of government and party were closely interrelated, although never completely synonymous. Beginning in the early 1990s, powerful social movements, the lifting of martial law, and the pluralization of politics made it politically untenable for the Nationalists to maintain such iron-fisted control. Governmental bodies exercised more autonomy, which led to the gradual separation of party and state.

Longtanlou, the Lu family ancestral shrine in Fujian.

Lu Hsiu-lien as a candidate
for national legislator in
1991.

The paddleboat that plied the East River adjacent to the United Nations headquarters to lobby for Taiwan's admittance as a member state in 1995.

Lu as a candidate for vice president in the 1995 Democratic Progressive Party primary.

At a celebration for Lu Hsiu-lien's inauguration as Taoyuan County chief executive in 1997, Jerome Cohen (right) remarked, "Many politicians go from public office to prison, but only extraordinary ones go from prison to public office!"

Lu, welcoming the Dalai Lama to Taoyuan County.

Campaign for vice president in 2000.

To celebrate Lu's inauguration as vice president in 2000, friends from Amnesty International presented her with a plaque reading, "We helped you walk out of the darkness of prison. On the journey to democracy you will lead the way."

Lu family cemetery in Taoyuan County, a site that holds the remains of more than 2,300 clan members.

Lu, campaigning with President Chen Shui-bian in 2004 before the assassination attempt on the eve of the presidential election, in which Chen and Lu were wounded by gunfire.

Lu, dancing in El Salvador as vice president in 2001.

Lu was accompanied by a police escort on Harley Davidson motorcycles during a visit to San Francisco in 2005.

Lu, videoconferencing with members of the Council on Foreign Relations in New York on January 17, 2007.

CHAPTER 8

KNOCKING AT THE GATE OF THE UN

THE HISTORY OF THE NATIONALISTS IN THE UNITED NATIONS goes back to the final months of World War II, when in a benevolent gesture the Americans gave China a seat on the UN Security Council. In late 1945, Chiang Kai-shek's troops still controlled much of China, but they were threatened by the Communist forces after the Chinese Civil War erupted in full force. A series of crushing military defeats and sharply declining economic conditions in China's cities forced Chiang Kai-shek to beat a hasty retreat to Taiwan. He promptly took up the trappings of Taiwan's Japanese colonial masters by moving into the colonial headquarters in Taipei and naming himself president of the Republic of China, despite the fact that he had resigned from the same post in China due to political pressure.

In time, Taiwan might also have fallen to the Chinese Communists had not the outbreak of the Korean War injected a Red Scare into the hearts of American opinion makers. For the next two decades, the United States supported Chiang Kai-shek's claims to represent China, with the protection of the Seventh Fleet in the Taiwan Strait, even though the Communists exercised total control over the Chinese mainland. Most countries followed the lead of the United States, calling Taiwan "Free China" and maintaining diplomatic relations with the Republic of China instead of the People's Republic. The Republic of China's representatives, not China's, were present at the signing of the UN Charter in San Francisco, and they held China's permanent seat on the UN Security Council.

National Security Advisor Henry Kissinger's visit to China in 1971 completely reversed the course of US policy. Interested in playing the China card to drive the Soviet Union toward détente, President Richard Nixon asked Kissinger to secretly arrange a summit with Chinese leaders Mao Zedong and Zhou Enlai in the early months of 1972. When Kissinger returned and revealed his clandestine dealings, a number of nations dropped their support for Taiwan in the United Nations, backing a General Assembly resolution for Beijing to take over the China seat on the Security Council. Realizing that support for the Republic of China was in free fall, the United States drafted its own resolution, to allow Taipei to retain membership in the United Nations and to hold a seat in the General Assembly.

In retrospect, the US resolution presented the best opportunity for UN membership that reflected Taiwan's actual status in the international community. But conflicting views within the US policy-making establishment and intransigence by Chiang Kai-shek's UN representatives scuttled this compromise arrangement. Unwilling to risk jeopardizing the fragile rapprochement with his Chinese counterparts, Kissinger visited China a second time. The timing of his visit—very near to that of the vote on the US proposal and an Albanian counterproposal in the General Assembly—resulted in rapid erosion of the US position. Kissinger's characteristic failure to coordinate with other diplomats left the US man on the floor of the UN General Assembly, George H. W. Bush, surprised and dismayed by weakening support for the US proposal. Bush attempted to elevate the question on Taiwan's UN membership to "important question," which would have necessitated a two-third's majority for approval and reduced the likelihood that the Albanian proposal would pass. The Albanian proposal called for the removal of Taiwan from the United Nations and granted Taipei's permanent Security Council seat to Beijing. Bush's strategy failed. A 50 percent majority vote would pass the Albanian proposal. Efforts by Taiwan's allies to delay the proceedings through filibuster were unsuccessful. Moments before the vote on the Albanian proposal, Liu Chieh, the ROC representative, announced from the rostrum that the Republic of China government would take no further part in the proceedings of the General Assembly. Chow received friendly applause from most delegations and led his delegation out of the hall. The Albanian proposal passed easily in the General Assembly and, as the result of Liu Chieh's walkout, was not subject to a veto in the Security Council, a power that Chiang Kai-shek could have exercised. Beijing took the permanent seat on the Security Council, and Taiwan's representatives and its citizens, with very few exceptions, have been barred from the United Nations ever since. George H. W. Bush described the passage of the Albanian proposal as "a moment of infamy," adding wistfully, "It's hard to believe that just a few hours ago we didn't think we had anything to worry about."

In February 1972 the United States and China signed the Shanghai Communiqué, culminating the rapprochement that Kissinger had worked to orchestrate. Oddly enough, the date of the signing was February 28, the date of the ill-fated uprising in Taiwan in 1947, and the same date that Lin Yi-hsiung's family would be murdered in 1980.

In the Shanghai Communiqué, the United States acknowledges that the "Chinese" on both sides of the Taiwan Straits "maintain that there is but one China and Taiwan is a part of China." Over time, the interpretation of this ambiguous position has shifted to imply that Taiwan is part of China and is represented internationally by the People's Republic. China interprets the Shanghai Communiqué as granting support to its claims of sovereignty over Taiwan, even though the US "acknowledgement" does not actually amount to agreement or acceptance of the Chinese position. Moreover, most Taiwanese do not identify themselves as "Chinese," nor do they believe Taiwan is part of the People's Republic of China.

Kissinger's real betrayal, however, was that Taiwanese were neither consulted nor represented during negotiations leading to the Shanghai Communiqué. The Taiwanese public never voted via a referendum to determine the status of their homeland's sovereignty. While the Nationalists maintained that Taiwan was part of China, this position did not reflect popular will or even the realities of international law.

Almost before the ink dried on the Shanghai Communiqué, other countries moved to switch their official diplomatic relations from the

Republic of China to the People's Republic of China. In 1971, sixty-eight countries had formal diplomatic relations with Taiwan. From 1971 to 1973 alone, this number was halved, as twenty-seven countries switched formal relations to China. By 1988, the number of Taiwan's allies had decreased by almost 90 percent. As of 2014, roughly twenty-two countries plus the Vatican maintain formal diplomatic relations with Taiwan. Beijing has actively suppressed the number of Taiwan's allies by abrogating diplomatic relations with any country that recognizes Taipei. Geostrategic concerns and the lure of China's vast market has trumped concerns over its poor human rights standards, nontransparent government, and nondemocratic rule in most countries' deliberations over whether to establish formal diplomatic relations with China.

In terms of international law, however, Chinese claims to Taiwan are shaky at best. In 1895, after losing the Sino-Japanese War, the Qing dynasty ceded Taiwan to Japan "in perpetuity." The signing of the Treaty of Shimonoseki by Beijing and Tokyo led to fifty-one years of Japanese rule in Taiwan. Throughout the 1920s and 1930s both the Chinese Communist Party and the Nationalist Party called for self-determination in Taiwan and not for reunification. Taiwan was seen as too "Japanese" to unify with China. The Nationalist Party changed its tune during World War II, when in the Cairo Declaration, the United States agreed to return Taiwan to China following Japan's surrender. Typically, such wartime statements bear no legal force. Yet geopolitics won out over morality. In spite of Franklin Delano Roosevelt's penchant for advocating self-determination for Japan's former colonies and possessions, Taiwanese were not allowed to choose their rulers nor decide their destiny.

In the San Francisco Peace Treaty of 1951, Japan renounced its sovereignty over Taiwan but did not specify a recipient, prompting a furious debate between Beijing and Taipei over which side held sovereignty over Taiwan. The Nationalist Party claimed sovereign rights to rule China from Taipei, and the Communists claimed sovereignty over Taiwan from Beijing. Both assertions were ridiculous. Chiang Kai-shek had lost political control over the mainland; Mao Zedong never controlled Taiwan. If justice and not Realpolitik had prevailed, Taiwanese citizens would have undisputed sovereignty over their homeland.

In the late 1980s, liberalization of the media in Taiwan and the lifting of martial law restrictions on travel and trade boosted awareness of the outside world. Taiwanese compared their society to other countries and decided that Taiwan's inferior status was unacceptable. By the 1990s, Taiwan's economic performance placed it among the world's top trading nations. Politically, its democracy was more advanced than many UN member states. Democratization and economic success were sources of pride, and Taiwan's diplomatic isolation was a source of shame. Meanwhile, rather than diminishing over time, the threat of a Chinese invasion increased with the election of a Taiwanese president and debates in Taiwan on the merits of formal independence. Thus, for Taiwan, entering the United Nations and joining the network of "normal" nations came to be seen as a diplomatic shield that could grant a measure of protection against Chinese aggression.

In June 1991, South Korea and North Korea were due to be admitted to the UN General Assembly simultaneously and with separate representation. Moscow and Beijing, seeking better relations with South Korea, refused to support North Korea's resistance to the South's admission. Because the parallels between the Korean situation and the China-Taiwan situation were obvious, this precedent sparked a debate within Taiwan over the prospects of Taipei's readmission to the United Nations. "If South Koreans can do it, why can't we?" many Taiwanese asked themselves. "What right does Beijing have to represent Taiwan? How can Taiwan gain its own representation?" For these questions, the Nationalists offered few satisfying answers.

The first person to propose that Taiwan apply to rejoin the United Nations was a Nationalist legislator from Taoyuan County, Huang Chu-wen. He described the government's policy of waiting for China to permit Taiwan's accession to the United Nations as "pressing Taiwan's hot cheek against China's cold ass." In June 1991, eighty-two legislators signed his resolution asking the Nationalist government to "immediately apply to rejoin the United Nations." I watched the debate with interest but the Nationalists appeared divided on the issue. Party conservatives saw membership as fueling a dangerous tendency toward Taiwan independence. Nationalist liberals, mostly native Taiwanese, recognized the necessity of seeking greater international recognition. As a result of this internal division, no action was taken.

In September, I left for the United States to attend an academic symposium hosted by Professor Parris Chang, who was then director of East Asian studies at Pennsylvania State University. At the symposium, I advocated pressuring the international community to allow Taiwan to join the United Nations. My words were met with derision by former ambassador to China James Lilley and former State Department Taiwan desk chief Harvey Feldman: "Mission Impossible," they told me. With their remarks stinging in my ears, I returned to Taipei resolved to attempt what they said I couldn't accomplish: win Taiwan's admission to the General Assembly. The process of applying to the international body, even if it did not immediately accomplish the goal, would improve Taiwan's international visibility, and thus the island's security in the face of the threat of Chinese military invasion.

At the time, the diplomatic isolation of Taiwan was so complete that it seemed as if the name appeared only on doorknobs, machine tools, and computer accessories. Chinese pressure forced international organizations to play a "name game" that forced Taiwan to compete in the Olympic games as "Taipei China" and to apply to the World Trade Organization as the "Separate Customs Territory of Taiwan, Penghu, Kinmen, and Matsu." It had taken the Communist People's Republic twenty-two years to join the United Nations and it had taken fifteen years for Korea. I wanted Taiwan to gain reentry in less than ten years.

Back in Taipei, President Lee Teng-hui had pardoned the defendants in the *Formosa* trial and restored my political rights. I discussed Taiwan's readmission to the United Nations with a number of Democratic Progressive Party politicians as I weighed running for a seat in the national legislature. I found that most DPP politicians had little interest in Taiwan's UN bid. "Forget the UN campaign," said Huang Hsin-chieh, then DPP party chair. "It's a lost cause. The National Assembly election is more important."

That year the DPP was participating in the first full election for National Assembly. The "old thieves" had been turned out, and the DPP was running on a pro–Taiwan independence platform. As the DPP focused its energy on the election, I decided to launch Taiwan's UN campaign on my own and placed an advertisement in Taipei newspapers asking for volunteers to go to New York to demonstrate in front of the UN headquarters.

The response to my advertisement took me and nearly everyone else by surprise. Although members of my delegation had to pay their own way, fifty volunteers signed up immediately. Most participants were wealthy businesspeople or intellectuals, but some were blue-collar folks, including one old man who ran a shop in a local vegetable market. Skinny and wizened by years of hard work, the man had never flown in an airplane or even gone out of the country. I later found out that he had also just undergone major surgery.

In order to prepare for the demonstration, I left Taipei for New York in advance of the delegation's departure. The small sum of funds I had raised in Taipei wasn't even enough to cover the cost of hotel accommodations, so I stayed in a friend's cramped Midtown apartment. The primary tool for my PR campaign was a fax machine in my friend's kitchen, which I also used as a telephone. I spent entire days standing in the kitchen contacting Taiwanese organizations and journalists on the East Coast. Because Taiwanese living overseas are acutely aware of their country's international isolation, hundreds of people agreed to take the day off to participate in our demonstration.

My plan was to run a *New York Times* advertisement announcing the protest, lead a march through downtown Manhattan, and send representatives to the embassies of all of the UN Security Council members. But upon arrival, I realized that we didn't have enough money to accomplish even these simple objectives. Friends from New Jersey suggested that I enlist the support of Trong Chai, a legislator who had led demonstrations in Taiwan urging for a referendum to decide whether Taiwan should reapply to join the United Nations. He agreed to share the funds from his war chest, giving me enough to cover half the cost of the *New York Times* advertisement. The other half of the funds was donated by Taiwanese living in the United States.

When my delegation arrived in New York, I heard that the old man from the vegetable market had had a medical emergency on the flight over from Taipei. Apparently, his recent surgery had affected his bladder. After the plane took off, he lost the ability to urinate and slipped into unconsciousness. Fortunately, a doctor on the flight used a tube from a set of earphones to fashion a life-saving catheter. The old man told me upon arriving, "Ms. Lu, if I had died on that plane and made the slightest contribution to my country, it would have been a great honor." To me, his heartfelt sentiment epitomized the intense fervor of Taiwanese who hope that one day their homeland will possess the international status of other nation-states.

Nearly 1,000 Taiwanese and a few sympathetic Americans turned out on the day of the march. We began the demonstration in front of the UN building with our bullhorns, chanting slogans, and with our banners waving in the autumn breeze. Then, the march approached several embassies located near the UN compound. Our representatives were received kindly by the Russians and coldly by the Americans, who met us at the door with frowns and armed guards. When our demonstration neared the Chinese Embassy to the United Nations, the New York Police Department stepped in to intervene, restricting the protest to a distance of one block from the embassy, where the Chinese could be seen watching us from the roof in horror.

Predictably, the Chinese saw the demonstration as a plot to "divide the motherland." On attempting to enter the embassy, I got into a standoff with flustered Chinese bureaucrats. I wanted to present a copy of our petition advocating UN membership for Taiwan. The Chinese insisted that they would only allow us to enter if I pledged that Taiwan was part of China, or submitted a revised petition to that effect. I politely refused, and the Chinese closed the embassy for the day.

Our demonstration, along with the advertisement in the *New York*

Times, which because of an editorial error ran a second day for free, transformed the "Taiwan for the UN" campaign into an instant media sensation. Magazines and newspapers from across the United States sought interviews. For once, Beijing was too surprised to react. China had never expected a nongovernmental attack on its policy of excluding Taiwan from international organizations.

Back in Taipei, I pushed the Nationalist government to apply for full membership in the UN General Assembly. The ruling party leadership was frightened. Vice Foreign Minister Chang Hsiao-yan, the son of Chiang Ching-kuo, had even proclaimed in a public debate that "to attempt such a thing is to invite insults upon oneself." Realizing that a Chinese veto in the Security Council could shoot down Taiwan's application for membership, the Nationalists worried that a confrontation with China would fail, resulting in a loss of face at home.

Yet the Taiwanese public was frustrated with Nationalist passivity. People saw the Nationalist reluctance to fight to improve Taiwan's international standing as a sign that it wasn't looking after the island's interests. Democratic Progressive Party politicians were swift to point out that ending Taiwan's isolation would improve its bargaining position vis-à-vis China in the event of bilateral negotiations on trade or sovereignty.

December 1991 marked the first time that the Taiwanese went to the polls to elect all members of the National Assembly. Mainlanders who had been in the National Assembly since 1947 were enticed into retirement with generous pensions. That year the DPP's main policy planks were domestic political reform and Taiwan independence. The Nationalist Party faced its most direct ideological challenge. The DPP took 27 percent of the popular vote in the National Assembly election, a slight reduction of support since the previous Legislative Yuan election for a smaller number of seats. DPP leaders viewed this as a rebuff of the party's pro-independence position, and they prepared to pose the independence agenda in a less combative manner. The Nationalists, realizing they would face stiff competition in the next Legislative Yuan election, sought a means of heading off criticism of their weak stance on sovereignty issues. Advancing Taiwan's bid to rejoin the

United Nations became one way that the DPP and the Nationalists could both pursue their political interests.

My success in leading the demonstration outside the United Nations in 1991 and the growing politicization of the issue made it easier to devote myself to promoting Taiwan internationally. On February 28, 1992, twenty years from the date of Richard Nixon's signing of the Shanghai Communiqué, I brought Taiwan's UN campaign back to the United States for a second time. Growing public support gave the demonstration more funds and volunteers. My target audience expanded from the international community in New York to the policy-making establishment in Washington, DC. This was reflected by the decision to run a full-page advertisement in the *Washington Post*, the newspaper of record "inside the Beltway," under the headline "Twenty years ago today, America betrayed Taiwan." By the 1990s, most politicians in the United States had forgotten the abrogation of diplomatic ties with Taiwan in January 1972 that had left Taiwan bereft of representation in the United Nations.

My activities abroad did not go unnoticed at home. Nearly all Taiwanese took pride in the international attention Taiwan received as a result of the advertisements and demonstrations. In the 1992 legislative election, the first in which I would participate since my 1978 campaign for National Assembly, I hoped to mobilize this popular support to win office. For fourteen years I had waited. Finally, I had my chance in December 1992. The Democratic Progressive Party nominated me for a legislative seat in Taoyuan County. I knew my chances were excellent, and I let the voters know that I planned to work for Taiwan's entry into the United Nations through the influential Legislative Foreign Affairs Committee. "Put me in the legislature and I'll put Taiwan in the United Nations," I often told voters.

"Ms. Lu," one Taoyuan man told me, "I've kept this vote for you in my pocket since 1978."

Based on the positive responses to Taiwan's UN campaign, I advocated the clarification of Taiwan's international status by pursuing the strategy of "One China, One Taiwan." In other words, we had to convince the nations of the world that Taiwan is distinct from China and a valuable diplomatic ally. While speeches can persuade or inspire, concrete action makes political objectives more relevant to the public. The plan that I hatched was an imaginative one.

October 1 is China's National Day, an occasion celebrating the establishment of the People's Republic in 1949. I wanted to lead a group of Taiwanese to Beijing to "celebrate" the occasion by unfolding a banner in Tiananmen Square with the slogan "Taiwan for the Taiwanese." Realizing that this could result in my spending the next few years in a Chinese prison instead of in the Taiwanese legislature, my supporters urged that I proceed with utmost caution.

With a small group of supporters to accompany me, I had my travel agent apply for the Taiwan Compatriot Permit necessary for travel to China. Beijing does not issue visas to Taiwanese. I was somewhat concerned that my request could be denied because of my role in the "Taiwan for the UN" campaign. Yet everyone in our group received the permit without any complications.

To avoid any interference prior to leaving for China, we proceeded to Tokyo, where we held a press conference explaining the nature of our visit to China. The date was September 28, the twentieth anniversary of the establishment of formal diplomatic relations between Japan and China. I pointed out that at that time, Japan had had a more important economic relationship with Taiwan, in terms of trade volume. Nevertheless, Japan had cut off diplomatic ties with Taipei in 1972 in favor of a communist dictatorship. As Taiwan's former colonial ruler, Japan owed Taiwan more respect.

I also released to the international media the names of five of the eighteen members of our group. Part of my strategy involved concealing the identity of the other thirteen delegates so they could enter China undetected.

Many of the reporters present were sympathetic to Taiwan's situation and showed friendly concern for our safety. The bloody crackdown in Tiananmen Square three years earlier had left a powerful impression of Chinese repression and ruthlessness.

"It won't be as easy as you think!" blurted out one reporter.

"Too dangerous," murmured another.

"Our delegation will be a peaceful one," I said. "We are going to celebrate the PRC's National Day; we go for the sake of Taiwan's future in international affairs."

With a nervous shuffling of his feet, one Japanese journalist stood up and addressed me, "I'm a close friend of Aung San Suu Kyi," he said. "When she first led the people in Myanmar's democratic movement, I was by her side reporting on the struggle." Gesturing to a battered Nikon camera at his side, the man continued, "Several times pictures from this camera saved her from harm at the hands of the military junta. To me, this camera is a special talisman. I want to give you this camera because I recognize the significance of your mission, and I pray that it will protect you from harm." I accepted the camera from the man and keep it to this day.

On the morning of September 29, we boarded a 9:00 A.M. flight and arrived during the noon hour in Beijing. Nothing appeared out of the ordinary as our group walked in the direction of customs. "How odd!" I remember thinking. "The Chinese don't seem very impressed by us, do they?" No one followed us. I didn't sense nervous tension among the security personnel or hear the crackle of walkie-talkies. Nothing.

In Tokyo, we had discussed a number of scenarios. If customs denied me entry, I had instructed my supporters, then they should go on ahead, an idea few of them liked. They joked that it would be no fun without me and said that if I was refused entry at customs, they wanted to return with me. One of the delegates, whose identity had not been revealed at the press conference, was in charge of contacting the international media if I was arrested.

When we were standing in the customs queue, an officer approached me. "Are you Ms. Lu Hsiu-lien from Taiwan?" he asked.

"Yes, I am."

"Please show me your passport. Ms. Lu, I am under instructions to send you back to Japan on the next available flight. Please come with me."

The man led me off to one side, where I watched as customs agents rounded up three delegates whose identities had been released at the press conference in Tokyo. Thirteen others, whose names had been kept secret, had already passed through customs. According to the PRC list, based on the four names released, only one person was missing—a Buddhist monk who used a religious name that was different from the one on his passport. After bringing the four of us chairs, a high-ranking police officer approached me.

"Ms. Lu, exactly how many people did you bring with you today?"

"A group of eighteen," I replied truthfully.

"Eighteen! Have they passed through customs already?"

"They certainly have."

I watched the officer reexamine his list and consult his subordinates. The physical appearance of Taiwanese and Chinese is nearly identical. There was really no way the authorities could catch someone who had already passed through. While we waited, one of my friends who had already passed through customs rushed back to within earshot. "Do you want us to notify the press?"

"Proceed as planned," I replied, smiling.

The Chinese officer frantically counted the number of our party, trying to match the names with the number of people who had passed through customs. Finally, he had no choice but to ask me if I would help him identify the remaining members.

"Sure," I said, "I'll help you find them."

When I strolled into the airport lobby, a large number of journalists stood waving to me from across the arrival hall.

"I've come to Beijing," I shouted, "but they won't let me leave the airport!"

The airport police walked around the passenger arrival area shouting the names I had given them, while I chatted with members of the media. Liao Yun-yi, the person in charge of notifying the press of my arrival, was on the telephone and oblivious to a policeman standing next to him calling out his name. "Mr. Liao Yun-yi, who is Mr. Liao Yun-yi?" I waved at Liao. He waved back and smiled when he heard the policeman calling his name. Then he finished his telephone conversation with a reporter and walked over.

After everyone was assembled, a policeman pulled out a piece of paper and read a prepared speech. "According to our intelligence reports, you have come to engage in subversive activities. You are unwelcome here. You are hereby asked to return to Japan on the next available flight."

We groaned in mock disappointment: "How extraordinary!" I exclaimed. "I was under the impression that the people in the People's Republic see Taiwanese as fellow countrymen. Tomorrow is the PRC's National Day and we have come to deliver our best wishes on this festive occasion. Sending us back just proves that Taiwanese are not your compatriots, we're foreigners." The policeman stiffened as if his spine had become an icicle and did not reply. Representatives from Japan Airlines rushed over to direct us toward the check-in counter.

As a kindly gesture, Japan Airlines upgraded me to first class for the flight back to Narita International Airport. Sitting near me were a number of senior Diet members and high-ranking government officials who had apparently attended the PRC National Day celebration. We walked out of the baggage claim area at approximately the same time. As we entered the passenger arrival area, a pack of journalists quickly shouldered their cameras and hustled over in our direction. I assumed they were waiting to interview the Diet members, but the Japanese journalists held placards written in Chinese characters saying, "The Honorable Lu Hsiu-lien." They were waiting to interview me.

I had originally intended to mobilize the Taiwanese community in Tokyo to protest in front of the PRC embassy, but China was one step ahead of me. Beijing demanded the Japanese government refuse to allow me to leave the airport or to take a transfer flight to Hong Kong, where I might have led a similar protest. I returned to Taipei on the first flight in the morning and arrived in Taiwan to a warm welcome, with media organizations calling from all over the world for interviews.

After my election to the national legislature that fall, I joined the Legislative Foreign Affairs Committee, where I served for six legislative sessions and was elected chair of the committee three times. Unlike in the United States, where leadership positions in congressional committees are based on seniority, the legislative committee chairs often rotate in Taiwan, changing with each biannual legislative session. Committee members, both from the DPP and the Nationalist Party, elected me because I devoted myself to foreign affairs.

After 1991, my activities to win Taiwan admission to the United Nations were coordinated from New York. I realized that to make greater progress, I had to create new inroads to the United Nations on a day-to-day basis. I wanted to push for Taiwan's entry through institutional channels by joining international organizations affiliated with the United Nations that might provide access to UN key leaders. Through a stroke of good fortune, after I delivered a speech at a rally in Taipei's New Park, a Taiwanese businessman offered me his Manhattan office free of charge. The office was just two blocks from the UN headquarters, and it became the US branch of the Taiwan International Alliance (TIA).

Registered as a nongovernmental organization in the United States, the TIA provided me with greater access to international organizations than any Taiwanese had enjoyed since the 1970s. The TIA's primary function was to improve awareness of Taiwan's diplomatic isolation. The extraordinarily talented TIA staff gave me the courage to attempt challenges that would have otherwise seemed impossible.

In early 1994, the program director of the Global Summit of Women, Irene Natividad, wrote a letter asking me whether I would be interested in hosting the 1994 Global Summit of Women in Taipei. Although I had attended the 1992 Global Summit of Women in Ireland hosted by that country's first woman president, Mary Robinson, the request came as a total surprise. Participants in the summit were women leaders who made significant contributions to advancing the cause of women in their countries, either through activism or by setting extraordinary examples in the field of politics. The participants included international human rights workers, senators, government ministers, and heads of state. Canada, the first country to host the summit, had spent four years preparing. The summit in Ireland had required more than two years of planning. Spain, originally scheduled to host the summit in 1994, had backed out of its commitment after one and a half years of preparation. My TIA staff advised me that, with eight months until the date of the summit, preparation time was woefully inadequate. But I knew that hosting the Global Summit of Women in Taipei would give Taiwan invaluable international exposure, so I told Ms. Natividad that I would investigate the feasibility of bringing the summit to Taipei.

Procuring enough funds was the first obstacle to overcome. By pointing out to Deputy Foreign Minister Chang Hsiao-yan that Beijing would host the UN Conference on Women the following year, I managed to win his promise that the Ministry of Foreign Affairs would cover half the cost of the summit. The selling point was that we had to make a pitch to the summit participants to end Taiwan's international exclusion, because many of the women would also attend the Beijing conference. After my meeting with Chang, I rushed back to the office and sent off a fax to the program director telling her "I would be delighted and honored to host the Global Summit of Women in Taipei." Just hours later, the Nationalist administration reshuffled the cabinet. Chang Hsiao-yen was made the head of the Overseas Chinese Affairs Commission. His successor refused to match the generosity of Chang's support. Not twenty-four hours after agreeing to host the event, I was scrambling to raise funds.

Most of the women leaders we invited hailed from countries that did not have formal diplomatic ties with Taiwan. This meant that Beijing brought great pressure to bear on their governments to dissuade them from attending the Taipei summit. A painful example of this was the decision by the speaker of the National Assembly in the Philippines to serve as a keynote speaker and her subsequent cancellation out of fear that it would antagonize China. The Nigerian parliament speaker also quailed in the face of Chinese pressure, along with a cabinet minister from England, and the wife of Nobel Peace Prize winner and Costa Rican president Oscar Arias. Many women, however, refused to bow in the face of Chinese threats. Lithuania's first prime minister Kazimiera Prunskiene may have spoken for many when she said, after her arrival in Taipei, "It's all men's fault that a nation as lovely as Taiwan has not been recognized by the international community. PRC pressure made coming here difficult, but I insisted on coming. Women have to correct all of men's mistakes."

In Taipei, criticism from conservative Nationalist factions also prevented governmental officials from attending the summit. At that time, politics was seen in black-and-white terms. One supported either the Nationalists or the DPP. There was little safe middle ground in between, even in the case of an international conference that ostensibly had little to do with domestic politics. After agreeing to come, President Lee Teng-hui found resistance too great to do so, simply because I was the summit host and a Democratic Progressive Party legislator. He did, however, receive fourteen women from the summit in the presidential office building, and he asked Vice President Lee Yuan-tsu to deliver an address on his behalf.

With assistance from the TIA staff in New York, we sent invitations to women leaders all over the world. My staff workers handled visa, travel, and hotel arrangements. I took care of fundraising and planning. Slowly, in the way that the artist's penciled sketch becomes a colorful oil painting, the 1994 Global Summit of Women went from a dream to a concrete reality, bringing nearly four hundred leaders from more than seventy different countries. Participants included Prime Minister Edith Cresson from France, Prime Minister Kazimiera Prunskiene from Lithuania, Minister of State Betty Bigombe from Uganda, and former Korean state minister for political affairs Yung-Chung Kim. Without a doubt, the summit became the largest and most important international event held in Taipei for years. The theme, "In the Home and in the World, Equality and Responsibility for all Women and Men," was the focus of my opening address as I stood before the assembled participants, attempting to put the difficulties of organizing the event behind me.

In 1980, UNESCO issued a world report stating that women make up half of the world's population, work two-thirds of the total working hours; yet they receive only one-tenth of the global income and own only one percent of the world's property. Later, in 1993, UN reports indicated that in the whole twentieth century, there have been only seven women elected as presidents, and sixteen appointed as prime ministers worldwide. Among the legislative bodies,

women, on average, occupy just 10 percent of the seats. As for the
cabinet level, the percentage is even lower—only 3.5 percent. . . .
 If politics is defined as public affairs, why are women
excluded? . . . You must know that if women can look beautiful, cook good meals, and manage a household, they can
also direct and administer public affairs. You must also
believe that if women are born to be mothers, they also possess inherent compassion for people and the Earth.

For Taiwanese women, the Global Summit of Women offered a
rare opportunity to gain international exposure. For the international participants, Chinese efforts to prevent them from attending
the summit attuned them to the injustice of Taiwan's plight.

Very soon I would profit immensely from the friendship I developed with one of the participants, the cochair of the UN Women's
Environment and Development Organization, Bella Abzug. For former congresswoman Bella Abzug, it seemed appropriate that, after
hosting the Global Summit of Women in Taipei, I should be invited
to attend the UN Conference on Women in Beijing the following year.
She saw me as a leading feminist in Asia and a true sister in the cause
of improving the status of women. After returning to New York, Bella
made arrangements to include me among her organization's members
at a preparatory meeting for the Beijing Conference on Women to be
held at the UN headquarters. She took a great risk in doing so, knowing that she might face condemnation from Chinese diplomats and
resistance from the UN leadership.

In March 1995, I showed my pass at the gate of the United Nations
and walked into the preparatory meeting. I was the first incumbent
politician from Taiwan to participate in a UN function since 1971. Since
Liu Chieh's walkout, all Taiwanese nationals had been barred from
UN activities. Chinese browbeating had cowed the United Nations to
the extent that not even Taiwanese students at American universities
could set foot inside the UN buildings as interns.

A glance at the meeting's agenda showed me that the vice president of the Chinese National Women's Association, Huang Qichao,

was scheduled to give the opening address. I knew her well. Huang had been my guide during my trip to China five years earlier. "On behalf of the People's Republic of China, I invite all sisters around the world to attend the UN Conference on Women in Beijing, regardless of their nationality and political orientation . . . ," she said.

"Will you allow Tibetan women to attend as well?" one woman from the floor wanted to know.

"This is a domestic issue. According to Chinese law, Tibet is part of the People's Republic of China. Treatment of women from these areas will be handled in accordance with Chinese domestic laws and regulations." Huang was clearly embarrassed.

The reaction on the floor was total outrage. Everyone suspected Beijing would exclude women from Tibet. The debate over attendance continued at the UN Asia-Pacific regional workshop I attended in the afternoon. "If we want to make the upcoming conference a success," said a woman from the Philippines, "we should make sure that all women are eligible to attend."

"This is especially true of women from Taiwan," a woman from Hong Kong chimed in. "The PRC government may make it difficult for them to participate in the conference."

"Women from Outer Mongolia might face political difficulties similar to those of Taiwanese and Tibetan women," said another participant. "The Chinese government has discriminated against them in the past."

I had stayed silent until this point, but the time had come to take some form of concrete action. "Let's pass a resolution," I suggested, speaking loudly, "that the PRC cannot, under any circumstances, prevent women from any region in the world from attending the conference, including Taiwan." To my surprise and delight, nearly everyone agreed and moved to put the matter to a vote.

"This is a formal resolution," said the rapporteur chairing the meeting. "Please be ready to reply 'yes,' 'no,' or 'I abstain.'" All those in attendance, with the exception of Huang Qichao, who didn't speak English and was awaiting a translation of the proceedings, responded with a unanimous "Yes." Only after the resolution passed did Huang understand what had transpired.

When I left the conference room, a member of Huang's staff was waiting for me outside. "Ms. Lu," she said, "would you consider joining Vice President Huang Qichao for coffee?"

The Communist Party had arranged for Huang to receive me at the National Women's Association during my visit to Beijing. I remembered that she had listened eagerly as I spoke of the modern feminism in the West and in Taiwan. Her positive impression of me, I hoped, had not worn off.

"Why not?" I replied.

"We're sisters; Taiwan and China are one nation," Huang said. "Why did you raise such an embarrassing issue in front of foreigners? You could have spoken with me privately."

"This conference is international," I said pleasantly, "so the issue of Taiwanese attendance is an international one."

The two of us returned to the preparatory conference together, where the rapporteurs read resolutions from the regional workshops to be voted on by the entire assembly. When the rapporteur from the Asia-Pacific group read my resolution, stating specifically that women from Tibet and Taiwan should not be excluded for any reason, the assembly applauded and voted unanimously to adopt the resolution.

"Now this is fun," I remember thinking to myself. "Not only have I been the first national-level politician to attend a UN function in two decades, but my intervention may have tipped the balance in favor of Taiwanese women attending the Beijing conference." Beijing did not take my attendance at the meeting lightly, however. China moved swiftly to orchestrate a counterstrike.

When I walked past the UN guards on the second day of the preparatory meeting, I saw Huang Qichao standing at the gate. "Good morning," I ventured politely, expecting her to comment on the resolution passed the day before.

"Ms. Lu, my government has ordered me to return to China this afternoon. I am afraid that I must bid you farewell."

"Goodbye!" I said. In my heart I wished her well.

From that point on, I encountered difficulties. Later that day, the deputy secretary general of the United Nations approached me to see if I had a legitimate ID for entering the United Nations. When I showed my ID, her face turned pale. "It doesn't look fake," she said, and then went to find Bella Abzug, whose organization had issued me the pass. Although Bella resolutely defended me, invitations to attend other UN functions were cancelled, including one sent to me, as the president of Taiwan International Alliance, to the official celebration of International Women's Day.

That spring, Taiwan International Alliance applied to attend the UN's Fourth World Conference on Women in Beijing as a nongovernmental organization incorporated in the United States, and we received UN accreditation to attend the preparatory meeting in Vienna. This "prepcom" was one of several meetings held at UN regional centers to prepare documents for the conference in Beijing. Too busy to attend myself, I asked two women from my New York office to go over. One of them was the TIA executive director, Margie Joy Walden, a woman of uncommon charm and good-natured tenacity.

At the prepcom, NGOs had the opportunity to distribute officially approved documents to all the attending delegations from Europe and North America. Margie received official permission to submit the final statement approved by the Global Summit of Women held in Taipei. Copies of the document were delivered to the UN Post Office and sent to each delegation by the UN staff.

The following morning, Margie and her assistant, Jo Ann Fan, happened to mention the statement to a representative from the official US delegation and were told that the statement was never received. When Margie inquired at the UN Post Office, she was told that the UN leadership had ordered the removal of the statement from all mailboxes. The UN commissioner's office had also asked for a list of all the delegations that had picked up the TIA document.

Margie met with the ambassador of the US delegation and convinced her to request an explanation from the United Nations and the prepcom leadership. Meanwhile, Jo Ann delivered copies of the document to each delegation individually, explaining the circumstances under which it had been withdrawn from circulation.

When the official UN list of NGOs at the prepcom was distributed the following day, TIA and the Tibetan Women's Association of Switzerland had been removed from the list. Both organizations had received accreditation to attend the prepcom. After the US and Swiss delegations demanded an investigation, UN officials said that there had been computer tampering with the official list. No one knew why the names had been removed or by whom. Waving a press release in her hand, Margie told the US and Swiss ambassadors that if a revised list was not distributed immediately, the whole world would know about this breach of security and removal of authorized documents from UN mailboxes. At 3:00 P.M., UN officials told Margie they would send out a new list. At 5:00 P.M., they said the list would be out shortly. At 8:00 P.M., Margie and Jo Ann waited, while the cleaning crews came in, finished work, and started turning off the lights in the building. Another UN official appeared to apologize. "Sorry for the delay," he said. "The computer printer has jammed." Finally, at 10:00 P.M. the UN leadership distributed the revised official list, including the names of the TIA and the Tibetan Women's Association, to each delegation.

In response to such underhanded Chinese tactics, the TIA redoubled its efforts to host international events that raised hackles in Beijing, to the delight of Taiwanese nationalists at home. In April 1995, I arranged an event in Japan called the Centennial Commemoration of the Treaty of Shimonoseki, bringing together Japanese and Taiwanese politicians, as well as Japanese who grew up in Taiwan and Taiwanese who were educated in Japan. The commemoration was held on the same day and at the same location as the signing of the Treaty of Shimonoseki a hundred years earlier that ceded Taiwan to Japan "in perpetuity." The idea was to improve the Japan-Taiwan bilateral relationship by highlighting the common history of the two island nations and to point out that China abandoned all sovereign rights to Taiwan in 1895.

Unlike Koreans and Chinese, who have horrific memories of Japanese imperial aggression, most Taiwanese who grew up under Japanese rule are nostalgic about the past, although no one denies that under Japanese rule Taiwanese were second-class citizens. The

Japanese were more honest and efficient than the ragtag Chinese carpetbaggers that ruled Taiwan after Japan's surrender to the Allies in World War II. Moreover, Japan's investments in Taiwan's ports, railways, and agricultural sector, in particular, have benefited generations of Taiwanese.

China responded to the Centennial Commemoration with a blue streak of condemnation prompted by fears that improving the international community's knowledge of history might threaten China's fragile claims to sovereignty over Taiwan. Even some pro-unification journalists in Taiwan accused me of "worshipping the Japanese emperor" by attending a religious ceremony at Shimonoseki related, in a distant manner, to the Japanese imperial household.

The following month, TIA sponsored another event in Linz, Austria, called "Focus on Taiwan," the largest Taiwan studies conference ever held in Europe. An Austrian university student had approached me the year before, expressing interest in organizing the event. He planned to feature presentations by political experts from Taiwan, Austria, Germany, England, and the United States; performances by Taiwanese musicians, including the rap artist "Pig Head" (Zhutou); literature presentations; and films from Taiwan. The poor student had no idea that the conference would attract the attention of Chinese diplomats in Europe, who tried to convince him to alter the agenda to remove "separatist elements."

Meanwhile, the Nationalist position on applying for UN membership had undergone a complete reversal. In 1993, Taiwan's Ministry of Foreign Affairs sent an application to the United Nations requesting that the General Assembly establish an ad hoc committee to study Taiwan's readmission to the United Nations. It was a move that revealed perhaps intentional ineptitude on the part of the ministry, which was a lukewarm supporter of Taiwan's application. Normally, proposals to the United Nations must be submitted six months before the fall session to ensure inclusion in the agenda of the General Assembly. The Ministry of Foreign Affairs (MOFA) submitted the proposal late, and it foundered in the General Committee, the UN body that determines the agenda. The next year, MOFA submitted the same proposal a few months earlier, only to see it die in the General Committee. I opposed these attempts, preferring instead to apply directly through the General Assembly. Bringing the issue to a vote before the General Assembly or the Security Council, even if the resolution failed, could fuel debates that would raise Taiwan's eventual chances at success.

By the spring of 1995, my patience with the Foreign Ministry had worn thin. I railroaded a resolution through the Legislative Yuan, requesting the government to formally apply to join the UN General Assembly by the fiftieth anniversary celebration of the signing of the UN Charter on June 26. Legislators in the Foreign Affairs Committee demanded the resignation of Foreign Minister Frederick Chien should he fail to submit the formal application on time. The wheels of the Nationalist bureaucracy began to grind into motion.

Working miracles in New York, TIA's Margie Joy Walden got me an invitation to attend the UN celebration of the signing of the United Nations Charter in San Francisco. This was extraordinary, considering the extent to which China sought to bar my participation in UN activities. I wanted to point out the irony that the United Nations denied membership to the Republic of China even though it had been among the first signatories of the UN Charter.

On the eve of the banquet, the Taiwanese media reported on my plans to attend the celebration. The Nationalists, reluctant to watch me win another diplomatic coup, sent the president of the legislature, Liu Song-fan, and a pack of journalists to San Francisco. Liu scheduled interviews with the press in front of the building hosting the celebration, in hopes of convincing people at home that he had joined the UN activities.

One significant development on the fiftieth anniversary of the United Nations was that the Ministry of Foreign Affairs sent a formal letter to UN Secretary-General Boutros Boutros Ghali requesting admission to the United Nations under the name Republic of China. The Foreign Ministry also published a series of advertisements in the *Washington Post* and in the *New York Times* emphasizing Taiwan's qualifications for membership. Secretary-General Ghali replied that the United Nations recognizes Taiwan as part of China, thus Taiwan is, in a sense, represented by Beijing in the United Nations. He encouraged Taiwan to settle the question of UN representation through negotiations with Beijing, and he said that the question of Taiwan's membership is a domestic, rather than international, affair. The Nationalist application did not succeed, but applying in a manner that was sincere, official, and representative of Taiwanese public opinion indicated progress.

Back in Taipei, I became entangled in another political struggle—not with the People's Republic or with the Nationalists, but with the Democratic Progressive Party. I was campaigning for the position of vice presidential candidate in Taiwan's first-ever nationwide presidential election. In the past, the National Assembly had elected the president, to six-year terms in office, and the president had selected a vice president. This practice had changed prior to the election of March 1996, and each presidential candidate would run on a ticket with a vice presidential candidate, and the victors would serve a four-year term.

My decision to compete for the vice presidential nomination grew out of my admiration for the DPP presidential candidate, Dr. Peng Ming-min. Educated at Tokyo Imperial University and a former politics professor at National Taiwan University, Peng had lived in exile for twenty-five years after his imprisonment for drafting a manifesto that advocated Taiwan independence. A gentle and insightful man, Peng was a generation my senior.

DPP bylaws called for all candidates to be selected through a party primary, including a poll to choose vice presidential candidates, separate from the poll to choose the presidential candidates. I planned to enter the party primary for vice president, as a means of testing the waters to see if voters were ready for national leadership by a woman. My campaign got off to a slow start, however.

On the day I announced my candidacy in front-page advertisements, newspapers ran the story of a restaurant fire in Taichung that killed sixty-seven. It was a bad day to talk politics, to say the least. The DPP leadership reacted to my announcement with shock and apprehension. Men controlled the top posts in the party, and none of them, it seemed, had considered the party bylaws or the possibility of an individual running for vice president.

Factions within the DPP, led by others seeking the vice presidential slot, quickly moved against my candidacy by voting to change the party bylaws to mirror the system in the United States, where the presidential candidate selects his or her running mate. Women's groups, my frequent allies in the past, started to criticize me for my willingness to play second fiddle. "If you are a real feminist, why don't you run for president?" they asked.

I fought back by leading a demonstration of "100 supporters of Lu Hsiu-lien" to the DPP headquarters during the party's Central Standing Committee meeting. My supporters included one of Lee Teng-hui's presidential advisors, legislators, artists, and professionals. I also released twenty letters signed by foreign dignitaries supporting my candidacy. Among these people were two of my guests at the Global Summit of Women, Prime Minister Kazimiera Prunskiene of Lithuania and Prime Minister Edith Cresson of France.

By midsummer, the United Nations had sent me a formal invitation to attend the Fourth World Conference on Women in Beijing. I was scheduled to chair an NGO panel discussion and had also been invited by a professor at the University of California at Berkeley to serve as a discussant on her human rights panel. When my travel agent went to Hong Kong to get my Taiwan Compatriot Permit, the officials at China's de facto consulate, the Xinhua News Agency, confiscated my documents.

"She is not welcome," they said. "She can't attend the conference."

"Please return her application and relevant documents," my travel agent replied.

"That's impossible."

Xinhua did not return my official invitation or my Taiwan ID card, so I notified the international news media. Reporters who called the Xinhua News Agency were told my application for a Taiwan Compatriot Permit (*taibaozheng*) had never been received. Later, I heard that the Communists had threatened all airlines flying to China that there would be "serious consequences" if they allowed me on a flight to Beijing.

In New York, Margie Joy Walden was experiencing similar difficulties. After she had taken her passport and official UN invitation to the Chinese consulate to apply for a visa, the consulate told her that the documentation had been lost. "I know that my passport is back there," Margie said, "and I won't leave without it. I want to see the consul or the head of the visa section down here in five minutes, and he had better be holding my passport in his hand."

"I'm sorry, Ms. Walden, but we can't find. . . ."

Margie had to think fast and decided to bluff her way through the encounter. "I have a close personal relationship with Senator Jesse Helms. Have you heard of him? He is waiting for my phone call right now to make sure that I can attend the conference. I'm going to call the senator now unless someone shows up with my documentation!" Margie knew that her threat was completely hollow. She didn't know Senator Helms personally and gambled that the Chinese would be impressed enough to back down. The consulate returned Margie's passport but not her UN invitation. It seemed there was little to be done to convince Beijing to allow Margie to attend the conference.

I knew I had a slim chance of attending the World Conference on Women, but I had to do something in response. My TIA staff and I made arrangements to host another event inviting key women leaders to Taipei for the Feminist Summit for Global Peace. The focus of the meeting was on women's contributions to peace worldwide. In Taiwan, avoiding war with China was a particularly popular topic after a Japanese newspaper printed what appeared to be a Chinese invasion plan for Taiwan and an influential book had predicted an imminent Chinese attack on the island.

More than thirty distinguished woman politicians attended, including the Liberian foreign minister. On the final night, while religious groups gathered to pray for peace, the Liberian foreign minister returned to her hotel and read a deeply moving fax from home. Liberia had just signed a peace treaty ending six years of civil war, a very pleasant coincidence, indeed! On the same night, I let my hair down:

In a speech to the participants, I discussed my disappointment that none of the Taiwanese presidential candidates, all men, had agreed to attend the Feminist Summit for Global Peace. "If the title of the event did not pertain to women," I said, "they certainly would have come." I called off my campaign to be the DPP's vice presidential candidate and warned, "If women's role in politics does not improve, look for me to come out again in four years, possibly as a presidential candidate!"

Several of the participants at our summit went immediately to the World Conference on Women in Beijing, taking with them the final resolution passed by our Feminist Summit for Global Peace. Later, I heard from these women that, although China barred me from attending, many participants in the conference had heard of my circumstances: a seat at each panel discussion I was scheduled to attend was left vacant in my honor.

On October 25, another major event honoring the fiftieth anniversary of the United Nations was held at the UN headquarters in New York. Heads of state from powerful nations around the world were present, including Bill Clinton and Jiang Zemin. This time, unlike in San Francisco, we were playing on Margie Joy Walden's home turf. Her leadership culminated in our most flamboyant demonstration yet for Taiwan's entry into the United Nations.

When I gave the order, our "forces" approached the United Nations from land and sea. Our demonstrators, one hundred strong from Taipei and several hundred from the New York area, chanted, sang, and marched as New York City tour buses drove past bearing the advertisement "Welcome Taiwan into the UN!" Riding on the deck of a Mississippi paddleboat, my "navy" sailed up the East River and anchored at the UN headquarters, so all the UN employees and journalists saw the boat's massive "Welcome Taiwan into the UN!" banner. By day, the paddleboat anchored in front of the United Nations, and by night the paddleboat moored near the heliport, where world leaders transiting from Newark and JFK airports could see it.

The Nicaraguan ambassador to the United Nations later told me that Chinese President Jiang Zemin had invited him to coffee after his speech to the General Assembly. Sitting in the delegates' dining room, Jiang Zemin had looked out the window at the "Welcome Taiwan into the UN!" sign on our paddleboat. With his face twisted into a frown, Jiang exclaimed, "They are wasting money!"

"Was it a waste of money?" I asked the ambassador.

"Certainly not!" he said, smiling.

The following year I brought the boat back for the party on the night the UN General Assembly went into session. We had scheduled a dinner cruise with a number of UN dignitaries. By early evening, heavy rains pounded down and lightning crackled in the sky. I feared that no one would show up. But by the time we set off, the boat had taken aboard some two hundred ambassadors, UN employees, Taiwan delegation members, and close friends for a night of dancing and live music. By sheer chance, the First Ladies' Party hosted by Hillary Clinton passed by and her guests gawked at our "Welcome Taiwan into the UN!" sign. Even years later, when I would arrive at a banquet in New York or Washington, someone would shout, "Where's the boat? Everyone misses the boat!"

By the winter of 1995, I had lost my taste for politics in the Legislative Yuan. I saw the legislature as a political circus where bitter criticism fueled media sensationalism and the prospects of cooperation foundered. The Legislative Yuan had become the site for fencing ill-gotten treasures and the smelting pot of justice. I was deeply exhausted and fantasized about retiring from politics completely. My speech "Farewell to the Legislative Yuan," which made it clear that I wouldn't run again, received a standing ovation from legislators on both sides of the aisle, who were appreciative of my contributions.

In the run-up to Taiwan's first direct presidential election, tensions with China reached the highest level since the two sides had last come to blows in 1960. Beijing's propaganda machine castigated President Lee Teng-hui as a "splittist dividing the motherland." The PRC leaders had been particularly concerned by Lee's vigorous diplomatic efforts to expand Taiwan's international space, his assertions that Taiwan's democracy was a model for China and the world, and his views that the Republic of China was a sovereign nation until reunification, which could only occur when China was a democracy.

In the summer of 1995, the People's Liberation Army held a series of military exercises and fired missiles into the sea off Taiwan. Then, just prior to Taiwan's first presidential election in March 1996, the Chinese fired missiles near Taiwan's two largest container ports, Kaohsiung and Keelung, in an attempt to unnerve Taiwanese voters and intimidate the United States, which had allowed Lee Teng-hui to visit his alma mater, Cornell, the year before.

Presumably, President Jiang Zemin hoped that this "Taiwan Strait Crisis" would cow Taiwanese into voting for pro-unification candidates Hau Puo-tsun and Lin Yang-gang. The plan backfired as Taiwan's military went on full alert and reservists readied themselves to fight a war. Taiwanese resentment of China soared as the stock market crashed. The United States, fearing imminent conflict, sent two aircraft carrier battle groups toward the area in the largest show of force since the Vietnam War. Surprised, and sensing that it had seriously miscalculated, Beijing backed down as Lee Teng-hui was elected to a third term in office with a resounding majority.

A calm in political activity followed the storm of the Taiwan Strait Crisis. Cooperation in Taiwan followed strife, a brief period of truce after the Nationalists and the DPP realized that their own differences were much smaller than those between Taipei and Beijing. In the days before his inauguration, Lee Teng-hui asked two senior figures in the DPP, including Huang Hsin-chieh, a *Formosa* trial codefendant, to serve as his presidential advisors. The DPP agreed to allow the union that once would have been considered unholy.

On May 19, one day before President Lee's inauguration, I was sitting at home in my Taipei apartment when I received a phone call from one of the president's close confidants. "The president has followed your career closely since you worked in the Executive Yuan. He was a minister of state at the time, and your work in feminism really impressed him. 'A little Taiwanese girl, this active and persuasive!' President Lee sympathized during the dark years of your imprisonment and appreciated your work in foreign affairs."

"That is very kind of you to say," I said, wondering where the conversation was going.

"Ms. Lu, President Lee would like to invite you to serve as a presidential advisor."

"Am I that old?" Typically, presidential advisors in Taiwan are very senior and do very little.

"No, no, it's because you are capable. Your position would have duties and receive a salary."

"You'll have to allow me to consult the DPP and my faction, the Justice Alliance."

"Please hurry."

The president's offer caught me off guard, but the DPP could not refuse after allowing Huang Hsin-chieh and Yu Chen Yue-ying to serve as advisors. I had, of course, followed the activities of President Lee closely, opposing his policies or supporting them at different junctures. The Western press has exaggerated Lee's contributions considerably, lauding him as the "Father of Taiwanese Democracy." I saw his role differently.

The real heroes of Taiwanese democracy are those who spent the prime of their life in prison for advocating political change like Shih Ming-teh, bought freedom of expression with their lives like Cheng Nan-rong, or lost their loved ones like Lin Yi-hsiung, and the hundreds of others who fought for liberalization and fostered a unique Taiwanese national identity. These people are the flowers of democracy. President Lee did not plant these flowers. He watched them bloom and arranged them into a beautiful bouquet. Lee has since acknowledged opposition leaders, such as Huang Hsin-chieh, as his teachers and inspiration. President Lee Teng-hui's invitation to serve as an advisor was an honor and the beginning of a friendship that I continue to cherish. I did not serve as his advisor for long, however. Another wave of destiny soon washed over me, carrying me in a new direction.

CHAPTER 9

POLITICAL TRASH

MID-MORNING ON NOVEMBER 29, 1996, I WAS AT THE LAI LAI Hotel coffee shop with someone from Washington, DC, chatting about US-China policy, when I excused myself to answer my cell phone. A reporter from the *Independent Morning Post* was on the line.

"Have you heard the news?" she asked.

"What news?"

"Taoyuan County chief executive Liu Bang-yiu was murdered this morning."

"What?"

"He was shot in his official residence. It is unclear how many others were killed." The news chilled me, but the reporter's second question was even more shocking. "Do you want to run for Taoyuan County chief executive?"

"You're not serious!" I admonished her.

A few minutes later another reporter called. He told me that a total of eight people had been shot, including the chief executive. Emergency efforts to save their lives continued at a hospital in Taoyuan County.

I rushed back to my office. My staff had just watched the latest television report and provided further details. Early that morning two men had overpowered the security guard at the gate, slashing his throat and taking his pistol. They shot the other guard and took his gun before making their way into Chief Executive Liu Bang-yiu's living room. There several local politicians and the chief executive had gathered for a breakfast meeting. The killers forced all eight people into the guardroom, and using surgical tape, bound and blindfolded the captives. Then, the execution began. Eight shots rang out; one bullet passed through the skull of each victim.

Residents of the neighborhood around the chief executive's residence mistook the gunfire for fireworks, the traditional means of frightening away evil spirits. The gunmen walked out the front door, wearing long rain ponchos that covered all but their eyes. One of the politicians' assistants sat in her car outside the chief executive's residence. The men got into her car and ordered the woman to drive to a deserted mountainous area, where they left her and escaped in another vehicle.

The chief executive's wife and the family's maid were upstairs when they heard the shots. Moments later, Mrs. Liu walked into a guardroom that resembled a slaughterhouse. Spattered blood and gore covered the walls and tiled floor. Her husband lay among the slain. Mrs. Liu immediately called for assistance. By the time ambulances arrived, only one of the eight victims showed vital signs. The others were dead on arrival at the hospital.

After a briefing from my staff, I left for Taoyuan immediately. Although my legislative constituency had been in Taoyuan County, I had never been a friend of Chief Executive Liu. He was a Nationalist with a reputation for corruption and he was a Hakka, who in Taoyuan County tended to be insular folk. I met the DPP chairman, Hsu Hsinliang, outside the hospital, where the doctor in charge led us into the emergency room. The scene was a grizzly one. The men lay on gurneys like pale wooden figures, while nurses attempted to resuscitate them.

"This one is dead," said the head doctor, pointing to the chief executive. "We should have announced his death already, but the provincial governor has ordered us to wait."

The hospital announced the deaths of five others, while a nurse stood over the chief executive's body, pumping on his chest mechanically. Only two weeks earlier, I had seen Liu Bang-yiu on a stage, addressing a crowd of thousands in the Taoyuan Dome. The occasion had, ironically, been a funeral for nine firefighters who had been killed in a factory explosion. Short and heavyset for a Taiwanese, and darkly handsome, he emanated a vibrant confidence and animal intensity. His life ended so suddenly. Until the end, he had struggled for money, for power.

I went to look at the other bodies, one of whom was a county assemblyman. I overheard the doctor say to his wife, "It's better to let him go. Your husband died this morning. If resuscitation efforts continue, we will break his ribs."

"Why bother to work so hard?" I asked myself. "Life is short and so unpredictable." It was like a part of me died, too, in this needless tragedy.

The killing of the chief executive cast Taoyuan County into confusion and depression. Liu Bang-yiu had many enemies. Investigators told me there could have been a hundred reasons for the murder. A notorious womanizer, Liu had led an administration infamous for corruption and excesses. Before his county council appearances, Liu would invite the county councilors scheduled to raise questions during interpolation to his home for breakfast, when he gave each one a red envelope containing cash. If they criticized his administration, he would say, "Wait a minute now, wait a minute! Do you want me to tell the council a few things about you, too?"

One time, protestors were demonstrating outside the county government building, and Chief Executive Liu happened to be passing by. "What kind of a chief executive are you anyway?" one man shouted at him. "You got elected by buying votes for NT$500 [US$16] apiece!"

"Who told you that you had to sell your vote to me anyway?" the chief executive retorted.

Tracking Liu Bang-yiu's killers would prove difficult, if not impossible. Police did not seal off the crime scene. Reporters and television cameramen had trampled through the bloody chambers of the chief executive's residence, spoiling the chance for a good forensic investigation and flooding television channels with gory images. Later, the floor was "accidentally" washed clean of bloodstains. False leads sent police running in different directions every day. Rumors abounded. "The killers were from mainland China," one taxi driver told me.

"Taiwanese could never be so cruel." A man claiming to be one of the gunmen even called a police hotline and demanded to speak to Liu Bang-yiu's wife. When the police went to get her, the line went dead. Reporters covering the investigation suspected that high-ranking Nationalist leaders had ordered Liu's execution and obstructed the investigation. To this day, the case remains unsolved.

In the weeks after the murder, supporters and DPP politicians pressed me to campaign for the vacant chief executive seat. "You're the only one who can solve Taoyuan's problems," they insisted. Yet, depression induced by the murder weighed upon me. Other DPP legislators expressed interest in the post. "Let them run," I told my friends. The DPP meanwhile conducted opinion surveys to determine which candidates had the most popular support. I led each poll by a large margin. Party chairman Hsu Hsin-liang even offered to cancel the party primary if I agreed to run.

"Enough, enough," I thought. "Taoyuan needs me, so I'll give it a shot. The entire nomination and campaign process was completed very quickly. Unsurprisingly, no prominent Nationalist politicians showed interest in competing in the by-election. For a corrupt politician, the spoils would be small: the replacement chief executive would serve only eight months, after which he or she would face a second expensive campaign for a four-year term. The Nationalist Party nominated Fang Li-hsiu, the Hakka mayor of Chungli, Taoyuan County's largest city.

In Taoyuan County's first chief executive elections, in the 1950s, the two major ethnic groups, Hoklo (Min-nan) and Hakka, had fought bloody battles over which group's candidate would head the county. Both Min-nan and Hakka were early settlers of Taiwan and are considered native Taiwanese, although the groups speak different languages and share different cultural traditions. The Min-nan and Hakka eventually came to a compromise that was stringently adhered to until I took office: A Hakka would lead for two terms as county chief executive while a Min-nan served as speaker of the county council. Then, the order would switch; a Min-nan chief executive would complete two terms while a Hakka served as speaker of the county council. Liu Bang-yiu had served over seven years. By nominating a Hakka candidate, the Nationalists gambled that Taoyuan County voters would insist upon completion of the "Hakka period" for county chief executive. This turned out to be a miscalculation.

The crowds that attended my speeches were in the thousands. When I traveled through Taoyuan County in a long train of campaign trucks, shopkeepers would run out and give bread and soft drinks to my campaign workers. "Elect Lu Hsiu-lien, elect Lu Hsiu-lien!" they cried. My opponent, Fang Li-hsiu, treated his guests to dinner but couldn't fill small venues. I had seen enough campaigns to know that mine was going well, but the Nationalists didn't see the storm on the horizon.

The election fell on March 18. Voting began at 8:00 A.M. and ended at 4:00 P.M. At 3 o'clock, Nationalist Party secretary-general Wu Puo-hsiung held a press conference at the Nationalist headquarters. He stunned everyone by announcing Fang Li-hsiu's victory.

"Originally, Fang was not favored in the election," said Secretary-General Wu. "But we have employed the most high-tech surveying system available to analyze today's returns. The results show that Fang Li-hsiu has pulled off a great victory, winning by two percentage points!"

Wu congratulated Fang and they toasted his good fortune until 4:30 P.M., when the first wave of actual results appeared on television. I led by tens of thousands of votes, and it was soon clear that the election was a blowout. I didn't receive twice the number of Fang's votes, but I came pretty close. The Nationalist secretary-general slipped quietly away (and was forced by the party to resign). When the final votes were tallied, the sprawling tents of Fang Li-hsiu's headquarters looked like a ghost town. Fang was nowhere to be found.

My return to Taoyuan demonstrates there is such a thing as fate. When I returned from Harvard in 1978 to run for a National Assembly seat, Hsu Hsin-liang had been the Taoyuan Country chief executive. After hearing me give a speech, Hsu had told everyone that I would be his successor. One of his secretaries had even came to my house and asked, "Ms. Lu, do you have a minute?"

"Yes, what do you have in mind?" I asked.

"Picking out wallpaper."

"What?" I gasped in surprise.

"The new official residence of the chief executive has just been completed and Hsu Hsin-liang wants you to pick out the wallpaper. You will be living there eventually."

"Come on," I laughed. "Without winning the election, how can I make myself county chief executive!" That was in 1979. Hsu Hsin-liang was right about my becoming his successor. I was the first opposition politician to follow him as county chief executive, although I never would reside in the chief executive's mansion. Murder investigators had declared it off-limits.

On the eve of my inauguration as Taoyuan County chief executive, the Dalai Lama held a religious service in the Taoyuan Dome. It was His Holiness's first visit to Taiwan and I was invited to see him. I had known the Dalai Lama for years and suggested that he visit Taiwan many times in the past. When he finally did arrive, he turned up in Taoyuan on the eve of my inauguration!

The county certainly needed His Holiness's blessings. When I took office, the country's environmental protection agency had rated Taoyuan the most polluted county in the nation. The defection of a scientist to the United States in the 1980s had led to the abortion of Taiwan's secret nuclear weapons program. Radioactive waste had been dumped into a streambed. Gravel from this polluted stream had been dug up and used to make asphalt to pave downtown Taoyuan. Eight streets in downtown Taoyuan had been paved with radioactive materials!

RCA, the American television manufacturer, had operated a factory in Taoyuan County for years, dumping toxic substances on-site. Chemicals had seeped into the groundwater. Hundreds of people had developed cancer and were sick or dying. A hoof-and-mouth epidemic had broken out among the county's hogs, and thousands of head had to be quarantined and slaughtered.

Garbage, however, presented the worst health crisis. Especially in Chungli, a city of 320,000 people, heaps of garbage lined street corners and alleyways. The stench of half-eaten squid-on-a-stick, mango skins, pineapple rind, and fish carcasses was unbelievable. Chungli was a boomtown for cockroaches, rats, and stray dogs.

A crime syndicate with a monopoly on garbage collection and close ties to the county council left mountains of garbage on the street as a means of extorting money from the government. Taoyuan County was forced to send the garbage, at very high cost, to landfills in other counties. The excuse for this persisting problem had been that local landfills were too full to accept more garbage. Yet nothing was done to build incinerators or to create new landfills. The "emergency handling" of garbage when it piled up uncollected permitted the syndicate to charge higher fees. As a result, the syndicate profited the most when Chungli citizens were the most miserable.

On the day of my inauguration, the director of the Nationalist Party county office ordered the Chungli mayor to stop trash collection. Because I could not command the Chungli sanitation department directly—it is administered at the local level—piles of garbage began to fester on the streets. With the next election eight months away, Nationalist politicians had an interest in demonstrating that I couldn't handle the garbage crisis.

The crime syndicate controlling garbage in the county was well organized and well connected. The Taoyuan County government's environmental protection agency advised me to attempt to dump the garbage in the landfill of the neighboring county of Miaoli because, they said, all the landfills in Taoyuan County were unavailable. However, when the garbage trucks arrived in Miaoli, several vehicles full of protestors blocked the road to the landfill. My aids later told me that the protestors drove trucks from a floral company in Chungli. In other words, either someone in the Taoyuan County government told the garbage cartel in advance or our phones were tapped. The protestors pretended to be from Miaoli, while the locals, it turned out, couldn't have cared less. In my next move, I sent one of my aides to Chiayi County to sign a contract to lease a landfill. When he arrived, the owner of the landfill said, "My apologies, but someone just came from Taoyuan County and bought the landfill from me."

These setbacks and the fear that garbage-covered streets could start an epidemic sent my staff scrambling to find a solution. They knew that if I couldn't remove Chungli's trash, I would have to resign. "Why don't you try the Longtan Township in Taoyuan County?" one of my aides suggested. "Their landfill is in a deep canyon, and the residents there all voted for you." Even assembling garbage truck drivers proved to be difficult because the syndicate had already made threatening phone calls to a number of them.

I spoke to the head of Longtan Township, and he agreed to let me dump the garbage in the landfill, if I didn't admit that he had prior knowledge. "Chief Executive Lu," he said. "I know you're having a rough time. Drive in late at night and everything should be fine."

That night, as the commander in chief of fifty-one garbage trucks, I felt like a cowgirl riding at the head of a stinky wagon train. It was 11:00 P.M. when the first truck approached the mountain village to dump a load of garbage into the landfill. The noise woke residents of the local village, and in minutes they had rushed out in a rage.

I waited until everyone had gathered around before speaking. "I'm sorry that I have disturbed your rest. I had no other choice. If the garbage continued to pile up on the streets, an epidemic could start and an affliction spread from which none of us would be safe. Since you have such a large landfill, I would like to use it on a regular basis. I'm willing to pay generously to do so. I'll maintain your landfill and spray it to cut down on bacteria and the stench."

"With more garbage, it will stink more!" someone shouted. "We've put up with the stink for twenty years!"

"If that's the case, let me fill the landfill up fast and close it so that it won't stink anymore. Otherwise you'll have to live with the stench for another twenty years."

"You lie! All lies!"

"How do you know that I'm lying?"

"All chief executives lie."

"Who did you vote for in the last election?"

"We voted for you."

"If you voted for me, then give me a chance."

"We're already disappointed. We voted for you because the Nationalists had lied to us for too long. We hoped you'd treat us a little better. You just sent us someone else's garbage."

Their words prompted a great surge of pity within me. All that I could do was apologize again and again. Then, for a moment, it was as if I stepped out of my body and could see the whole scene from a distance. The valley of Longtan was green from spring rains, and the lights from farmhouses twinkled brightly. The landfill lay on the edge of a great canyon, with a full moon shining down. Garbage trucks were parked along the roadside with their lights aglow. Villagers, young and old, stood back a few paces from a small woman, a mixture of emotions coloring their faces with anger, doubt, thinly veiled sympathy. "No, I'm not imagining this," I thought. "I am here arguing about garbage in the moonlight."

There were several trucks lined up and full of garbage. I had to get them unloaded; if I returned without dumping them, the Nationalists would never let me hear the end of it. Pretending that I agreed to leave, I had my car slowly pull away from the villagers and go down the mountain. Several of my aides remained behind to keep an eye on the situation at the landfill, while I called the Taoyuan County chief of police. It was already 2:30 A.M.

"Got a little problem here and I need to make a show of force," I said.

When I knew what I must do, I hated myself from the bottom of my heart. I hated that I had to use force against innocent people. After all, I had more experience protesting the use of government coercion than using the powers of government to coerce angry citizens.

Within an hour, the police chief assembled a force of 180 police officers. "Leave your guns behind," I told the officers. "These people haven't done anything wrong. The batons that you carry must not be used. We'll get this garbage dumped without bloodshed! Understand?"

My cell phone rang. It was my lookout at the edge of the canyon. "Most of the villagers have gone home," he said.

"Let's go," I shouted, waving to the police officers.

Dozens of squad cars, with lights flashing blue and red, led the way back up the canyon. The villagers had suspected a trick and blocked the road with cars and a coffin. When I arrived with the cavalry, the villagers were so frightened that they burst into tears and prostrated themselves in the dirt road before me. I pulled them to their feet, but they lay down again screaming and bawling. I gave the police a nod. Four officers stepped forward and lifted each of the villagers away from the road. The garbage trucks moved up the line and dumped their loads. I shook hands with each of the garbage collectors and police officers before going home. It was 7 A.M. when I returned to the apartment I shared with Eldest Sister and turned on the television to watch the news coverage of my handling of Taoyuan's garbage crisis.

Because the township government had refused to accept payment for the garbage, I sent my staff around to every household in Longtan to explain the nature of the county's need to use the township's landfill temporarily. Each household would be paid individually for the garbage we had dumped. And after a series of township meetings, the villagers voted in a referendum to take payment in the future and to allow regular dumping. However, one morning about 11:00 A.M., the head of Longtan Township called me at the office.

"Chief Executive Lu, you're dumping garbage in Longtan and everyone's really upset."

"What do you mean? Longtan had a public referendum, and the villagers supported me."

"But you didn't ask permission from the township chief, the township representatives, and the county councilors. They lost face badly. We're having a meeting right now and we want you to come over. You can't dump garbage without our permission."

"I'll be over immediately."

No one saw me arrive, so I stood in the back of the room listening to the officials rant. "It's a complete mystery," said a township representative. "Our villagers are unbelievable! When the landfill was built twenty years ago, they beat the township chief senseless. In the history of Taiwan's environmental movement, that was the first time people rioted against government policy. I've no idea what Chief Executive Lu did to get them to agree with her. I just don't understand."

"I'll tell you what Chief Executive Lu did," I said, stepping forward. "The chief executives in the past have never respected them. What I did was to hold a public referendum and show them that they had my respect."

A shocked silence filled the room before the officials responded angrily. "How about us? You never asked our opinion. You never gave us your respect. You didn't let us save face. Today you can't dump garbage!"

I knew that if I backed down, I would have more trouble in the future. "The garbage will be dumped today as planned," I said, leaving the meeting.

That afternoon, my secretary called me with urgent news. "Chief Executive Lu," she said, "the speaker of the county council just announced that County Councilor Yeh Fa-hai has committed suicide at the site of the Longtan landfill. He said that Councilor Yeh chose to die rather than allow more dumping of garbage. The speaker declared a recess and has sent the entire Taoyuan County Council to Longtan."

My heart was pounding. What if the fool really had killed himself? On the way I called the county police chief, but he was already on the scene with several officers. Yeh Fa-hai, it turned out, had not committed suicide. Instead, he sat in the road stripped down to the waist. His legs were folded into the lotus position, and he held a broken beer bottle in his hand. Yeh made gestures toward his midriff that suggested a samurai warrior preparing to commit hara-kiri. "I'm going to kill myself! I'm really going to kill myself!" he shouted.

When my black Mercedes Benz approached, the speaker of the county council whispered something into Councilor Yeh's ear. Yeh jumped into the landfill, a short drop, and made a small cut on his arm with the bottle. "Do you see this?" he shouted to me, pointing to the cut. "If you insist on dumping garbage here, I'm going to commit suicide! If you let us save face and don't send police with the trucks, we'll allow you to dump garbage." The speaker of the county council swore Yeh's words were true.

"OK," I said, trying not to laugh. "No dumping today; we'll send the trucks tomorrow."

This compromise avoided further confrontations in Longtan, but different garbage crises took place in the districts of Yangmei, Daxi, and Taoyuan City. Clearly, the construction of a landfill was a necessary first step, with the addition of incineration plants as a long-term solution. I handled Taoyuan County's garbage problems step by step, misadventure by misadventure, town meeting after town meeting.

On my birthday, June 6, I signed a contract to buy a piece of land for the disposal of Chungli's trash. "Do you want a commission?" the landlord asked. "Chief executives in the past always took a commission."

"No, we just want a low price," my aide told him.

"Really? I've never heard of this before. . . ."

"I can assure you that Chief Executive Lu won't take a commission."

"If she doesn't want a commission, we can negotiate price reductions." The man dropped his price by 30 percent.

Later, I insisted that each township and city be responsible for its own landfill and enforced strict regulations on maintenance. The one-company monopoly on garbage collection was dismantled and its business given to several companies. After setting up a build-own-operate (BOO) plan paid for entirely by the private sector, I decided to construct two large incinerators to secure future garbage-processing capability. The first incineration plant, built by the Hsin Yung Enterprise Corporation, utilized state-of-the-art German technology for converting garbage into electricity. Eventually, the plant was so successful that it produced energy for industries and households in the surrounding vicinity, and plans to build a second incineration plant were put on hold. The garbage problem was gone.

The Taoyuan County Council's history resembles a dystopian crime novel. The council speaker was usually the gangster who spent the most money buying the votes of the other councilors, and the deputy speaker was his chief lieutenant. Councilors elected the speaker, and the speaker used his office to manipulate county government policy for financial gain. Kidnapping one's opponents was common, and inviting councilors on trips overseas was a typical means of buying loyalty. Accidents did occur, however, in the vote-buying process. Once, the chief lieutenant proved better at buying votes than his "Big Brother" and won the council speakership. The Big Brother got upset, and evidence of vote buying wound up in the hands of the county prosecutor. The lieutenant went to prison, the Big Brother escaped to China, and over 90 percent of the county council members were indicted on bribery charges. The Nationalist government, hoping to minimize damage to the party's image, leaned on the judicial system to suspend the charges.

My opponent in the second election for chief executive was the county council speaker Chen Gen-de. Unlike my first race for county chief executive when I campaigned for three months, in the second race I campaigned for three weeks. Chen Gen-de knew his chances were slim, so he waged a no-holds-barred campaign. The Nationalist Party spent a huge sum of money televising county council sessions, where councilors leveled preposterous charges against me. The goal was to make me burst into tears, which would look bad on television, or to frighten me so much that I wouldn't even go to the county council. The harder they attacked me, the more fiercely I responded.

On each councilor's desk in the county council sat a telephone, which constituents could use to call in and make comments. When the television coverage of the council session aired, the councilors' phones rang off the hook. "Your comments made no sense at all!" a constituent might say, or, "How can you say that about my county chief executive!" One councilor told me that he had to stop criticizing me because every time he did, he lost fifty votes. The result of the television coverage was the opposite of the Nationalists' intent: I got a lot of free media exposure.

On the day of one scheduled appearance before the county council, I had a terrible head cold with a runny nose, a fever, and a wracking cough. The Nationalist councilors arranged for the temperature in the council chamber to be as low as possible. The room was freezing. Just before I left the house for the county council, my phone rang. "Chief

Executive Lu," an unknown voice said, "wear extra clothes today." The Nationalist foul play had brought new supporters to my camp.

President Lee Teng-hui, the Nationalists' most popular patriarch figure, was the most sought-after speaker for campaign rallies. Standing on stage for a rally at Chen Gen-de's campaign headquarters and looking out at a massive poster of me that I had erected nearby, President Lee mispronounced Chen Gen-de's name. The president's most critical remark was that "if someone only understands foreign affairs, she'll never make a good county chief executive." When the election results came out, I had won by a higher margin than in my first campaign, gaining 55,000 new votes.

A few months after my reelection, I was visiting a Catholic hospital in Taoyuan when I noticed that a clearly agitated man was following me. "What's up?" I asked him.

He looked desperate. "Chief Executive Lu," the man said, "my wife is Hsu Hui-ling, a journalist from the *Liberty Times Newspaper*. She's in the maternity ward about to give birth. My wife was really happy when she heard you were in the hospital. She sent me to ask if you could stop by to see her."

"Hsu Hui-ling—she reports on the Taoyuan County government. It would be my pleasure."

The president of the hospital told me that Hsu Hui-ling was already in the birthing room. "Usually we don't allow anyone inside besides the husband," he said. "But the chief executive is a woman, so we'll make an exception." The maternity ward staff asked me to put on a green hospital robe, gloves, and a hat. "She's been in there for thirty minutes but the baby won't come out," the doctor said.

Hsu Hui-ling was screaming and crying. I reached out and held her hands. She looked really happy when she saw me. Five minutes later, bong, the baby popped right out. A beautiful baby girl! Witnessing her birth was better than the most spectacular sunrise. I felt blessed. The father eagerly picked up his camera; the doctor handed me the baby girl, umbilical cord still attached, and I stood there holding her with tears of joy.

In the daily drama of local politics, I never knew what to expect. On

February 16, 1998, I was at a meeting in Taipei when I received a phone call. "A China Airlines plane has crashed," a reporter told me. "Have you heard?" The reporter didn't know where the plane had crashed, and I didn't know how the tragedy might concern me. I resumed the meeting. Minutes later, I got another phone call: "A China Airlines plane crashed! How come you haven't gone back to Taoyuan?"

"Why should I go back?"

"The crash occurred in Dayuan Township, Taoyuan County, a couple of miles from Chiang Kai-shek Airport."

I sped to the scene of the crash to find the area cloaked in darkness and smoke. The airplane had exploded on impact and knocked out power lines. All of the streetlights were out. We borrowed the front room of a first-floor apartment to set up an emergency command center and brought in generators to power lights and computers. Police, firefighters, and prosecutors arrived while emergency workers briefed me.

The China Airlines Airbus A-300 had crashed at around 8:15 P.M. after returning from Bali, Indonesia. All 202 passengers aboard were killed on impact. Arms, legs, and decapitated bodies littered the roadway where the plane had gone down. Later we learned that many of the bodies had been eviscerated by the impact and become a tangled mess.

I knew families of the deceased would come to the crash site, and I acted fast to make preparations. I told the police to clean up a section of the crash site, and I put emergency workers to the task of erecting a tent in the event of rain. "We should have tables, chairs, and hot ginger tea for the families," I told them. I asked my staff to locate all the coffins in the county. I even made arrangements for the delivery of white flowers, which in Taiwanese culture are displayed during mourning. When the preparations were complete, I asked to meet the victims' families.

"They're all at the Transit Hotel outside the airport," I was informed. "China Airlines hasn't told them that everyone is dead."

At this, I hurried to the hotel, where family members ran around wailing, "Is my brother alive? My husband? Is everyone dead?"

"This isn't right!" I said. "I've got to tell them." I asked the family members to sit down.

"Ladies and gentlemen, I am Taoyuan County chief executive Lu Hsiu-lien. A horrible thing has happened. Please prepare yourself psychologically for what I have to say. I'm not ready to say this but I must. Everyone is dead. Your family members, your friends are gone. The worst has happened. Hopes of a miracle are in vain."

For a moment I thought the screams of grief would shatter windows and bring down the roof. It took several minutes for anyone to regain composure. "I will tell you the truth about the days ahead. They will be unimaginable, but you must find the strength to handle the parting ceremonies for your loved ones."

"We've got to go to the crash site!" people shouted.

"You can't do that now. The crash site is very chaotic. Prosecutors are identifying bodies. Later, I will come back and take you over to look. Now you must comfort each other and quiet the horror and shock in your souls. Each of you has a room in the hotel here. It may be best to go back to your hotel room. If you must weep, then weep. If you must scream, then scream. When you're done, take a rest. Eat something, if you can. I will return to help you face this tragedy."

"We want to know what's happening!"

"If you must, then watch the live television news coverage, but you can't go to the crash site at this time."

When I finished speaking, a middle-aged man approached me. "Chief Executive Lu," he said, "I'm the son of Sheu Yuan-dong, the chairman of the Taiwan Central Bank. My mother and father were both on that plane. I'd like to go early, if possible, to identify their remains, and do what I can to find the remains of my father's senior advisors."

The chairman of the Central Bank in Taiwan had the prominence of a man like Alan Greenspan in the United States. I took the chairman's son along with me in my car. The prosecutors had identified his father but did not find the remains of his mother for twenty-four hours. Eventually, they found one of her arms, identifiable only by a scar from surgery years before.

In the dead of night, several Buddhist groups arrived in Dayuan Township. The police wouldn't let them approach the crash site. I rushed back to negotiate. Buddhists believe that scriptures must be read over the dead so the spirit will depart quickly to heaven and not linger as a ghost. "Let the Buddhists come in," I told the police. "This will calm the families watching the cleanup on television."

The prosecutors cleared off a section of the crash site. Buddhist monks were allowed to light lily flower lamps, pray, and read scriptures. When the tents were erected, and tables and chairs in place, I brought over the families. Fathers and mothers, wives and husbands, grandmothers and grandfathers clung to me weeping. When prosecutors called out the names of the dead, I accompanied family members to identify the bodies.

The China Airlines staff needed comforting, too. "If we try to help, people yell at us," the employees said. "Chief Executive, please help us handle things."

"I can't do everything. I've just about done all that I can. What about these bodies?" I said.

"We'll just leave them here."

"Impossible! There's no refrigeration here, no storage facilities. When the sun comes, up the stench will be unbelievable. You need to get these bodies in mortuaries by dawn." Fortunately, at 4:00 A.M. it started to rain and the temperature dropped. Otherwise, the stench might have been unbearable by dawn.

There was not enough space in the Taoyuan County mortuaries, so the bodies were sent to Taipei County. By 5:00 A.M., refrigerated trucks were shipping the bodies. By 9:00 A.M., workers had removed the bodies from the crash site.

On my way home, I read about the crash in the newspapers. An article in the *China Times* focused on the efforts of Premier Vincent Siew to lead disaster relief and cleanup efforts. One paragraph even described how the premier was directing affairs from the crash site. Reporters who had spent the night in Dayuan with me asked if Premier Siew had really come to Taoyuan County to give assistance. "I'd like to know myself," I said, "because I didn't see the premier once last night."

As soon as I got back home and took a hot shower, the telephone rang. It was one of my personal secretaries. "Chief Executive, the provincial governor James Soong will arrive at the crash site at 3:00 P.M. this afternoon. He has asked that you accompany him."

"There isn't anything to see at the crash site. It has been cleaned up. If he wanted to come, he should have been there in the middle of the night with the rest of us. How is it that when all the hard work is done, he wants to come and express his concern?"

If either the premier or the provincial governor had been present, they could have issued executive orders to bring in additional prosecutors from neighboring counties. This would have reduced the workload for the eleven Taoyuan prosecutors working through the night to record body parts and identify the deceased.

In accordance with Taiwan's Criminal Procedure Law (*xing-shi susong fa*), the county chief executive had powers to assist in criminal investigations. In 1996, however, the national legislature eliminated this authority. Therefore, it wasn't possible for me to participate in the investigation of the murder of my predecessor, Liu Bang-yiu. His case joined other famous political murders in Taiwan that remain unsolved. Instead, I did what I could to improve the morale of the Taoyuan police force by clarifying rules governing rewards (and disciplinary actions) within the force. Police performance improved to the point that they cracked 95 percent of major criminal cases.

Because county government employees had served Nationalists for twenty years, they had an almost instinctive dislike of the Democratic Progressive Party. To break the ice and facilitate collaboration, I made a habit of weekly meetings over coffee with employees from all branches of the county government. In addition, I established a collaborative program with Tamkang University for employees to expand their horizons by attending night classes that led to postgraduate degrees. I also arranged for delegations of county government workers to visit Japan, the United States, and Europe.

As my relations with county employees improved, a transformation took place in the county council. I stated publicly that the days of red-envelope bribery and commissions for construction projects were over: "If you're in politics, don't do business; if you're in business, don't do politics." Then, only half of the county councilors ran for reelection. Nineteen councilors were reelected, but thirty-five new councilors were elected, resulting in a comprehensive "change of blood" that dealt a blow to the culture of corruption. My job as chief executive was getting easier.

In my second term, I had a series of strange encounters that prompted me to consider the role that I would have in the upcoming presidential election. On one occasion, I went to the coastal town of Hualien in eastern Taiwan, where I visited a gallery full of "spirit rocks" and fossils crafted by nature's hands. The man who ran the shop led me off into a separate room with some of his best pieces. For a moment the two of us were alone.

"Could you please tell Mr. Chen Shui-bian that he needs to walk more slowly in order to demonstrate poise and stability," the man said. "He also needs to get dental work done to improve his teeth. Chen Shui-bian will lose when he runs for reelection as Taipei mayor. But he may run for president. Chief Executive Lu, you had better get ready. If you campaign as his vice presidential candidate, you will bring him good fortune, and Chen Shui-bian will win." The man's words set my spine to tingling as they echoed among the stones.

Later, I was traveling in the south of Taiwan when my tour bus stopped briefly at a rest area. I went to wash my hands, and when I emerged from the lavatory, a middle-aged man seated at a low table called out my name. "Chief Executive Lu, wait a minute," he said, tapping on the table emphatically. "Have a cup of tea." The man sat alone brewing "old man's tea" in the traditional style with a small pot and tiny porcelain cups. When he saw that I had paused, he poured tea into two cups. "You've got to get ready for the election," he said.

"I have just finished my second election in a year."

"You have to get ready for the 2000 election," he said. "This time you'll run for vice president."

"We shall see," I said smiling. "Thanks for the tea!"

On the Mid-autumn Festival in 1998, President Lee Teng-hui

invited me to his home in Taoyuan County for dinner. A number of his cronies were there as well, including Premier Vincent Siew, the Nobel Prize–winning physicist Lee Yuan-tseh, and the secretary-general of the president's office, Huang Kun-hui. In front of everyone, President Lee pointed to me and said, "She is the hope of Taiwan. Just look at what she has accomplished in international affairs and in Taoyuan County. Chief Executive Lu, I think you should prepare to run for president or vice president."

President Lee recited a list of my successes while Lee Yuan-tseh looked on in surprise. Taiwan's most famous scholar had been called back from a conference in Indonesia and did not understand why. Lee's compliments continued for half of the evening until Premier Siew, who the president barely mentioned, was green in the face.

Just months after President Lee's dinner invitation, a power struggle broke out within the DPP over who would represent the party in the presidential election. The two front-runners were men to whom I owed a debt of gratitude. Hsu Hsin-liang, the former DPP chair from Taoyuan County, had arranged for me to run for Taoyuan County chief executive without an intraparty primary that I might not have won. Taipei mayor Chen Shui-bian, by far the opposition's most popular figure, had campaigned tirelessly on my behalf prior to both of my elections in Taoyuan. I hoped that Hsu and Chen would work out their differences and campaign on the same ticket.

In March 1999, I was scheduled to visit New York and to attend several events in Washington, DC, including a conference on the twentieth anniversary of the Taiwan Relations Act. This is a US law that articulates the policy of maintaining unofficial relations with Taiwan, mandates the sales of defensive weaponry, and states that a threat to Taiwan's security is a matter of grave concern to the United States.

I had just left home and was on the way to the airport when my personal secretary rang my cell phone. "Chief Executive, Chief Executive," he said excitedly, "Chen Shui-bian wants to meet with you."

"I'm just about to get on the airplane." As members of the DPP's Justice Alliance faction, Chen Shui-bian and I had been on reasonably good terms but had little personal contact. Chen had never asked to meet with me privately before. "What does he want to discuss?"

"I don't know. Chen Shui-bian says he wants to chat."

"I'll meet with him after I return from the United States," I said, assuming that Chen wanted to talk about his dispute with Hsu Hsin-liang.

At the panel discussion hosted by the Heritage Foundation, a scholar stuck up his hand and said, "Ms. Lu, what is this we hear about you preparing to run for vice president?"

"A rumor that I haven't heard!"

When I met with Richard Bush, formerly a national intelligence officer for East Asia and at this point the head of the American Institute in Taiwan, he said, "We've heard that you'll be Chen Shui-bian's vice presidential candidate if he wins the party nomination."

"No kidding? It's news to me." But I began to wonder if Richard Bush had better sources of information on Taiwan politics than I did.

In New York, several of the ambassadors representing Taiwan's diplomatic allies in the United Nations asked about my participation in the election. "If you ran for president," one said, "it would be great for Taiwan in international affairs. You should give it some serious thought." With all this fuss about a presidential race to which I had given little thought, I decided that maybe it was time to start playing along. At the UN Plaza Hotel I held a press conference where I announced that I would not be absent from the lineup in the presidential election.

The day after I arrived back in Taipei, it was Chen Shui-bian's turn to go overseas on a trip to South Korea and Mongolia. "We'll speak when he comes back," I told his staff.

When Chen returned, he asked me to meet him at a private club in the Far East Plaza Hotel. Our conversation was casual and polite. We chatted about international affairs and the current state of US-Taiwan relations. Chen Shui-bian told me that he planned to go to Washington, DC, so I assumed he wanted to seek my advice on foreign affairs.

"What do you think about the presidential election?" he asked.

"I think the DPP is too divided by internal conflict. You and Hsu Hsin-liang should find a way to run on the same ticket. If there's anything I can do, please let me know. I'm grateful to both of you for assistance in the past."

"Do you think it's possible?" he said.

"Why not?"

"The situation is too complicated. It wouldn't work." I could tell that he wasn't considering a rapprochement with Hsu.

"The conflict is bad for the party's image," I said. "I would be happy to speak to Hsu Hsin-liang on your behalf." Chen Shui-bian did not reply. He seemed to want to change the subject.

"I'm not really ready to run for president," he said. "But after losing the Taipei mayoral election to Ma Ying-jeou, I am out of a job. On top of it all, I'm not even certain that I could win the DPP nomination. If I can work out the dispute with Hsu Hsin-liang and I become the presidential candidate, would you join me as the vice presidential candidate?"

"Why me?" I asked, recalling Richard Bush's surprising query.

"My wife supports you. You are one of the Kaohsiung Eight and senior to me. You have a good record in international affairs. You've worked as a legislator, a presidential advisor. You served with distinction as the Taoyuan County chief executive. Besides, I'm from the south, and you are from the north. I'm a man and you are a woman. Women voters support you."

"Lots of other people could run with you," I said.

"Like who?"

"Tainan County chief executive Chen Tang-shan or Legislator Yeh Chu-lan." I suggested several prospects and he rejected them all. Chen's manner was polite, even deferential.

"Lu Hsiu-lien," Chen said, "I feel bad even suggesting that you join me as vice presidential candidate, because you are more senior in the opposition movement. But please consider it."

By summer, the Democratic Progressive Party had nominated Chen Shui-bian as its presidential candidate. Hsu Hsin-liang, realizing that his defeat was imminent, quit the DPP to run as an independent. The same regulation that led to my defeat as vice presidential candidate in 1995 now meant that Chen Shui-bian could choose me as his running mate without a party primary. But there were some DPP faction leaders who didn't support my candidacy. They advised Chen to choose a running mate from outside the party, and a debate ensued over who should be the vice presidential candidate.

The logic behind the DPP faction leaders' pushing Chen to run with an outsider was simple. They thought there was little chance that Chen would win the race and hoped that his political career would end in defeat; then, with no rising star to lead the party, they could secure the presidential nomination for the next election. On the other hand, if Chen picked me, even if we lost the election, my political stature would grow and I might become a rival in future power struggles.

Not surprisingly, Chen saw things differently. With me as his running mate, his chances of winning the presidential race increased. After Chen's defeat in the Taipei mayoral race, the presidential campaign was the ultimate test of Chen Shui-bian's political fortunes, an all-or-nothing struggle in which he sought to mobilize the strongest possible team.

On July 9, 1999, Chen Shui-bian officially received the DPP nomination. A week later, I accepted Chen Shui-bian's invitation and promised to keep my commitment a secret. He wanted to delay the announcement of our candidacy until he had visited every county and village in Taiwan and had the opportunity to allay the fears of DPP elders. Meanwhile, media pressure to announce whether we would run together continued to mount.

The Nationalists' candidate, Vice President Lien Chan, had already announced that he would run with Premier Vincent Siew as his running mate. The front-runner in the presidential race, former Nationalist provincial governor James Soong, had sent several emissaries to see me as well, to test the waters for possible cooperation. The head of the Legislative Yuan, Liu Song-fan, even told journalists publicly that I was James Soong's best choice for a vice presidential candidate.

Chen Shui-bian had hoped to announce our joint candidacy on September 19 at a major DPP rally in Taoyuan. However, I suggested waiting until I came back from a trip to Qatar and France. "Who should I choose as vice presidential candidate?" he asked a crowd of 100,000 supporters at the rally.

"Lu Hsiu-lien!" the crowd shouted.

"Who?"

"Lu Hsiu-lien!"

Secret opinion polls conducted by the DPP and Chen's campaign showed that I was the running mate that most elevated his popular support. Chen and I made plans to formally announce our candidacy shortly thereafter.

After the Taoyuan rally, I led a delegation to the oil-producing country of Qatar. The president of Exxon Mobil Corporation had invited me to visit a liquid natural gas plant there that was similar to one that Mobil wanted to construct in Taoyuan County. At a banquet hosted by the crown prince, an aide rushed in with horrible news.

In the early morning hours on September 21, the country's largest earthquake in history hit the center of the island. Hundreds of people had been killed instantly. An international disaster relief effort was being launched. I told my host and my delegation that I would return to Taiwan at once. By the time my plane touched down in Taoyuan County's Chiang Kai-shek International Airport, the death total had risen to over 2,000.

Within one week, I raised the equivalent of one million US dollars to aid the thousands of Taiwanese whose homes had been crushed, by encouraging officials in the county government to donate one day's salary. In the disaster area, thousands of people lived in hastily erected tents; hundreds of children were made orphans overnight. In the midst of such tragedy, partisan politics seemed irrelevant. Chen Shui-bian rightly decided to downplay the upcoming presidential race, while the Nationalist central government struggled to enact disaster relief legislation. The formal announcement of our candidacy was put on hold.

In the days that followed, international organizations helped to free people trapped under buildings and to feed and house those whose homes lay in ruins. Taiwanese from around the world donated funds to assist relief efforts. Only China played politics as usual by insisting that relief funds pass through the Chinese representatives in the United Nations rather than going directly to Taiwan. Beijing even denied Russian relief workers the right to fly through Chinese airspace on route to Taiwan.

It was not until November that campaigning resumed, with the announcement by Nationalist-maverick-turned-independent James Soong that his running mate would be Chang Chao-hsiung, the dean of a university in southern Taiwan. At this, Chen Shui-bian grew eager to release the identity of his vice presidential candidate, but I asked him to wait until the Taoyuan County Council went into recess in December. I still had to handle matters in Taoyuan County, and at word of my candidacy, the Nationalist county councilors would call for my resignation. Chen Shui-bian and I decided to announce our joint candidacy in December.

CHAPTER 10

THE GLORIOUS REVOLUTION

ON DECEMBER 10, 1999, TWENTY YEARS TO THE DAY SINCE THE *Formosa* Incident, two decades since the night of tear gas and strife, Chen Shui-bian and I shared the stage in a much different venue. With several hundred of Taiwan's most famous women and political leaders, we gathered in a ballroom at the Grand Hyatt Taipei for an event celebrating the transformation in Taiwan politics that gave us the opportunity to compete for the country's highest office. The glittering ballroom and the banquet-style tables of the hotel to me symbolized the transition that we hoped would take place with our election, to complete the change from nascent opposition to ruling party, to move from the street protests of twenty years ago toward the consolidation of democracy.

With Chen Shui-bian's position already well established, the event focused on me and the historic significance of the election. In preparing my speech that evening, I remembered the words a former political prisoner had told me following my release from prison: "I served fifteen years for an essay I wrote in college," the man had said. "The government released me in time for the Kaohsiung Incident, where I heard you speak to the people at the rally. You said everything I've wanted to say my whole life and served less than six years in prison!"

It was a personal goal not to disappoint such comrades on accepting Chen Shui-bian's offer to run for vice president:

It was twenty years ago that I faced court martial on charges of sedition and Chen Shui-bian served as one of the defense attorneys for those of us on trial. Today, I am honored that Mr. Chen has invited me to be his running mate in the election for Taiwan's president and vice president. Far more than joy, I feel a sense of deep gratitude, gratitude toward all those in my party who have gone before me, and gratitude toward Chen Shui-bian for his confidence in me. In accepting this invitation, I pledge to throw my whole heart and mind into working with Chen Shui-bian. With his election as president we will not only win a sacred battle for democracy but throw open the doors to a new era for Taiwan.

Every election has its historical significance. This year, in September's earthquake, Taiwan experienced the worst natural disaster to hit our country in living memory. Bitter rivalries within the Nationalists between the camps of Vice President Lien Chan and former provincial governor James Soong added political turmoil to natural disaster. Facing political turmoil and natural disaster, the Taiwanese people must realize the historical significance of the 2000 presidential election.

This historical significance is to put an end to political rule imposed from outside; it is to return political power to the people of Taiwan. Taiwan has been ruthlessly ruled by a succession of foreign regimes: the Dutch, the Spanish, the Manchus of the Qing dynasty, the Japanese, and the Nationalists. Only by voting into office the Democratic Progressive Party, a party born and nurtured in Taiwan, will democracy be realized in our nation. Only then will the people of Taiwan become masters of their home.

The historic mission of this presidential election is to put an end to the politics and dirty money; it is to return power and resources to the people. For fifty years now, the Nationalist Party has created for itself a system of special privileges and monopolized control over the country's resources. Rampant corruption, vote buying, and collusion have characterized Nationalist rule. Only with the removal of the Nationalists from power can we eliminate the politics of corruption and dirty money that have so long burdened our shoulders.

The presidential election is to put an end to the old order of incompetent bureaucratic rule; it is to create a new progressive government to lead Taiwan into the twenty-first century. By insisting that it represented the whole of China, the Nationalist Party lost Taiwan's seat in the United Nations and in other international organizations. The "one China" policy left Taiwan mired in the mud of diplomatic isolation, unable to participate in world affairs in the manner it deserves. In recent years public safety has declined, the state's financial situation has deteriorated, and human error has spawned environmental disasters. Only by removing the old order of bureaucrats—only by bringing in fresh leaders with vision and energy—can we create the bright future Taiwan deserves.

This presidential election is to put an end to the enmity between the Nationalists and the Chinese Communist Party; it is to build lasting peace between Taiwan and China. The hostility and military tension between China and Taiwan is a relic of the Chinese Civil War between the Nationalists and the Communists. Only when the Nationalist Party is removed from power will China realize that Taiwan belongs to Taiwanese. Only then can Taiwan and China forge peaceful coexistence and foster a special relationship as distant relatives and close neighbors.

This presidential election is to put an end to government solely by men; it is to usher in an era of gender equality in which women and men administer national affairs together. Throughout history . . . the half of our population that is female has been ruled by men and denied a voice in many of the decisions that affect their lives and well-being. Government has traditionally been of men, by men, for men. By electing Chen Shui-bian and me, Taiwan can move toward real gender equality in society and politics. We can create a government of women, by women, and for women—side by side with men. . . .

Two weeks before the announcement of our candidacy, a television station put together a very special program. Each member of the *Formosa Magazine* group was asked to return to the old *Formosa* headquarters in Taipei to film a retrospective looking back at the twenty years since the magazine led the Dangwai movement. The weather that day was grim and overcast. By the time I arrived at the old office on Jenai Road, a cold rain had begun to fall. I showed up first and sat waiting in my official limousine. Soon, the Dangwai patriarch Huang Hsin-chieh arrived, and I got out of the car to greet him. Huang looked old and frail but he had come despite deteriorating health, to show solidarity on this historic occasion. As the rest of our opposition comrades arrived, I marveled at how much we had changed over the years. My old comrades had come to represent a "who's who" of opposition politicians. Lin Yi-hsiung, whose twin daughters and mother had been murdered during the *Formosa* trial, was the chairman of the Democratic Progressive Party and a key strategist in the Chen-Lu campaign. Chen Chu, my cell mate for nearly five years, was serving as social affairs director for the City of Kaohsiung. While we had a special bond, Chen Chu and I had drifted apart over the years. Yao Chia-wen, the man who had resisted my entry into the Dangwai ranks, had become a legislator and a great source of assistance to me on numerous occasions. His black hair gone white, Yao still had the warm smile of his youth. Chang Chun-hung, once depicted in a cartoon as the bellowing lungs of the Dangwai for his skill as an orator, joined his former comrades but had little to say. Chang had recently lost to Lin Yi-hsiung in the election for party chair. Hsu Hsin-liang, the former DPP chairman and Taoyuan County chief executive, showed up too. Hsu had left the DPP after losing out to Chen Shui-bian for the presidential nomination and was running for president with a New Party supporter of unification with China. Ideologically, Hsu had changed most since the early days of the opposition. He had sent his son to Peking University and advocated expanded trade ties to improve relations with China. Having gone bald, Hsu shaved his head and declared himself a devout Buddhist.

The only one of us missing was Shih Ming-teh. Taiwan's former Errol Flynn character who had served nearly twenty-five years in prison. He overslept that morning and everyone waited for him in the drizzle. A member of my staff finally contacted Shih at home to wake him up; an hour later, the ever dapper Shih arrived looking disheveled and chagrined at the inconvenience he had caused.

The interviews were uneventful, but I could see that waiting outside in the cold had taken its toll on elderly Huang Hsin-chieh. That night, after going south to participate in election activities in Kaohsiung, I learned that Huang had checked into Taiwan National University Hospital, and I went to see him immediately. He was nearly in a coma, but when he saw me, his eyes lit up for an instant. Huang Hsin-chieh couldn't speak, so I just held his hand and smiled, realizing that I might never see him again. He had meant so much to me over the years. From the early days, when I hosted fund-raisers for women's crisis clinics in Taipei, Huang Hsin-chieh had bought tickets, purchased my books, and attended events to lend support. In 1978, after my return from the United States, Huang had been the only major Dangwai politician who believed in me. When DPP leaders had opposed Chen Shui-bian's selection of me as his running mate, Huang had announced publicly, "There is no one more suitable to run with Chen than Lu Hsiu-lien. I'm willing to burn out my old life in support of their campaign." Dozens of reporters were waiting outside Huang's hospital room when I walked out. At the sight of the TV cameras and journalists, I burst into tears, knowing he would not be with us long.

Huang Hsin-chieh's death on November 30 of a coronary thrombosis shortly after his hospitalization was a blow to the Chen-Lu campaign and to the supporters of the Democratic Progressive Party. He had been the one individual who could unite rival factions within the party. He had been a teacher-father figure for a generation of politicians who took inspiration from his courage during martial law. Huang had survived as a Taipei city councilor by virtue of his popularity, and then later in the Legislative Yuan, he had used the legal immunities of that office to shield Dangwai activities. Serving as Huang Hsin-chieh's defense lawyer in the *Formosa* trial was Chen Shui-bian's entrée into opposition politics. "Ah Bian," as he was often called, would never have existed as a political figure without Huang Hsin-chieh. On the night of the Kaohsiung Incident, as always, Huang had played the role of peacemaker. Huang negotiated with the authorities, even trying to halt the demonstration when conflict appeared imminent. Within the DPP, Huang made his final appearance as peacemaker by trying to smooth over differences between Chen Shui-bian and Hsu Hsin-liang to preserve party unity. At a time when factionalism had riven party unity, the peacemaker had finally found peace and his protégés had inherited the responsibility to bring peace among themselves.

With the announcement of me as Chen Shui-bian's running mate in the presidential election, Ah Bian's standing in the polls shot up several percentage points, surpassing for the first time the popularity of his rival, James Soong. The difference in Chen's attractiveness to voters with me on board was considerable. Every poll ranked me as the voters' number-one choice among vice presidential candidates, the primary reasons being my attractiveness to women voters, young supporters of improving Taiwan's image abroad, and older voters who remembered my contributions to the democracy movement.

It was a strange coincidence that the background of our main competitor, James Soong, who served for years as a Nationalist leader, was nearly opposite to that of Ah Bian and me. While I stood trial for sedition in 1980 and Chen served as defense attorney, Soong had been the director of the Government Information Office and had held press conferences to convince the world that the Dangwai were a vicious element. He had presided over a bureaucracy that discouraged speaking the Taiwanese language, a restriction against which I had fought.

Yet Soong's image in the minds of many Taiwanese was that of a clean politician who had fallen out of favor with the Nationalist mainstream led by Lee Teng-hui. They saw Soong as a loyal general who cared for the people and had been aggrieved by those he faithfully served. A mainlander, Soong had been close to Chiang Ching-kuo; after Chiang's death Soong threw his weight behind Lee Teng-hui, when the Chiang family had strong reservations about devolving power to a native Taiwanese. After Lee Teng-hui consolidated his power as president in the early 1990s, the two men had a close relationship. Many people assumed that Lee owed Soong a debt for his early support of Lee's presidency. In 1994, Lee nominated Soong to run for provincial governor, at the time the highest elected office in the land; amid allegations of widespread vote buying, Soong beat his DPP rival Chen Ting-nan by a large margin.

But in 1996, in anticipation of the transition of Hong Kong to Chinese rule, the DPP pushed the Nationalists to eliminate the provincial government, to demonstrate that Taiwan was not a province of China and that the "one country, two systems" model that Beijing proposed to unify Hong Kong and China would be unacceptable for Taipei. Additional reasons to eliminate or downsize the provincial government abounded. The constituency of the president and the provincial governor were nearly the same, presenting the possibility that a dangerous rivalry could emerge. Part of the legacy of Chiang Kai-shek's old government, which was designed for ruling China, the provincial government was slow, expensive, inefficient, and corrupt. The Nationalists had little choice but to bow to popular demands for downsizing that eliminated the entire provincial government. James Soong, as the first and only popularly elected provincial governor, saw the move to dismantle his government as a personal attack. Soong resigned from his post on the Nationalist Party Central Standing Committee and held tearful press conferences criticizing party policies. In the 2000 election, Soong knew that he had little chance of winning the Nationalist presidential nomination and maneuvered to run as an independent. The party expelled Soong from the party for running against the officially nominated candidates, Vice President Lien Chan and Premier Vincent Siew; James Soong became the front-runner, according to nearly all opinion polls.

In late November, one of Ah Bian's key strategists, Chiu Yi-jen, received a black file highlighting investments in the Taiwanese stock market by James Soong's son, then a recent college graduate. Estimates of the amount invested approached US$30 million. Unable to locate proof of the transactions, Chiu Yi-jen resisted releasing the information to the press. On December 9, Nationalist legislator Yang Chi-hsiung held a press conference at which he asked how James Soong's son could have acquired such a large sum by honest means. The imbroglio that followed, known as the Xingpiao investment case, changed the outcome of the presidential election.

At first, Soong's reaction to media's queries was to deny any allegations. In subsequent press conferences, however, Soong admitted he had received the funds from an "elder" in the Nationalist Party. Later, he claimed that Lee Teng-hui had given him the funds to take care of Chiang Ching-kuo's widow and to pay for party activities, a charge that Lee Teng-hui vehemently denied. Explaining how these funds ended up invested on the stock market under his son's name proved more difficult. The Nationalists threatened to take legal action to retrieve the party's misappropriated funds. Soong's popularity nose-dived. The decline in Soong's political fortunes did not, as some DPP feared, lead to a spike in support for the Nationalist candidate, Vice President Lien Chan. Instead, with two months remaining before the election, Chen Shui-bian and I took the lead.

Lien Chan had a PhD from the University of Chicago and was the heir to a vast family fortune. Born in Xian, China, in the 1940s, he never developed a feel for Taiwan's common people. After serving as both premier and vice president under Lee Teng-hui, Lien Chan had resigned from the former post after massive demonstrations criticized his handling of high-profile crime cases. In the presidential race, Lien's vice presidential candidate was Vincent Siew, his successor as premier in the Lee Teng-hui administration. The Lien-Siew campaign had real advantages. It had tremendous financial resources. As the sitting vice president, Lien had opportunities to look "presidential," greeting foreign dignitaries, making policy proclamations, and handling disaster relief following the September 21 quake.

Chen Shui-bian and I offered a new alternative to five decades of Nationalist rule. DPP legislators and county and city administrators were known to be less corrupt than their Nationalist counterparts. In addition, Ah Bian and I had played a key role in Taiwan's democratization; we had both suffered to change Taiwan through democratic means.

Chen's wife, Wu Shu-chen, was the symbol of his sacrifice. She had been run down by a truck after Chen Shui-bian's unsuccessful campaign for Tainan County chief executive, in what many people believe was a politically motivated act. She had been in a wheelchair since, while remaining her husband's trusted advisor. My own imprisonment and the cause of Mother's death were known to many, but the fact that I was a woman and had foreign affairs expertise and experience in local government were additional selling points. Perhaps equally important, my roots were in northern Taiwan and Chen's were in the south, giving our candidacy national appeal.

To emphasize our compatibility, and to soften Ah Bian's image a bit, I took the middle character of Chen Shui-bian's name meaning "water" and put it together with the Chinese character in my name meaning "lily," naming our political supporters the "Water-Lily Association." Our campaign slogan, *shui xing taiping, lian kai sheng shi*, was another of my creations: "With water there is happiness and great peace; when the lily blossoms, the nation prospers." Water in this case symbolizes life and purity, and the lily represents beauty and dignity rising from muddy soil.

The disadvantage we faced was the checkered legacy of the DPP. In the minds of moderate voters, the DPP had been overly violent in the early days of Taiwan's democratization, when fisticuffs in the legislature were as common as meaningful debate. Although most county- and city-level governments were run by DPP administrators, voters worried that a DPP presidency would fuel tensions with China.

Beijing made no secret that it hoped a non-independence-leaning candidate would win. Thus, James Soong and Lien Chan attempted to convince voters that a vote for the DPP would push the country down the slippery slope toward war with China. Their campaign advertisements emphasized Chen Shui-bian's ties to the independence movement, although his position on unification and independence had in fact moderated with the announcement of his "New Middle Path." The idea of a New Middle Path was designed to appeal to moderate voters who disapproved of the DPP's advocacy of de jure independence. It proposed flexibility on the question of unification.

In stump speeches around the island, I placed the New Middle Path in historical context. Taiwan's tension with China results from the legacy of the Chinese Civil War between the Nationalists and the Chinese Communists. Chiang Kai-shek's retreat from the mainland transported this conflict to Taiwan. If Chiang had surrendered in China, Taiwan would have sought autonomy and the current impasse wouldn't exist. If Chiang had retreated to Burma, he might have stayed there, formed a base for his government to the southeast of China, or been defeated. But Chiang came to Taiwan. As two individuals with ties to the Nationalist Party and to this conflict, Lien Chan and James Soong could not offer a fresh start with China. Their victory would prolong five decades of animosity. If the DPP won, the historic conflict between the Nationalist Party and the Chinese Communist Party could come to an end. Chen and I hoped to mediate Taiwan's domestic differences from the middle of the spectrum on Taiwan's sovereignty and thereby have the credibility to truly represent Taiwan's interests in new dialogue with China.

The sheer work of running a national campaign, even in a country the size of Taiwan, was unbelievable. The campaign headquarters focused on grand strategy and electioneering; the local headquarters helped to schedule events, spread the word of campaign activities, and mobilize volunteers. There were activities every day and political rallies at night all across the island. My single-day record was eighteen speeches in five different cities and counties. I went from Taipei County up to Keelung, down to Taichung, Nantou, and Chiayi, from the north to the south of the island. During the course of the campaign, I lost my voice repeatedly and had to scale back my activities. I lost six kilograms and my tailor had to sew new outfits.

One rainy morning in Taipei County, I stood for hours waving at local residents from the back of a campaign truck. Although I wore rain gear, I got soaked whenever I lifted my arm to wave to the crowds. That afternoon I flew south to speak at rallies in Chiayi and Kaohsiung. By nightfall, I was horribly ill with a high fever. I checked into National Taiwan University Hospital, where I spent a couple of hours on a bed of ice packs to reduce my body temperature. The following day, the doctors removed the intravenous needle from my arm so that I could keep a lunchtime speaking engagement. Two hours later, I checked back into the hospital, and later, despite a phone call from Chen Shui-bian urging me to rest, I attended evening campaign rallies as usual. I didn't want to miss anything.

During the final weeks of the campaign, tension among the competing candidates reached an unprecedented level of intensity. The Nationalists could see that the survival of their regime, if not the party itself, was at stake. Lien Chan denied that the Nationalist Party's wealth gave him an unfair advantage and announced the party would henceforth place its assets in a trust fund. The support Lien had hoped to win went instead to James Soong's camp, as Soong portrayed himself as a capable reformer and Nationalist outsider loyal to the party legacy. In February, however, the discovery that James Soong's twenty-nine-year-old son owned five houses in the United States damaged Soong's ability to portray himself as clean.

Chen Shui-bian's strategists sought to make Ah Bian appear friendly and approachable. They sold cartoon-like Ah Bian dolls, Ah Bian hats, and trinkets for children that flashed and glowed. The intended effect was to make Chen seem cute, personable, and safe. I didn't approve of this transformation of Chen Shui-bian into an adorable commodity, but it was an innovative way of giving people the means to show their support.

Out on the campaign trail, I got a different perspective than the strategists did from their air-conditioned conference rooms. I sensed the time had come to take the kid gloves off and knock our opponents down for the count. The moment to make people realize the historic importance of their vote had arrived. I reminded voters that in the United States, people who are not born in the country cannot run for the office of president. "Neither Lien Chan nor James Soong was born in Taiwan," I said. "Their children are US citizens. If their children don't want the ROC nationality, what does this say about the loyalty of the Lien and Soong families to Taiwan? What does this say about their confidence in the future of this beautiful and treasured island? A vote for Lien or Soong is a vote to make the 'father of Americans' your president." I emphasized James Soong's role as the director of the Government Information Office during the *Formosa* trial, and I told him to apologize for restricting the use of Taiwanese, Hakka, and aboriginal languages. I also assembled a team of experts to analyze pork barrel spending during Soong's tenure as provincial governor.

Mobilizing women voters was another key strategy. On March 8, ten days before people went to the polls, we chartered an entire train and took 2,000 prominent women on a one-day tour of the island beginning in Taipei and traveling to Taichung, in the center of the island, and to Kaohsiung in the south. At each stop, we disembarked and joined a rally with cheering supporters. Each car of the train featured workshops on a topic pertaining to women, with twelve different topics in the twelve different cars. Media, riding along on the train with us, broadcast the event live on radio and television. The reaction among women who attended the events was inspiring. I saw clearly that women were playing an influential role in national politics.

The narrowing of the gap between the Soong camp and ours made ethnicity and the DPP's anticorruption stance key issues. Soong is a mainlander. His pronunciation when speaking in standard Chinese reminds older generations of Nationalist repression and the era when mainlanders denigrated Taiwanese culture. People saw the election as a contest between Taiwan's former oppressors and the Taiwanese who fought to make Taiwan free; votes tended to split along ethnic lines. Mainlanders were James Soong's core supporters, and ours were Taiwanese. This was especially true in southern Taiwan. In Tainan and Kaohsiung there are fewer mainlanders, and identification with Taiwan as a nation runs deep. Mainlanders supported James Soong based on the calculation that, if elected, he would protect their interests.

With a history of fighting organized crime, illegal gambling, prostitution, and corruption, Ah Bian and I had credibility as reformers that Soong and Lien couldn't match. Our commitment to rule of law, free and fair economic activity, and internationalizing Taiwan's economy appealed to the business community. Proof of this emerged in the number of prominent business leaders that publicly supported us, including the head of the Evergreen Shipping Group, Chang Jung-fa; the high-tech tycoon Hsu Wen-lung; and the head of the Acer computer corporation, Stanley Shih.

It was not seen as coincidence that Chang Jung-fa, Hsu Wen-lung, and the Nobel Prize–winning chemist and president of Academia Sinica, Lee Yuan-tseh, were close advisors and associates of President Lee Teng-hui. Although President Lee ostensibly supported

Lien Chan, many Taiwanese believed Chen-Lu, and not the Lien-Siew team, were Lee Teng-hui's preferred successors.

Nobel Prize winner Lee Yuan-tseh's support had a huge influence on our fortunes. Without question, Lee Yuan-tseh is Taiwan's most respected academic figure, revered even more because he had eschewed politics in the past. After a series of private meetings, Lee Yuan-tseh accepted an offer to head a national political advisory committee if we won the election. To demonstrate his commitment, Lee Yuan-tseh declared his intent to resign as president of Academia Sinica, Taiwan's most prestigious research institution, "so as not to bring any inconvenience" to his colleagues.

It is illegal in Taiwan to release the results of opinion polls during the last ten days of the campaign. In truth, each of the candidate's camps conducted secret polls, and spies in each campaign made this information available. Every night Chen Shui-bian and I discussed the events of the day, and he showed me poll results suggesting we held the edge in the secret polls. We sensed that after years of struggle our "glorious revolution" was at hand.

The yawning gap between the number of people attending our political rallies and those who attended the rallies of Soong and Lien confirmed that we were pulling away. At a huge rally in Taichung a week before the election, an estimated 350,000 people turned out to cheer us on. Then, with the cresting wave of popular support behind us, two major crises occurred.

On Monday, March 13, the Taiwan stock market took a record one-day nosedive, losing 7 percent of its value. Some analysts accused the Nationalists of orchestrating a massive sell-off to frighten voters who intended to vote for the Chen-Lu ticket. Each campaign headquarters put its own political spin on the stock market crash. The Soong camp blamed the lack of investor confidence in the Nationalist government, saying, "This shows the Nationalist Party's credibility is bankrupt and that President Lee Teng-hui's administration is out of touch with public sentiment." Lien Chan retorted that "everyone knows who is endangering national stability and development," implying that a DPP victory would lead to financial ruin. Our official position was that "the Nationalist Party is sacrificing investors' interests to win votes." The central government, under pressure to remain nonpartisan, was forced to intervene to shield the market from further shocks.

On March 15, three days before the polls opened, Chinese premier Zhu Rongji warned Taiwanese voters not to elect the "wrong candidate." "Let me advise all these people in Taiwan," Zhu said in a threatening tone, "not to act on impulse at this juncture, which will decide the future course that China and Taiwan will follow. Otherwise I am afraid you won't get another opportunity to regret [the choice]." In effect, Zhu Rongji was telling the Taiwanese not to vote for the Chen-Lu ticket; if they did, they might never have the chance to elect their leaders again.

By pointing his finger directly at the TV cameras, Zhu seemed to be directing his threat at every household in Taiwan. "We believe in the political wisdom of the people of Taiwan," Zhu said, "and we trust that our Taiwan compatriots will make the right historical choice."

Zhu Rongji's remarks, like the lobbing of missiles into the Taiwan Strait in the prior presidential election, had a pronounced impact on Taiwanese voters. Most Taiwanese had two reactions: strong resentment of Chinese intervention in Taiwanese politics, and genuine concern that relations with China would worsen if Ah Bian and I won the presidential palace. Among people who abhorred Beijing's attempt to intervene in the election, Zhu's remarks backfired; their resentment crystallized support for our candidacy. For those voters who feared tensions with China more than they cared about ending corrupt government, James Soong appeared the better choice because he was a mainlander and favored unification, a plus for improving ties with China. Either way, votes that might have gone to Lien Chan were split between these two positions in roughly even numbers. The Chinese Communists had certainly confirmed the sense that the election was historic and absolutely crucial.

In a final DPP rally at the Zhongshan Soccer Stadium in Taipei, the enthusiasm of our supporters reached a fever pitch. The stadium was packed, from the athletic field to the grandstands. Halfway through the program there were so many folks present that dozens stood craning their necks in the stairwells to catch a glimpse of the stage. It was nearly impossible to get inside the stadium; tens of thousands of flag-waving supporters milled around outside, watching the speeches on large movie screens. Never in Taiwan had so much seemed to be at stake or had the opportunity of real change appeared so close at hand.

When my turn came to speak at the rally, thousands screamed, "Elect Lu Hsiu-lien! Elect Chen Shui-bian! Elect Lu Hsiu-lien!" My message was one of history. It was to retell the story of my sacrifice and the sacrifices that so many others had made to make this moment possible. People who were living testament to the truth of my words stood with me on the stage: Yao Chia-wen, Chang Chun-hung, Peng Min-ming, Lin Yi-hsiung, and others who had fought for Taiwan's democratization. Even Shih Ming-teh cheered us on.

On China's attempt to coerce Taiwanese voters, I pulled no punches: Zhu Rongji's threat had revealed Beijing's "one country, two systems" model for unifying China and Taiwan to be utterly false. How could such a system be possible, with political autonomy for Taiwan, if China sought to force the Taiwanese to accede to its wishes? Zhu Rongji had shown that Beijing really sought "one country, one system," under Communist Party rule.

"Zhu Rongji was the world's ugliest man when he threatened Taiwan's democracy," I said, referring to his mottled complexion and finger-pointing antics. "We don't need to glare across the Straits at one another. We can use sweet and intimate language to reduce the tension between the sides. But Zhu Rongji was right about one thing: he was right to believe in the wisdom of the people of Taiwan and to trust that they will make the right historic choice. I share this belief and this trust. Tomorrow marks the beginning of a glorious revolution."

Taiwan is a small country. Sometimes it seems like a single-celled organism that reacts to an event that affects it powerfully, whether this be a disaster such as the September 21 earthquake or the 2000 presidential campaign. There is a definite social contagion. The intensity of our supporters and their fierce determination to vote for change proved infectious. A sense of excitement in the election's final days brought many undecided voters into our camp.

On the eve of the election, I returned to the apartment that I had shared with Eldest Sister since her husband had passed away. Strangely, I felt relaxed and empty of worry and anxiety. In the morning, I awoke early to vote at a polling station near my home in Taoyuan County. Mid morning, I went to the campaign headquarters in Taipei, where I joined other staff members waiting for the results. By early afternoon the tallies indicated the race was close, but returns consistently showed that Chen Shui-bien and I were the front-runners. By early evening, the results were confirmed, and James Soong and Lien Chan held rallies to concede defeat.

With the highest rate of voter turnout ever recorded, 82 percent of Taiwanese voters had given Ah Bian and me victory by a narrow margin. With 39.3 percent of the popular vote, we beat James Soong by just 2 percent. He won many northern counties but fell far behind in the southern heartland. The difference was just over 310,000 votes. Lien Chan finished with an embarrassing 23 percent.

Our advisors held a series of hurried conferences to prepare our response to Taiwanese voters, the international community, and the host of international media assembled. Our statement had to reflect the gravity of our responsibility and the need to reach out to foster unity in a polarized electorate. It was decided that Ah Bian would speak with DPP chairman Lin Yi-hsiung during the press conference and I would address the foreign media in English at the rally held afterward.

As I took the stage, Brother, my childhood protector and role model, stood next to me. In my heart were thoughts of gratitude to Father, who had taught me to have confidence and to deal with others justly; thoughts of Mother, who had given me unconditional love and paid a horrible price for my misfortunes; and thoughts of Eldest Sister, who had been my most dedicated source of support throughout my imprisonment and now cheerfully witnessed the joy of our triumph.

After the Central Election Commission confirmed our victory, the chief of staff of the military, Tang Yao-ming, announced his unconditional support of the election results. In the days that followed, discontented Nationalists gathered around the party headquarters. The angry protestors became a riotous mob demanding the resignation of Lee Teng-hui as party chairman. Lee retreated into his residence and later resigned as party chairman to take responsibility for his party's defeat. The reign of the party that had ruled Taiwan for fifty-four years had gradually collapsed from within.

Yet the storm of energy that had been unleashed by our victory lingered over me. China's leaders seemed content, at first, to adopt the attitude of "listening to the words and watching the actions" of Chen Shui-bian. They chose me, however, as the lightning rod for their condemnation. Beijing criticized my position that the relationship between Taiwan and China was that of "close neighbors and distant relatives"—an idea I had developed during the campaign. An article in the *Asian Wall Street Journal* explained it well:

> We must admit that there is a special relationship between Taiwan and China. Namely, ethnically, we are relatives. Because our ancestors came from China, we are more than happy to admit we are relatives. And geographically, we are neighbors. By such a definition, we wish that there were no hatred between the two peoples. There shouldn't be any war. We should enhance peaceful coexistence for mutual substantial development. . . . A new era has approached. We cannot live in the past. All the Chinese leaders have been talking as if Taiwan is part of China. . . . But now we are approaching [an era of] globalization. If China really wants to stand up, as a leading country in the 21st century, its leaders must share global values, must abide by global norms. We have never done anything wrong. We are by no means troublemakers; we are peacemakers.

Attacks in China's state-run press covered the front pages of major Chinese newspapers and were broadcast on China Central Television. Xinhua News Agency reports accused me of advocating "the notorious discourse of Taiwan independence" with the "ferocity of a wolf." The *People's Daily* suggested that I had forgotten my ancestors and that my advocacy of Taiwan independence betrayed Lu family ties to Fujian going back centuries. These screeds insisted that Taiwan is an inalienable part of Chinese territory and Taiwanese are inseparable from the Chinese nation; my view that China and Taiwan were "distant relatives and close neighbors" courted destruction and threatened to spark a world war.

This sort of vitriol from Chinese media was not without precedent. One year earlier, Beijing had labeled Lee Teng-hui the "sinner in history" for his position that Taiwan had a special international relationship with China, asserting that Lee's pursuit of independence was a "road to death." Similarly, Britain's final governor in Hong Kong, Chris Patton, was "called a 'liar', a 'snake', a 'prostitute', and a 'tango dancer'" for his support of democracy in the former colony.

Sadly, Beijing responded to the expression of free will in Taiwan with the knee-jerk reaction of Chinese nationalists. Thus, governments in North America and Europe, fearful of offending China, greeted the election results with caution and concern. Nevertheless, I couldn't help finding the attention that China devoted to castigating me a little flattering—sentiment that I shared with the Associated Press: "The ugliest language in the world has been heaped on me. I'm not angry. Such a big country has to use all its resources to insult Annette Lu. Isn't that an honor?" Beijing's polemics seemed like a throwback to the tactics employed by the Nationalists to quash the Dangwai movement in the 1970s. President Chen Shui-bian defended me in the face of these Chinese propaganda attacks, saying that my statements had gone no further than his own and that an attack against me was an attack on the whole administration.

The month before I was sworn in, one morning in early April, Brother met me at my Taoyuan residence, and in the company of close relatives, we went together to pay a visit to the Lu family cemetery, a place that holds the bones of over 2,300 people. The visit was a solemn occasion but one filled with gratitude for all that Father and Mother had given me. With tears in my eyes, I presented the official certificate of my election as the Republic of China's tenth vice president to the spirits of my parents in heaven. A man who only attended elementary school, Father educated himself enough to teach me Chinese philosophy and had interested me in world affairs. But it was Mother who had the wisdom to bring me into the world on the exact date that I would be inaugurated as vice president! As it turned out, the inauguration happened to fall on my birthday according to the lunar calendar. Before I left the cemetery, I whispered to her, "Mother, the pain that you suffered twenty years ago has received compensation!"

On May 20, Chen Shui-bian and I took our formal oaths of office and stepped into the spring sunshine. Standing next to Ah Bian and listening to his inaugural address, I hoped that Beijing would receive his offerings of peace and join us in ending decades of tension. Because the DPP owed its success to the Taiwanese people, we were glad that they could join the celebration: Thousands of spectators cheered and threw their hats into the air as we walked back into the presidential palace on a long red carpet.

EPILOGUE

AS THE FIRST WOMAN TO BE ELECTED VICE PRESIDENT OF TAI-
wan, Lu Hsiu-lien personally participated in what many pundits saw
as the final stage of Taiwan's democratic transition. Yet euphoria over
the electoral victory and the transition of power from the Nationalists to the Democratic Progressive Party government was short-lived.
While forming the first non–Nationalist Party administration since
World War II, Lu's government was also the country's first without a
majority of seats in the national parliament. The passage of any major
governmental initiatives would require compromise.

To facilitate bipartisan cooperation, President Chen Shui-bian
appointed a number of Nationalists to senior positions in his government. These cabinet appointments included China-born Tang Fei
as the premier and head of the executive branch. A member of the
Nationalist Party, Tang had served as defense minister under Lee
Teng-hui and was committed to a peaceful transition under Chen
Shui-bian. This unprecedented attempt to form a two-party cabinet,
however, collapsed over a dispute concerning the construction of a
nuclear power plant in northern Taiwan.

The Fourth Nuclear Power Plant had been the subject of intense
controversy since the early 1990s. During his presidential campaign, Chen Shui-bian had opposed the plant's completion, reflecting widely held public concern over its safety. Located in a densely
populated area, the power plant lies atop a fault zone and is proxi-
mate to volcanic activity in the nearby sea. Nationalist politicians
had supported the plant from the outset. Reflecting the Nationalist position on nuclear energy and plagued by ill health, Premier
Tang Fei clashed with Chen Shui-bian over the future of the Fourth

Nuclear Plant and resigned within five months of the presidential inauguration.

In an effort to reduce tensions, President Chen Shui-bian and Nationalist Party chairman Lien Chan had coffee at the presidential palace to discuss their differences. Lien pressed Chen to support the plant's construction; Chen remained cordial and did not commit to a course of action. The atmosphere of bipartisan civility their meeting created was punctured by new premier Chang Chun-hsiung's announcement a few hours later that the government would halt construction on the plant. Humiliated at his loss of face, Lien Chan mended fences with his former rival James Soong. Together they called for the impeachment of both Chen Shui-bian *and* Lu Hsiu-lien, an act that would necessitate a new election for the head of state and give Lien Chan another chance to win the presidency.

With the survival of her government threatened, Lu Hsiu-lien struggled to define her role as vice president. Unlike in the United States, where the vice president is also president of the senate, in Taiwan the vice president has no such role. The vice president is the "backup president," serving only if the president becomes unfit to continue. No other role is clearly specified in the constitution. Vice President Lee Yuan-tsu, who had served under Lee Teng-hui, had characterized himself as a "vice president without a voice." In addition, when a president encountered difficulties, suspicions were directed toward the vice president, who stood to benefit by ascending to the presidency if the president was forced to step down. To make matters worse, mass media portrayed Lu Hsiu-lien as the president's "political wife" and suggested she was an "unhappy concubine in the depths of the castle" (*shengong yuanfu*). For Lu Hsiu-lien, these attacks revealed the almost feudal reluctance of some compatriots to accept a woman's authority.

In her first year in office, a sex scandal exacerbated Lu's difficulties when *The Journalist* (Xinxinwen) magazine published a report suggesting that Lu Hsiu-lien was the source of a leak that President Chen was having an affair with his staff member Bi-khim Hsiao. Lu Hsiu-lien saw the report as simply another Nationalist attempt to generate pressure for Chen's impeachment. Lu had never spoken to the reporter about the alleged romance, and she sued *The Journalist* for libel, winning the case after a four-year legal battle.

Meanwhile, the Council of Grand Justices issued a ruling on the Fourth Nuclear Plant that defused the impeachment crisis. Deciding against President Chen, the court ruled that the executive branch did not possess the authority to halt a project for which the legislature had already approved the budget. President Chen Shui-bian bowed to the wishes of the court, and construction on the plant went forward.

In her first years as vice president, Lu Hsiu-lien focused her energies on foreign relations, emphasizing the need for Taiwan to increase its "soft power"—the ability to attract and persuade. She founded the Democratic Pacific Union, an organization of democratic states on the Pacific Rim, which included Taiwan's formal diplomatic allies in Latin America. Barred from traveling to many countries, including the United States, except for brief transit visits, Lu Hsiu-lien made state visits to Latin America, where she received honorary doctorates for her achievements in the promotion of peace and democracy, and gave speeches via the Web to audiences in Prague, Tokyo, and New York. On a visit to Paraguay, she met Fidel Castro and succeeded in convincing him that Taiwan had the right to join the United Nations—a position that Castro later asserted in an interview with Cuban state media.

As Lu's first term as vice president drew to a close, she and Chen Shui-bian faced off against their opponents from the 2000 election, Lien Chan and James Soong, now united as presidential and vice presidential candidates, respectively. Internecine political conflict had diminished opportunity for concrete political accomplishment and contributed to Taiwan's mediocre economic performance. The 2004 presidential election proved even closer than the race in 2000.

On March 19, the eve of the election, disaster struck. While campaigning in the city of Tainan, Lu Hsiu-lien was hit in the knee by an assassin's bullet. Another shot ripped across President Chen's abdomen. As their injuries were not mortal, the election went ahead as scheduled. When the votes were tallied, Chen and Lu had won a second term in office by less than one percent of the popular vote.

Enraged at his defeat, Lien Chan launched a protest movement and demanded a recount. Nationalist supporters were convinced that Chen Shui-bian had staged the shooting as a means of winning a "sympathy vote." Senior military officers, including Minister of Defense Tang Yao-ming, offered their resignations, suggesting that prominent military figures opposed Chen Shui-bian's reelection. Fears of a coup circulated among Chen administration insiders. A congratulatory message from President George W. Bush, however, turned the tide of Nationalist-led resistance to the outcome. The Central Election Commission certified the election results, and angry crowds dispersed.

The investigation into the assassination attempt satisfied almost no one. Tainan-area investigators concluded that a disgruntled fisherman, Chen Yi-hsiung, had used a crudely made pistol to fire two shots at the campaign jeep in which Chen Shui-bian and Lu Hsiu-lien traveled. Chen Yi-hsiung was unable to respond to these charges, because he was discovered drowned in his fishing net. Many unanswered questions remained, even after forensic studies of the crime scene refuted suspicions of President Chen Shui-bian's involvement in the shooting.

In a book written after leaving office, *Penetrating 319: One Reality, One Taiwan* (Toushi 319: Yige zhenxiang yige Taiwan), Lu Hsiu-lien argued that investigators failed to directly connect Chen Yi-hsiung to the assassination attempt, despite extensive review of photos and video surveillance in the area. The pistol that investigators claimed Chen Yi-hsiung had fired was never found. Moreover, investigators found that the manufacture of the bullets used in the shooting differed from that of the bullets made by the supplier of Chen Yi-hsiung's gun, casting doubt on assumptions about the source of the illegal weapon and its ammunition. Lu Hsiu-lien's review of the case argued that authorities had wrongly attributed the crime to Chen Yi-hsiung as the sole perpetrator. She suspected that two or more assailants may have committed the crime and murdered Chen Yi-hsiung to hide the truth.

In Chen Shui-bian's second term, Nationalist legislators continued to hold a majority in parliament. As a result, the Chen administration focused on tasks that it could accomplish without bipartisan support: education reform to strengthen students' identification with Taiwan (as opposed to China), the renaming of streets and public spaces to emphasize Taiwan's aboriginal culture, and applying to join the United Nations as "Taiwan" (rather than as the Republic of China). Lu Hsiu-lien's greatest successes stemmed from her emphasis on women's rights and her championing of women's participation in politics. She hosted the Women's National Affairs Conference and invited former Japanese sex slaves known as "comfort women" to visit the presidential palace. During Lu's tenure in office, thirty-five women were appointed to positions as minister or vice minister and two women served as premier. She also led the Office of the President's Advisory Committee on Human Rights in conducting research on Taiwan's decades under martial law and headed the President's Advisory Committee on Science and Technology, which focused on sustainable energy, marine industries, cultural and creative innovation, and national defense.

Midway through Chen Shui-bian's second term, rumors emerged that members of Chen's family and staff had engaged in various forms of corruption. The alleged offenses included misuse of special presidential funds (*guowu jiyaofei*), large sums of money stashed in overseas bank accounts, influence peddling by First Lady Wu Shu-chen, and insider trading by Chen Shui-bian's son in law, Chao Chien-min, whom many people referred to simply as "the emperor's son in law" (*fumaye*).

In August 2006, former Dangwai leader and longtime political prisoner Shih Ming-teh wrote a letter to Chen Shui-bian imploring him to resign for the good of Taiwan and the Democratic Progressive Party. This was the first salvo in a groundswell of opposition by demonstrators known as the Red Shirt Army (*Hongsanjun*), who would demand Chen's ouster in demonstrations surrounding the presidential palace for weeks. According to Shih Ming-teh's memoir, "Commander in Chief Tells All" (*Zongzhihui de gaobai*), Shih and Taipei mayor Ma Ying-jeou (who served as president of the Republic of China after Chen Shui-bian) held a secret meeting in which they agreed the best arrangement for Taiwan would be for Chen Shui-bian to resign and for Lu Hsiu-lien, serving as president, to pardon Chen and his family. Mayor Ma agreed to back the protests on the condition that Shih Ming-teh promise not to run for the presidency in 2008. Ma's support for the demonstrations was crucial, as special permission was required for overnight protests within city limits.

Till the end of his second term, Chen Shui-bian insisted on his innocence and refused to resign. As a political candidate, Chen had vowed to fight corruption but had proven incapable of preventing his family members' involvement in shady financial dealings. Chen's wife, son, and daughter-in-law admitted to money laundering. Chen's wife, Wu Shu-chen, confessed to forgery. Chen's son-in-law, Chao Chien-min, was convicted of insider trading.

In Lu Hsiu-lien's eyes, Chen Shui-bian's trial amounted to political persecution by the Nationalist-dominated judiciary. At a banquet celebrating Law Day (Sifa Jie) attended by Nationalist Minister of Justice Wang Ching-feng before Chen's trial, a group of prosecutors performed a skit depicting Chen Shui-bian's arrest, with a female prosecutor waving handcuffed arms and exclaiming, "I have been beaten by the police! Judicial persecution!" (*Fajing daren! Sifa pohai!*) The minister of justice defended the performance as "reflecting a few of the people's opinions" and denied the skit represented the views of the Ministry of Justice. This lampooning of the subject of an ongoing investigation horrified the public and suggested that legal proceedings against Chen would be neither fair nor impartial.

Members of Chen Shui-bian's family had shown extremely poor values and worse judgment. Yet the courts revealed impropriety and inconsistency in their evaluation of expenditures from President Chen's special budget, using standards never applied to previous administrations, which had considerable discretionary use of the funds. Chen argued that the large sums of money discovered in Swiss bank accounts—the source of money-laundering allegations—were leftover campaign funds and, in accordance with Taiwanese law, his to dispose of in the manner he deemed fit. The judiciary's treatment of Chen Shui-bian after he left office seemed tailored for the persecution of the former president, as courts had not ruled similarly in other cases in which Taiwanese politicians had been suspected of graft. The transition from power to prison took a tremendous toll on the former president. While serving the first four years of a twenty-year sentence, Chen developed severe depression, non-typical Parkinson's disease, a speech disorder, and sleep apnea. He attempted suicide in 2013.

Lu Hsiu-lien's years after the vice presidency have been free from the taint of corruption charges. While in office, Lu had maintained a distance from Chen Shui-bian's family, kept watch on her personal finances, and avoided conflicts of interest. In retirement, Lu has chosen a simple life. She managed a weekly newspaper, became a vegetarian, and lives alone in an apartment near Taipei. Lu has traveled extensively in places once off limits to her as the vice president, including the United States, Japan, and Europe. At home in Taiwan, she has rekindled a passion for activism. Lu's recent work has included advocacy for the environmental benefits of vegetarianism, opposition to completion of the Fourth Nuclear Power Plant, promotion of natural and nuclear disaster preparedness, and support for organizations that elevate the status of women around the world.

NOTES

INTRODUCTION

5 *Taiwan was subjected to "Japanization" policies for five decades:* For accounts of Taiwan's cultural assimilation under Japanese rule, see Leo T. S. Ching, *Becoming "Japanese:" Colonial Taiwan and the Politics of Identity Formation* (Los Angeles: University of California Press, 2001) and George H. Kerr, *Formosa: Licensed Revolution and the Home Rule Movement 1895–1945* (Honolulu: University of Hawaii Press, 1974).

7 *The number of countries around the world officially recognizing the Republic of China:* Hung-Mao Tien, ed., *Taiwan's Electoral Politics and Democratic Transition: Riding the Third Wave* (Armonk, NY: M.E. Sharpe, 1996).

7 *Taiwan's economy grew at "miraculous" rates of over 10 percent per year:* Thomas B. Gold, *State and Society in the Taiwan Miracle* (Armonk, NY: M.E. Sharpe, 1986), 4.

7 *Lu Hsiu-lien condemned traditional biases against women:* Hsiu-lien Lu, "Women's Liberation: The Taiwan Experience," in *The Other Taiwan: 1945 to the Present*, ed. Murray A. Rubinstein (Armonk, NY: M.E. Sharpe, 1994), 289–304.

8 *Placing Taiwan (and not China) at the center of the Republic of China's political priorities:* For an excellent account of intellectuals in the 1970s, including the writing of Lu Hsiu-lien, see A-chin Hsiau, *Huigui xianshi: Taiwan 1970 niandai de zhanhou shidai yu wenhua zhengzhi bianqian* (Return to reality: Political and cultural change in Taiwan's 1970s, postwar generation) [Taipei: Zhongyang yanjiuyuan shehui yanjiusuo (Academia Sinica Institute of Sociology), 2010]. Another valuable resource on this period is Mab Huang, *Intellectual Ferment for Political Reforms in Taiwan, 1971–1973* (Ann Arbor: Center for Chinese Studies, University of Michigan, 1976).

10 *The following year, Chiang ended thirty-eight years of martial law:* For a
scholarly account of the evolution of Chiang Ching-kuo's views toward
democratization, which as of the 1980s he saw as a global trend, see
Linda Chao and Ramon H. Myers, *The First Chinese Democracy: Political Life in the Republic of China on Taiwan* (Baltimore: Johns Hopkins
University Press, 1998).

11 *Chinese Premier Zhu Rongji held a press conference at which he threatened
those pursuing Taiwan independence:* BBC News, "China Ups Pressure
on Taiwan," March 15, 2000, at http://news.bbc.co.uk/2/hi/asia-
pacific/678155.stm; see also Steven M. Goldstein and Julian Chang,
ed., *Presidential Politics in Taiwan: The Administration of Chen Shui-bian*
(Norwalk, CT: EastBridge, 2008), 16.

2. TAIWANESE DAUGHTER

19 *When they were newly married:* Lu Hsiu-lien's close family members are
referred to throughout the book, not by their proper names, but as
they would be in colloquial Taiwanese.

22 *Two years after the 2-28 Incident:* For an account of the establishment of
Nationalist Party rule in Taiwan and the party's subsequent adapta-
tion, see Bruce J. Dickson, *Democratization in China and Taiwan* (New
York: Oxford University Press, 1997).

22 *Chiang called his new regime in Taiwan "Free China":* The classic account
of the February 28 Incident was written by the former US State
Department analyst George Kerr. In the 1960s, many Taiwanese
studying overseas learned much about their history by reading George
H. Kerr, *Formosa Betrayed* (New York: Houghton Mifflin, 1965). See
also Tse-Han Lai, Ramon H. Myers, and Wou Wei, *A Tragic Beginning:
The Taiwan Uprising of February 28, 1947* (Stanford, CA: Stanford University Press, 1991).

22 *"Free China" was neither free nor in China:* Readers seeking more
background on Taiwan's political transformation in the nineteenth
and twentieth centuries should consider reading Denny Roy, *Taiwan:
A Political History* (Ithaca, NY: Cornell University Press, 2003). For
a recent and highly accessible introduction to Taiwan politics, see
Dafydd Fell, *Government and Politics in Taiwan* (New York: Routledge,
2012).

3. LIFTING HALF THE SKY

47 *In April 1970, former chairman of the National Taiwan University:* Peng Ming-min's account of his transition from scholar to activist and of his arrest, interrogation, and flight overseas appeared as Ming-min Peng, *A Taste of Freedom* (New York: Holt, Rinehart, & Winston, 1972).

53 *Commentary in the China Times newspaper on the value of life and chastity:* Lu Hsiu-lien, *"Cong Zhongqiman shaqi tanqi"* ("Starting the Conversation from Chung Chao Man's Killing of His Wife," Zhongguo shibao (China Times), September 24, 1972.

4. A MOTH FLYING TOWARD FLAME

76 *I began writing the book* Taiwan: Past and Future: A version of the book was later reprinted as *Taiwan: guoqu yu weilai* [Taipei: Zhibenjia chubanshe (Intellectual Capitalist Publishing House), 2003].

78 *I knew that convincing democracy activists:* For a scholarly account of the early *Dangwai* political organization and watershed elections in the 1980s, see Shelley Rigger, *Politics in Taiwan: Voting for Democracy* (New York: Routledge, 1999).

94 *US diplomatic relations with both China and Taiwan:* Nancy Tucker offers a detailed analysis of Cold War–era US-Taiwan relations in Nancy Bernkopf Tucker, *Strait Talk: United States–Taiwan Relations and the Crisis with China* (Cambridge, MA: Harvard University Press, 2009).

121 *Even the non-Nationalist mayors of Tainan and Taichung drew a clear line separating themselves:* See *Chongshen meilidao* (Re-trying the *Formosa* case) [Taipei: Zili wanbao chubanshe (Independent Evening Post Publishing), 1991], 206.

6. PATRIOTISM IMPRISONED

129 *As soon as I entered the Jingmei Detention Center:* The transcript of a lengthy interview with Lu Hsiu-lien after her release from prison conducted by Dr. Linda Arrigo was invaluable for the writing of chapter 6.

142 *Suspicion of government involvement:* Bruce Jacobs went on to become a renowned expert of Taiwan politics. For an excellent review of

Taiwan's democratization, see J. Bruce Jacobs, *Democratizing Taiwan* (Leiden: Brill Academic Publishers, 2012).

150 *The foreign press brought international pressure to bear on the National-ists*: Edith M. Lederer, "Dissident Denies Advocating Force to Topple Government, Associated Press, March 19, 1980.

152 *The government's decision to hold an open trial:* Years later, a Nationalist insider told Lu Hsiu-lien that Chiang Ching-kuo had been puzzled by the *Formosa* case and sought to learn the truth, as he suspected that his supporters had hatched a plot to entrap the *Dangwai* opposition. Two years after the trial, General Wang Sheng, who had headed the General Political Warfare College and was President Chiang Ching-kuo's confidant, was appointed ambassador to Paraguay to deprive him of power over domestic affairs. General Wang Sheng was thought by some to have ordered the murder of Lin's family in retaliation for the bombing of his son's residence in Mission Valley, CA, by overseas Taiwanese.

152 *Shih Ming-teh was sentenced:* A full account of Shih Ming-teh's fasci-nating life as a dissident and twenty-five years in prison has yet to appear in English. Some of his recent political views can be found in Ming-te Shih, *Political Will: The Final Statement of Innocence from a Devotee* [New Taipei City: Shih Ming-teh jiangzuo jijinhui (Shih Ming-teh Lecture Foundation), 2012]. See also Ming-teh Shih, *Chang-shi* (Common sense) [New Taipei City: Shih Ming-teh jiangzuo jijinhui (Shih Ming-teh Lecture Foundation), 2011].

163 *Persistent lobbying by overseas Taiwanese:* Former Taiwan Foreign Minister Mark Chen (Chen Tang-shan) published a moving tribute to Ted Kennedy in the *Taipei Times* in which he notes the importance of Kennedy and Congressional colleagues such as Stephen Solarz and Jim Leach in pressuring the Chiang Ching-kuo administration to end martial law and embrace democratization. See Mark Chen, "Senator Ted Kennedy: A True Friend of Taiwan," *Taipei Times*, September 5, 2009. , on January 18, 2013, at www.taipeitimes.com/News/editorials/archives/2009/09/05/2003452786.

164 *In prison, I had no idea that Amnesty International was lobbying for my release:* Columbia University senior research scholar James Seymour shared with Ashley Esarey his impressions of Amnesty International's advocacy to free the imprisoned Lu Hsiu-lien and explained his role

in translating letters sent by Eldest Sister (Lu Hsiu-rong) for Amnesty International.

167   *Jack Anderson decided to make my imprisonment the focus of his syn-dicated column:* Jack Anderson, "In Taiwan Jail, Woman Suffers for Rights Tract," *Washington Post*, May 20, 1982.

173   *The Liu murder had generated a wrath of criticism from the media and the Congress: New York Times*, "The Long Arm of Taiwan," February 11, 1985.

7. IN SEARCH OF DESTINY

178   *I felt a responsibility to put all the pieces together:* Hsiu-lien Lu, *Chong-shen meilidao* (Re-trying the *Formosa* case) [Taipei: Zili wanbao chubanshe (Independent Evening Post Publishing), 1991]. *Chongshen meilidao* was one of the first authoritative accounts of the *Formosa Magazine* trial.

185   *Dynamic political change in Taiwan in the late 1980s prompted my decision to return home:* For an account of the founding of the Democratic Pro-gressive Party and its route to prominence, see Shelley Rigger, *From Opposition to Power: Taiwan's Democratic Progressive Party* (Boulder, CO: Lynne Rienner Publishers, 2001).

186   *This sweeping recognition of Taiwanese identity:* In the 1990s and 2000s, many scholars in Taiwan, the United States, the United Kingdom, and Australia researched the evolution of political identities in Taiwan. The late Alan Wachman wrote an influential early study on the sub-ject: Alan M. Wachman, *Taiwan: National Identity and Democratization* (Armonk, NY: M.E. Sharpe, 1994). For a more recent account of the evolution of identities in Taiwan, see Melissa J. Brown, *Is Taiwan Chi-nese? The Impact of Culture, Power, and Migration on Changing Identities* (Berkeley: University of California Press, 2004).

196   *After attending the first day of the National Affairs Conference:* A schol-arly study that gives more credit for success at the National Affairs Conference to the DPP and to Lee Teng-hui's leadership is C. L. Chiou, *Democratizing Oriental Despotism: China from 4 May 1919 to 4 June 1989 and Taiwan from 28 February 1947 to 28 June 1990* (London: St. Martin's Press, 1995).

8. KNOCKING AT THE GATE OF THE UN

205 George H. W. Bush described the passage of the Albanian proposal: Henry Tanner, "Session is Tense: Washington Loses Its Battle for Taipei by 76 to 35," *New York Times,* October 26, 1971.

205 *In the Shanghai Communiqué:* For insightful analysis of the Shanghai Communiqué, see Robert S. Ross, *Negotiating Cooperation: The United States and China 1969–1989* (Stanford, CA: Stanford University Press, 1995).

9. POLITICAL TRASH

237 *The Nationalist Party nominated Fang Li-hsiu:* Although nominated by the DPP, Lu Hsiu-lien selected Lin Yung-gui, a Nationalist, as her campaign manager in the race against Fang Li-Hsiu for Taoyuan County chief executive. Lin was the former chair of the Chungli City Council and had been a critic of Mayor Fang Li-hsiu and the cartel that controlled garbage collection. One night, two men visited Lin's home and presented him with two items: A pistol and a bag containing NT$300 million (over US$1 million) in cash. They urged him to get bullets or take the money and stop criticizing the garbage cartel! Instead, Lin resigned as chair of the Chungli City Council. He visited Lu when she declared her intention to run for magistrate. After Lu expressed her determination to fight the garbage cartel, Lin Yung-gui agreed to serve as her campaign manager. Readers interested in learning more about the role of organized crime in Taiwan politics might consider Ko-lin Chin, *Heijin: Organized Crime, Business, and Politics in Taiwan* (Armonk, NY: M.E. Sharpe Publishers, 2003).

245 *I handled Taoyuan County's garbage problems step by step:* Few foreign scholars have conducted research on local politics in Taiwan. An exception is Benjamin Read, whose fascinating work on the "ultra-local" politics of urban neighborhoods has helped to shed light on the lowest levels of political contestation in Taiwan and in China. See Benjamin L. Read, *Roots of the State: Neighborhood Organization and Social Networks in Beijing and Taipei* (Stanford, CA: Stanford University Press, 2012).

272 *Zhu Rongji warned Taiwanese voters not to elect the "wrong candidate":*

BBC News, "China Ups Pressure on Taiwan," March 15, 2000, accessed November 9, 2013, at http://news.bbc.co.uk/2/hi/asia-pacific/678155.stm.

275 *"Close neighbors and distant relatives"*: *Asian Wall Street Journal*, "Taiwan's Outspoken Vice President," April 10, 2000.

275 *"The ugliest language in the world"*: William Foreman, "Taiwan Flattered by Chinese Insults," Associated Press, April 13, 2000.

275 *Attacks in China's state-run press*: Xinhua News Agency (Xinhuashe), "Lu Xiulian shudian wangzu 'Taidu' lun choumingzhaozhu" (Lu Hsiulien Forgets Ancestors with Notorious Taiwan Independence Discourse), April 14, 2000.

275 *The* People's Daily *suggested*: People's Daily, "Wangji jiushi beipan: Fujian Nanjing Lüshi zongqin tongze Lü xiulian" (Forgetting Is Betrayal: Lu Ancestors in Nanjing, Fujian Bitterly Rebuke Lu Hsiulian), April 14, 2000.

276 *This sort of vitriol from Chinese media*: Xinhua News Agency (Xinhuashe), "Fenlie guojia jiushi lishizuiren: Zaiping Lee Denghui de fenlie yanlun" (Dividing the Country Is to Become a Criminal in History: Further Criticism of Lee Teng-hui's Separatist Rhetoric), July 16, 1999.

276 *Chris Patton*: BBC News, "Politics 97," accessed November 10, 2013, at www.bbc.co.uk/news/special/politics97/hk/patten.shtml.

GLOSSARY OF NAMES

NAMES IN TAIWAN ARE INFREQUENTLY ROMANIZED IN SUCH standard formats as Wade-Giles or the pinyin system used in China. During the twentieth century most Taiwanese used the Wade-Giles system as a basis for rendering their names in English, although with slight modifications by people seeking to enable pronunciation by non-Chinese speakers. Throughout this book the authors have chosen to respect common spellings of names in Taiwan in modified Wade-Giles, or the spelling preferred by each individual, rather than force conformity with any one romanization system. For the reader's convenience, this glossary provides the names of key figures as they appear in the narrative, along with the pinyin romanizations, traditional Chinese characters, and a brief description of each individual. The names listed below appear surname first, as is customary in Chinese, followed by given names. For further details on many of the individuals listed here, see J. Bruce Jacobs, *Democratizing Taiwan* (Leiden: Brill Academic Publishers, 2012).

CHANG CHUN-HUNG, ZHANG JUNHONG, 張俊宏. Founder of such magazines as *Daxue* (University) and *Taiwan Zhenglun* (Taiwan Political Forum), Dangwai activist, Taiwan provincial assemblyman, editor in chief of *Formosa Magazine*, and political prisoner after the *Formosa* trial. After release from prison in 1988, Chang was a member of the National Assembly, a national legislator, and acting chair of the Democratic Progressive Party.

CHANG CHUN-NAN, ZHANG CHUNNAN, 張春男. Member of the National Assembly, Dangwai activist, cofounder of the Dangwai

Candidate Association, and political prisoner. He defected to the People's Republic of China and was later named to the standing committee of the Chinese People's Political Consultative Conference.

CHANG FU-MEI, ZHANG FUMEI, 張富美. Received her doctorate from Harvard and later returned to Taiwan to run for the National Assembly, in which she served two terms. Chang Fu-mei headed the Overseas Community Affairs Commission (*Qiaowu weiyuanhui*) from 2000 to 2008.

CHANG HSI-TIAN, ZHANG XIDIAN, 張希典. Also known as "Bruce Lee," Amnesty International Chapter 101 volunteer who kept in contact with Eldest Sister during Lu Hsiu-lien's years in prison.

CHANG WEI-CHIA, ZHANG WEIJIA, 張維嘉. Graduate of National Taiwan University Law Department, foreign student in France, and advocate of Taiwan independence in Europe in the 1970s.

CHEN CHU, CHEN JU, 陳菊. Dangwai activist and political prisoner after the Kaohsiung Incident (Lu Hsiu-lien's cell mate), director of the Bureau of Social Affairs in both Taipei and Kaohsiung, chairwoman of the Democratic Progressive Party, and mayor of Kaohsiung from 2006 to 2014.

CHEN SHUI-BIAN, CHEN SHUIBIAN, 陳水扁. Defense lawyer for Huang Hsin-chieh during the *Formosa Magazine* trial, Taipei city councilor, national legislator, Taipei mayor, Democratic Progressive Party chairman, and president of Taiwan from 2000 to 2008. He was later sentenced to twenty years in prison for corruption and money laundering.

CHENG NAN-RONG (CHENG NAN-JUNG), ZHENG NANRONG, 鄭南榕. Taiwan independence advocate and magazine publisher. Cheng committed suicide by self-immolation in defense of the freedom of speech and of the press in April 1989. Cheng was the husband of Yeh Chu-lan.

CHIANG CHING-KUO, JIANG JINGGUO, 蔣經國. Son of Chiang Kai-shek, premier, and president of the Republic of China from 1978 until his death in 1988. He was succeeded as president by Lee Teng-hui.

CHIANG CHUN-NAN (also ANTONIO CHIANG or 司馬文武), JIANG CHUNNAN, 江春男. Prominent Dangwai writer, founding member of the Democratic Progressive Party, media entrepreneur, and *Apple Daily* columnist.

CHIANG KAI-SHEK, JIANG JIESHI, 蔣介石 or 蔣中正. Militarist and leader of the Republic of China prior to the Nationalist defeat in the Chinese Civil War (1946–49). Chiang relocated the ROC central government to Taiwan and served as the paramount leader until his death in 1975.

CHIU CHUE-CHEN, QIU CHUEZHEN, 邱垂貞. Dangwai activist and folksinger imprisoned for singing a banned song at the Kaohsiung Incident in 1979. Chiu subsequently served as national legislator.

HAU PUO-TSUN (or HAU PEI-TSUN), HAO BOCUN, 郝柏村. Chief of the general staff (1981–89), minister of defense (1989–90), premier under president Lee Teng-hui, and vice presidential candidate in 1996.

HSU HSIN-LIANG, XU XINLIANG, 許信良. Taoyuan County chief executive from 1977 to 1979, when Nationalists removed him from office. Hsu was publisher of *Formosa Magazine* but left Taiwan prior to the Kaohsiung Incident in 1980. An advocate of Taiwan independence from abroad, Hsu returned to Taiwan in 1989 and was imprisoned before being pardoned by President Lee Teng-hui. Hsu Hsin-liang later served as the chairman of the Democratic Progressive Party, but he left the DPP and ran for president as an independent in 2000.

HUANG HSIN-CHIEH, HUANG XINJIE, 黃信介. Taipei city councilor, Dangwai campaigner, national legislator, *Formosa Magazine* founder, and political prisoner after the *Formosa* trial. Huang Hsin-chieh subsequently served as chairman of the Democratic Progressive Party and advisor to President Lee Teng-hui.

KANG NING-HSIANG, KANG NINGXIANG, 康寧祥. Early Dangwai politician, Taipei city councilor, national legislator, founder of the magazines *Taiwan Political Forum* (Taiwan Zhenglun) and *The Eighties* (Bashi niandai), and of the *Capital Morning Post* newspaper (Shoudu zaobao).

LEE TENG-HUI, LI DENGHUI, 李登輝. Agricultural economist educated at Cornell University, Nationalist mayor of Taipei, governor of Taiwan Province, chairman of the Nationalist Party, and vice president and president of the Republic of China from 1988 to 2000.

LEE YUAN-TSU, LI YUANCU, 李元簇. Minister of education, minister of justice, and vice president of the Republic of China.

LEE YUAN-TSEH, LI YUANZHE, 李遠哲. Winner of the Nobel Prize in Chemistry in 1986 and professor of chemistry at the University of California at Berkeley. Lee returned to Taiwan to serve as president of the national research academy Academia Sinica from 1994 to 2006.

LIEN CHAN, LIAN ZHAN, 連戰. Received his doctorate in political science from the University of Chicago before becoming a Nationalist Party politician. Lien Chan served as minister of foreign affairs, premier, chairman of the Nationalist Party, vice president of the Republic of China, and presidential candidate in 2000 and 2004.

LIN YANG-GANG, LIN YANGGANG, 林洋港. Nationalist Nantou County magistrate, mayor of Taipei, governor of Taiwan Province, minister of the interior, and presidential candidate in the 1996 general election.

LIN YI-HSIUNG, LIN YIXIONG, 林義雄. Provincial assemblyman, Dangwai politician, and political prisoner after the Kaohsiung Incident. Lin Yi-hsiung's mother and twin daughters were murdered in his home on February 28, 1980. In the late 1990s, he served as chairman of the Democratic Progressive Party.

LIU BANG-YIU, LIU BANGYOU, 劉邦友. Nationalist Taoyuan County chief executive from 1989 to 1996. Liu was murdered in his official residence along with seven others.

LU HSIU-LIEN, LÜ XIULIAN, 呂秀蓮. Feminist, author, novelist, Dangwai activist, national legislator, Taoyuan County chief executive, and two-term vice president of Taiwan.

MA YING-JEOU, MA YINGJIU, 馬英九. Lawyer educated at Harvard and New York universities. Ma Ying-jeou served in the Office of the President during the Chiang Ching-kuo administration. He was minister of justice and minister without portfolio under President Lee Teng-hui and later Nationalist Party chairman and the president of the Republic of China from 2008 to 2012. President Ma was reelected to a second term in 2012.

PENG MING-MIN, PENG MINGMIN, 彭明敏. Educated at Tokyo Imperial University. Peng became a well-known professor at National Taiwan University and one of the most high-profile advocates of Taiwan independence. After imprisonment and lengthy exile, Peng returned to Taiwan and ran as the Democratic Progressive Party candidate for president of the Republic of China in 1996.

SHIH MING-TEH (or SHIH MING-TE), SHI MINGDE, 施明德. Early advocate of Taiwan independence and Dangwai activist prior to the Kaohsiung Incident. Shih spent over twenty-five years in prison for advocacy of sedition and Taiwan independence and later served as chairman of the Democratic Progressive Party, legislator, and organizer of the 2006 *Hongsanjun* (Red Shirt Army) protests against the Chen-Lu administration.

SIEW WAN-CHANG (VINCENT SIEW), XIAO WANCHANG, 蕭萬長. First Taiwan-born premier, vice chairman of the Nationalist Party, and vice president of the Republic of China from 2008 to 2012.

SOONG CHU-YU (JAMES SOONG), SONG CHUYU, 宋楚瑜. Nationalist Party director of the Government Information Office from 1979 to 1984, Taiwan's only elected provincial governor, presidential candidate in 2000, founder of People First Party, vice presidential candidate in 2004, and presidential candidate in 2008.

SUN YAT-SEN, SUN ZHONGSHAN (or SUN YIXIAN), 孫中山 or 孫逸仙. Chinese revolutionary who undermined Qing dynasty rule, raised funds for revolutionary causes in the United States and Europe, and served as first president of the Republic of China.

WANG SHENG, WANG SHENG, 王昇. Commander of the Garrison Command at the time of the Kaohsiung Incident in 1979. Wang was a proponent of taking a hard line vis-à-vis the Dangwai. Wang was suspected of orchestrating attacks on opponents of Nationalist Party rule, named as ambassador of Paraguay, and politically marginalized.

WU SHU-CHEN, WU SHUZHEN, 吳淑珍. Wife of Chen Shui-bian and champion of people with handicaps in Taiwan after she became the victim of a political attack in 1985 that left her wheelchair bound. Wu was national legislator and first lady of Taiwan prior to her incarceration for perjury, money laundering, and corruption.

YAO CHIA-WEN, YAO JIAWEN, 姚嘉文. Lawyer, Dangwai activist, political prisoner, professor, and president of the Examination Yuan from 2002 to 2008.

YEH CHU-LAN, YE JULAN, 葉菊蘭. Wife of Cheng Nan-rong who entered politics after his death. She was a Democratic Progressive Party legislator, minister of transportation, chair of the Council for Hakka Affairs, vice premier during the Chen Shui-bian administration, acting mayor of Kaohsiung in 2005, and secretary-general of the Office of the President in 2007 to 2008.

YU TENG-FA, YU DENGFA, 余登發. National assemblyman, Kaohsiung County chief executive, and political prisoner who was falsely convicted of sedition in a 1979 show trial. Sentenced to eight years in prison and released on medical parole, Yu died at home in 1991 under circumstances deemed suspicious by members of his family.

INDEX

Aborigines (Yuanzhumin), 5, 88, 169, 201, 269, 282
Abzug, Bella, 220, 223
Academia Sinica, ix, 253, 270. *See also* Lee Yuan-tseh
Acer, 270
African National Congress, 16
Albuquerque, New Mexico, 164, 183
Alice in Wonderland, 41
Ambassador Hotel, 79, 81
Amnesty International, 157, 163–67, 175, 180–184, 288–89; adoption of Kaohsiung Eight as prisoners of conscience, 164; Chapter 70 in Erlangen, West Germany, 167, 184; Chapter 101 in Albuquerque, New Mexico, 163–66, 182–83; International Secretariat, 163; campaign seeking Lu Hsiu-lien's release, 166–67
Amsterdam, 184
Andersen, Hans Christian, 193–94
Anderson, Jack, 167, 289
Apple Daily, 295
Arias, Oscar, 218
Arrigo, Linda, 105, 125–28, 183, 287. *See also* Shih Ming-teh

Asia Foundation, 62–63, 65–67
Asian Wall Street Journal, 172, 275
Associated Press (AP), 150–51, 288
astrology, 36. *See also* fortune telling
Aung San Suu Kyi

Baez, Joan, 182
Bali, Indonesia, 248
Bamboo Union (Zhulianbang), 173
Beauvoir, Simone, 64
beifen rank, 78
Benevolence Rehabilitation Institute, 155, 159–62, 167–70, 173–74; Mandarin Chinese language policy, 169
Berlin, East, 184
Berlin Wall, 201
Bigombe, Betty, 219
Bookwalter, Karyl, 42
brother of Lu Hsiu-lien. *See* Lu Chuan-sheng
Buddhism, 158, 215
Bureau of Investigation, 48–49, 58–59, 65, 89–91, 104, 147–48, 159, 182. *See also* martial law; Nationalist Party
Burma (*see* Myanmar)
Bush, George H. W., 204–5

Bush, George, W., 281
Bush, Richard, 254–55

Cairo Declaration, 206
Cambridge, Massachusetts, 180, 184. *See* Harvard University
Canada, 217
Capital Morning Post (Shoudu zaobao), 186–88. *See also* Kang Ning-hsiang
Carter, Jimmy, vi, 75, 94–95, 109
Castro, Fidel, 280
Cathay Hotel, 106–09
Central Daily News, 156, 170
Central Intelligence Agency (CIA), 98, 133, 148
Chai, Trong, 209–10
Chang Chao-hsiung, 258
Chang Chi-hsiu, 119–20
Chang Chun-hsiung, 279
Chang Chun-hung, 92, 262, 273, 293; *Formosa Magazine* staff member, 100, 105, 108, 113; Formosa trial defendant, 144, 152–53. *See also* Dangwai
Chang Chun-nan, 100, 103, 105, 112–13, 196, 293. *See also* Dang-wai Candidate Association
Chang Fu-mei, 73, 180, 294
Chang, George, 47
Chang Gung Hospital, 159–60
Chang Hsiao-yan, 211, 218
Chang Hsi-tian, 163, 183, 294
Chang Jung-fa, 270
Chang, Parris, 208
Chang Teh-min, 78
Chang Te-ming, 95–96, 99

Chang Tse-yuan, 191
Chang Wei-chia, 44–45, 63, 132, 294. *See also* Taiwan Independence Movement
Chao Ben-li, 155, 159, 161–62
Chao Chang-ping, 88–89, 94
Chao Chien-min, 282–83
Chen Chu, 80, 118, 125–26, 136–37, 139, 144, 158, 164–67, 170, 174, 262, 294; arrest, 127; prison sentence, 152; cell mate of Lu Hsiu-lien, 153–55; release from prison, 177. *See also* Dangwai; Kaohsiung Incident; Benevolence Rehabilitation Institute
Chen Gen-de, 246–47
Chen Hen-chieh, 41, 47
Chen Shui-bian, 10, 298; accused of corruption, 282; attempted assassination, 280–81; defense attorney for Huang Hsin-chieh, 146; imprisonment, 284, president, 278–84, 294; presidential candidate, 11–12, 17, 252–77. *See also* Wu Shu-chen
Chen Tang-shan (Mark Chen), 255, 288
Chen Ting-nan, 264
Chen Wan-chen, 107
Chen Yi-hsiung, 281
Cheng Nan-rong, 233, 294
Chiang, Antonio (Chiang Chun-nan or Sima wenwu), 187–88, 295
Chiang Ching-kuo, vii, 9, 47, 95–96, 99, 107, 116, 144, 150, 152, 162–64, 172–73, 179, 183, 185, 193, 202, 211, 264, 266, 288, 295;

attempted assassination, 47; political identities, 186. *See also* Nationalist Party

Chiang Hsiao-wu, 173

Chiang Kai-shek, 14, 21–23, 28, 46, 74, 86, 142, 190, 193, 203–6, 267–68, 295; role in Taiwan's exit from the United Nations, 75, 204. *See also* Nationalist Party

Chiang Kai-shek International Airport, 248, 257. *See also* Taoyuan County

Chiang Kai-shek Memorial Hall, 194

Chiang Kai-Shek, Madame. *See* Soong Mei-ling

Chiayi, 25, 268

Chiayi County, 240

Chien, Frederick, 180, 226

Chien Jian-chu, 66

China, 41, 47, 94, 124, 196–97; 200–205, 208, 210, 221, 224; Civil War, 6, 22, 28, 193, 203, 261, 267; claims to sovereignty over Taiwan, 206; National Day, 213–14; "one country, two systems" model, 265, 273; possibility of war with Taiwan, 98, 208; relations with Taiwan, 187, 198, 218; Taiwan experts, 198–99; territorial expansionism, 187; United Front Work Department, 197. *See also* Chinese Communist Party (CCP)

China Airlines, 248–50

China Central Television (CCTV), 275

China Times Newspaper (Zhongguo shibao), 7, 53, 69–70, 250, 287

Chinese Association for Human Rights, 166. *See also* human rights; Amnesty International

Chinese Civil War. *See* China

Chinese Communist Party (CCP), 15, 17, 74, 94, 116, 198, 203, 222, 261, 267–68, 272; support for Taiwan's self-determination, 206. *See also* China

Chinese National Women's Association, 220

Chinese People's Political Consultative Conference, 294

Chinese Women's Anti-Communist League, 66

Chiu Chue-chen, 104, 115, 184–85, 295. *See also* Dangwai

Chiu Mao-nan, 118

Chiu Yi-ping, 136–37

Chiu Yi-ren, 265

Chongqing, 199

Chuang Ah-teng, 85, 91

Chung Chao-man, 52–53

Chungli, 92, 237, 290; Chungli Incident, 92–93; garbage crisis, 239–45. *See also* Nationalist Party

Clean Election Coalition (CEC), 9, 188–92

Clinton, Bill, 230

Clinton, Hillary, 231

Coalition for Democracy, 192–95

Cohen, Jerome A., 73, 76, 78, 139, 171–73, 175, 179. *See also* Henry Liu

eldest sister of Lu Hsiu-lien. *See* Lu
  Hsiu-rong
Empathy (Qing), 162
England, 225
Evergreen Shipping Group, 270
Executive Yuan, 7–8, 56, 60, 102,
  164, 232, 257, 272; Executive Yuan
  Council, 50; Law and Regula-
  tions Commission, 49–50, 62, 65
Exxon Mobil Corporation, 257

Fan, Jo Ann, 223
Fang Li-hsiu, 237–38, 290. *See also*
  Nationalist Party
Far East Plaza Hotel, 254
father of Lu Hsiu-lien. *See* Lu
  Shi-sheng
February 28 Incident (2–28 Inci-
  dent), 5, 22, 28, 44, 139, 150, 205,
  286. *See also* Chiang Kai-shek
Federal Bureau of Investigation
  (FBI), 48
Feldman, Harvey, 208
feminism, 64, 222. *See also* Lu
  Hsiu-lien and *New Feminism*
Feminist Summit for Global Peace,
  229–30
Focus on Taiwan, 225
Forbidden City, 202. *See also*
  National Palace Museum
Formosa Incident. *See* Kaohsiung
  Incident
Formosa Magazine (Meilidao zazhi),
  8–9, 99–102, 106–9, 111–12,
  114–15, 126, 134, 137, 186, 261–63;
  arrest of staff members, 127;
  response to Kaohsiung Incident,

119–25; trial in military court,
  138–41, 143–53, 163–64, 179,
  195–96, 208, 232, 262–63, 269
fortune telling, 19, 112, 168, 252
Fourth Nuclear Power Plant, 278,
  280, 284
France, 257
Friedan, Betty, 64
Fujian, 20, 199–101, 276. *See also*
  Zhangzhou
fumaye ("emperor's son in law"),
  282. *See* Chao Chien-min

Garrison Command, 23, 106, 119,
  121, 125, 160, 170, 179, 182, 298.
  See also Wang Sheng; martial law
General Agreement on Tariffs and
  Trade, 75
Geneva, 184
Georgetown University, 180
Germany, 225
Ghali, Boutros Boutros, 226
Global Summit of Women, 217–20,
  223, 228
Government Information Office,
  151, 163, 166, 264, 269. *See also*
  James Soong
Grand Canyon, 180
Grand Hotel, 164
Grand Hyatt Taipei, 259
Guanyin, 158
guowu jiyaofei ("secret national
  affairs budget"), 282

Hague, The, 184
Hakka, 25, 235, 237–38; identity and
  language, 92–93, 269

Harvard University, 75, 78, 117, 171, 180, 184, 186, 238; H.C. Fung Library xii; Harvard Law School, vii, 8, 73, 163, 172, 186; Harvard-Yenching Library, 76

Hau Puo-tsun (Hau Pei-tsun), 194, 196, 232, 295. *See also* Nationalist Party; Lee Teng-hui

Helms, Jesse, 229

Heritage Foundation, 254

Ho Hsiu-tze, 70–71

Hoklo (Heluo or Min-nan), 4, 86, 92, 237

Homstad, Gail, 43

hongbao, 34–35

Hong Kong, 216, 276

Hongsanjun (Red Shirt Army), 282–83, 298. *See also* Shih Ming-teh

Houston, Texas, 184

Hsiao, Bi-khim, 279

Hsinchu, 22, 68

Hsin Yung Enterprise Corporation, 245

Hsu Hsin-liang, 83, 89, 92–93, 95, 99–102, 106–8, 144, 159–60, 235, 237–39, 253–56, 262, 264, 295; decision to leave Taiwan for the United States, 112. *See also* Democratic Progressive Party

Hsu Hui-ling, 247

Hsu Wen-lung, 270

Hualien, 252

Huang Chu-wen, 207

Huang Hsin-chieh, 81, 91–92, 99–100, 102, 109, 119–24, 140, 143, 146–47, 152, 195–96, 209,

232–33, 262–264, 296. *See also* Dangwai; *Formosa Magazine*; Democratic Progressive Party; Kaohsiung Incident

Huang Kun-hui, 253

Huang Qichao, 197, 220–22

Huang Yu-chiao, 84–85

Hu Fo, 110

Hu Kai-cheng, 61–63

human rights, 12, 116–18, 124, 157, 162–64, 181. *See also* Amnesty International, International Human Rights Day; President's Advisory Committee on Human Rights

Independent Morning Post (Zili wanbao), 234

International Federation of Business and Professional Women (BWP), 7, 57–58, 62

International Herald Tribune, 151

International Human Rights Day, 9, 13, 116, 122–23, 178–79, 183

International Women's Day, 223

International Women's Year, 62

Ireland, Northern, 158

Ithaca, New York, 184

Jacobs, J. Bruce, 142, 287, 293

Jane Eyre, 182

Japan, 187, 251, 284; colonial rule of Taiwan, 14, 17, 20, 25, 70, 87, 169, 186, 197, 203, 206, 213, 224–25, 260, 285; diplomatic relations with Taiwan, 46, 213, 224–25. *See also* Treaty of Shimonoseki

Sun Yat-sen (Sun Zhongshan or Sun Yixian), 23, 27, 116, 298; Sun Yat-sen Memorial Hall, 110

Sun Yun-suan, 116, 164

Taichung, 104–6, 187, 191, 227, 268, 270–71

Tainan, 119, 270

Taipei, 5, 26, 28, 32, 38, 53, 68, 71, 82, 106, 111, 119, 123, 129, 156, 161, 164–165, 171, 187, 211, 216, 219, 223, 270, 272, 284; New Park, 217; Taipei City Council, 55–56; Taipei First Girls' High School, 32; Taipei First Girls' Middle School, 28; Taipei Municipal Mortuary, 142. See also Chen Shui-bian; Ma Ying-jeou

Taipei China, 208

Taipei County, 268

Taiwan, 222; attitudes concerning unification with China, 197–98; central government (see Executive Yuan); Criminal Procedure Law (Xingshi susongfa), 251; diplomatic relationships, 206; economic development, 7, 51, 285; environmental pollution, 18; as "Free China," 22, 74, 203; independence, vii, ix, 47, 108, 143, 148, 150, 152–153, 192, 198, 208, 210, 211, 286; isolation in international affairs, 187, 285; legislature (see Legislative Yuan); political (and ethnic) identities, 5–6, 186, 201–2, 205, 233, 289; relations with China,

187, 290–91 (see also China); Sinification, 6; United Nations readmission campaign, 207–17, 225–27, 230–231, 282; university entrance examinations, 31; women's legal rights in, 68. See also Taiwan Independence Movement

Taiwan Compatriot Permit (Taibaozheng), 213, 228

Taiwan Independence Movement, 45, 47, 49, 62, 64–65, 71, 75, 78, 96, 130, 132, 137, 154, 227, 267. See also Presbyterian Church; Dangwai; Democratic Progressive Party

Taiwan International Alliance, 217, 219, 223–26, 229

Taiwan: Past and Future (Taiwan: guoqu yu weilai), 8, 76, 101, 287

Taiwan Relations Act, 253

Taiwan Strait, 205; Taiwan Strait Crisis, 11, 232

Taiwan Studies Institute, 199

Taiwan Sugar Corporation, 57

Taiwan United Battlefront, 143. See Shih Ming-teh

Tamkang University, 251

Tang Hsueh-pin, 71

Tang Ming-yu, 52–53

Tao Pai-chuan, 81, 110

Taoyuan, 19, 23, 48, 84, 174, 245; Jingfu Temple, 23

Taoyuan County, 77–79, 82–84, 88, 101–2, 212, 240, 253; chief executive, x, 10, 83, 89, 92–93, 102, 159–60, 234–39, 253 (see also Hsu